Cooking and Stealing

Cooking and Stealing

The *Tin House* Nonfiction Reader

A
TIN HOUSE
BLOOMSBURY
BOOK

Published by Bloomsbury Publishing, New York and London
Distributed to the trade by Holtzbrinck Publishers

All papers used by Bloomsbury Publishing are natural,
recyclable products made from wood grown in well-managed
forests. The manufacturing processes conform to the
environmental regulations of the country of origin.

Library of Congress Cataloging-in-Publication Data

Cooking and Stealing : the Tin House nonfiction reader. — 1st U.S. ed.
        p. cm.
"A Tin House Book."
ISBN 1-58234-486-8 (pbk.)
  1. American essays—20th century. 2. American prose literature—20th century. 3.
American prose literature—21st century. 4. American essays—21st century.
PS681.C66 2004
814'.508—dc22

                                                2004012917

First U.S. Edition 2004

1 3 5 7 9 10 8 6 4 2

Typeset by Hewer Text Ltd, Edinburgh
Printed in the United States of America
by Quebecor World Fairfield

CONTENTS

Charles D'Ambrosio
Introduction
1

Jean Nathan
The Lonely Doll
7

David Gates
Possum Living
25

Elissa Schappell
Sex and the Single Squirrel
27

Panagiotis Gianopoulos
Arachnophilia
43

Amy Bloom
Cooking and Stealing
50

Rick Moody
Fractal Love of Brian Eno
57

Jo Ann Beard
Undertaker Please Drive Slow
64

Kathryn Harrison
Nit-Pickers
100

Eliot Weinberger
The Laughing Fish
119

Francine Prose
A Train of Powder
122

Jeffrey Eugenides
The Bunker
126

Katie Roiphe
Graham Greene's Vietnam
132

Russell Banks
No, But I Saw the Movie
147

Abigail Thomas
The Magnificent Frigate Bird
162

David Shields
The Only Solution to the Soul Is the Senses:
A Meditation on Bill Murray and Myself
168

Ann Hood
Little Audrey
188

Gerry Howard
The Mandarin and the Hipster
206

Richard McCann
The Resurrectionist
212

Lisa Zeidner
No Mo Po-Mo
222

Ken Tucker
Webb Pierce's ``There Stands the Glass´´
227

Sara Roahen
Drinking My Inheritance
231

Christopher Merrill
After You
238

Sallie Tisdale
Violation
244

Gary Greenberg
Little Brown Shack
257

Michael Lowenthal
You Don't See the Other Person Looking Back
280

Albert Mobilio
For Keeps: The Christian C. Sanderson Museum
306

Contributors
315

Copyright Notes
323

INTRODUCTION
Charles D'Ambrosio

There's an old bus stop in Seattle that's maybe the loneliest place in the world for me, and it was there, reading in the vague light, that I first discovered the essay. Even now when I drive by, I still check that stop, looking for one of my brothers or sisters, even though the stop has been moved and the family I might give a lift to is gone. By the standards of the day it was an excellent place to wait for the bus, really the stoop of an apartment, with a marble stairway that was cold but covered, offering shelter from the wind and the rain and a lighted entry that was bright enough to read by. You had to sit on the top step and slouch just right and futz with the book to get the angle, but once you had it, the words resolved on the page, like something taking shape through a telescope. Across the intersection was a bookstore that stayed open late. It was one of those small places that made up for a lack of inventory with sensibility, a bookstore you could trust, and the first that I knew of to hand out free bookmarks, which I thought at the time was infinitely clever. I had just figured out, rather naively, that I could buy my own books, and then almost instantly I became a prig about their condition, so much so that I wouldn't lend them to anyone, at least not without a solemn lecture about their proper handling—no breaking the spines, no dog-earring the pages, no greasy thumbprints. At home, I had my own somewhat wobbly arrangement of brick-and-board shelves, two and then three tiers of ugly pressboard, painted brown and laddered up against the wall, my first piece of furniture. In private, I thought of those shelves with enormous pride, as something I was building, book by book and brick by brick, and I often looked at them, vaguely satisfied, like a worker inspecting the progress of a job. I wanted the shelves to rise up and reach the ceiling, and for that to happen, all I had to do, I realized, was read.

My sense of the essay as a genre or form isn't something I can separate from my experience of those early encounters. I bought my first collection from that little bookstore, on the staff's recommendation, and fell in love with the writer M.F.K. Fisher, whose works on gastronomy couldn't have been more foreign to me—growing up, as I did, in a big family where we boiled everything in vats and drank powdered milk; my father, fielding a complaint about food, would clench the fist of his free hand and stab his fork at the offending item on his plate and say, "Eat it. Your stomach doesn't care." For years I was too shy to pepper food at a restaurant, afraid that it would insult the cook. Anyway, it was at family meals that we learned indifference to our bodies, but it was in prose, particularly the kind I found in the personal essay, that a relationship to that body began to be restored, at least for me. One of my earliest ideas about writing was that the rhythms of prose came from the body, although I still don't know what I was thinking. I would discover, eventually, that some of Fisher's love of food was a celebratory rebellion against a similar tyranny at home, a rejection of the dulling rules and sumptuary restrictions of the dinner table set by her grandmother. Prose moves so mysteriously that I believe I heard this unstated fact in the rhythm of her sentences, long before her biography confirmed it. It came to me sotto voce, whispered on a lower frequency. And so, while the superficial subject of Fisher's essays may have drawn me in, offering a fantasy world in which fois gras and Dom Perignon mattered, soon enough it was language itself, and more specifically, the right she assumed to be exact about her life, that won me completely. It was prose more than the wonders of Provence or tureens of whatever that taught me how to pay attention, and it was the essay, as a form, that was the container, the thing that caught and held like holy water the words, showing the concern, the intensity, the care a person might bring to life.

Other essayists followed, and I read them in great passionate jags— all of Joan Didion and George Orwell, all of Susan Sontag and Samuel

Johnson, living for weeks at a time with the sentences of a single writer, excluding other authors, other kinds of reading. I didn't read poems that way, or novels. Something in the nature of the personal essay must have instructed me and informed this pattern. And I must have needed that sort of fast attachment, that guidance, the voice holding steady in the face of doubt, the flawed man revealing his flaws, the older brother or sister—for essays were never a father to me, nor a mother. Essays were the work of equals, confiding, uncertain, solitary, free, and even the best of them had an unfinished feel, a tentative note, that made them approachable. A good essay questions itself in a way that a novel or short story does not—perhaps it's simply that an essay leaves its questions on the page, there for everyone to see; it is a forum for self-doubt, for an attempt whose outcome isn't assured. It seems to me we've lost so much to the expert and the confident authority that expressions of doubt or honest ignorance have become, to the demotic mind, a kind of recreancy, a failure of loyalty. Our public space has become a matter of allegiances, always a prelude to ugly business, and I sometimes wonder, in my uncertainty, where all the other people are who don't know, who don't understand. Are we all alone? Removing the engine of the essay—doubt and the unknown, let's say—leaves us with articles and theses, facts and positions, our side and their side, dreary optimism and even drearier pessimism, but nowhere to turn in a moment of true need.

For a definition, I would like to quote from an essay by Patricia Hampl:

On the first page of the *Confessions* [Augustine] poses a problem that has a familiar modern ring: "it would seem clear that no one can call upon Thee without knowing Thee." There is, in other words, the problem of God's notorious absence. Augustine takes the next step West; he seeks his faith with his doubt: "may it be that a man must implore Thee before he can know Thee?" The assumption here is that faith is not to be confused with certainty; the only thing people can really count on is longing and the occult directives of desire. So, Augustine wonders, does that mean prayer must come before faith? Illogical as it is, perhaps not-knowing is the first condition of prayer, rather than its negation. Can that be?

Seeking faith with doubt, that's definition enough for me. Or strike faith, and leave it at seeking with doubt. And longing. And the occult directives of desire.

And now the part of this introduction that I've been dreading, where I note some of the essays in this wonderful anthology, and fail to mention the rest. For an entire catalog, of course, there's the table of contents and the book itself, but here, without slighting anyone, I want only to connect a few dots, trying, in two or three strokes, to coax out the larger shape of this collection, the body of it.

The self as defined in this anthology is elusive and protean. From Elissa Schappell's comic misadventures at a furrie convention (in a raccoon suit, rented) to Richard McCann's haunting, lost considera- tion of "the body in which I carried what I called 'myself' " (after a liver transplant, donated)—the self we encounter is hardly stable, and often, as is the case with McCann's spooky piece, seems held together only for the fleeting length of the essay. The fragility of the self shows up elsewhere too, notably in Abigail Thomas's tremendously sweet and painful essay on her husband, institutionalized with brain damage after an accident, dreamily removed from the shared mem- ories that make social and personal cohesion possible. There is death—Amy Bloom's "Cooking and Stealing"—and there is birth— Gary Greenberg's "Little Brown Shack." This last, an essay on the writer's difficult road to adoption, takes the reader so deeply into the logic of the process, moving through the past and present tenses into the future, that the grammar itself conveys the dodgy, intangible nature of the self, unable to rest at some idealized or defined moment. It is a remarkable piece of work, honest and true and full of doubt, and I came away from the final line and the last lovely image feeling released until I read the line again, and was drawn back down into the open and unsure future.

When the self is in doubt, obsession or seeking in general animates the writer. Jeffrey Eugenides ("The Bunker") can't seem to get past the word itself—*bunker*, which turns strange to the ear with enough repetition, losing its meaning, so that his brief essay is partly about the failure of the word, and all it implies, to yield understanding. "What do we seek by going to the sites of atrocity?" he asks, down in a bunker that Hitler may have inspected. The essay considers the huge evil of the Holocaust before returning to the mundane, the cold and the dust and the candlelight, the knowable world. Katie Roiphe takes a literary pilgrimage into the Vietnam of Graham Greene, and her essay, like Eugenides's, partly turns by unpacking the power of a word—in this case *seedy*, a word that no one who's read Greene can escape. An obsession with Greene leads Roiphe on a journey and story of her own; freed from the word and the imprint of Greene, her transactions in the land of *The Quiet American* acquire their own sinister energy. And in opening lines that might stand in for all the obsessions in this anthology, Jean Nathan writes: "It was in the spring of 1997 that the oddest image floated into my mind: the cover of a children's book I hadn't seen or even thought of in more than thirty years. There it lodged, and there it remained." Nathan's essay is about Dare Wright and her strange children's book *The Lonely Doll*. It's absolutely fascinating, and offers, along the way, a model for the obsessed writer and the rewards of seeking.

I'd like to close with a word about an essay that surprised me. For reasons that aren't really reasons—prejudices, I guess—I didn't expect to like David Shields's essay, "A Meditation on Bill Murray and Myself." It takes the most oblique and fractured approach to its subject and yet does so with sentences that are so measured and confident and reasonable that I lost sight of my objections. Shields somehow does for Bill Murray what Samuel Johnson did for Shakespeare, articulating the resonance of a known figure, making him new and relevant again. And he, like Johnson, captures and sums up something important about the age, too. After reading the essay, I felt connected to the culture, relieved of my constant, nagging dissatisfaction, because someone else had done the very difficult work of wading through their uncertainties and doubts, carefully approaching a small portion of our world to see if, even tentatively, a direct relation was possible. "An unfortunate fact," Shields says about his own stuttering, "is that it prevents you from ever entirely losing self-consciousness when expressing such traditional and truly important emotions as love, hate, joy, and deep pain." His essay gives the feel of a solitary at work, and yet it has what I've always looked for in the form, since the days at the bus stop, when I sought essays for fellowship. And what is an anthology but such a gathering?

THE LONELY DOLL
Jean Nathan

I t was in the spring of 1997 that the oddest image floated into my mind: the cover of a children's book I hadn't seen or even thought of in more than thirty years. There it lodged, and there it remained. It felt as if it were a message, and its insistence startled me. Maybe it wasn't even meant for me. I tried to tromp it down. I live among the grown-ups now. I don't even have any children. I am a writer. A deadline looms. I have work to do.

But the image just kept flashing in my mind: a pink-and-white gingham field inset with a black-and-white portrait of Edith, the lonely doll, an open book between her spread, outstretched legs.

My own copy of *The Lonely Doll* was long lost, and I soon learned from a bookstore clerk who did give me the name of the author, Dare Wright, that the book was out of print. The New York Public Library's computer listed three copies, all damaged or missing. (I didn't know then that Houghton Mifflin was planning the book's reissue in September 1998.)

When I called a children's-book searcher listed in the phone book, she said she knew the book well and would add my name to her waiting list. I remember feeling almost a childish sense of disappointment at more delay, but also astonishment to learn that Edith lived on in other people's consciousnesses.

Meaning to close the phone book, I found myself turning distractedly to "Wright." And there, jumping out at me from blurred columns of typeface, was "Wright, Dare, 11 East 80th Street. 249–6965." I don't think I could have been any more amazed if the address given had been, say: "Second to the right and then straight on till morning," Peter Pan's address on the island of Neverland.

But there she was, evidently real. In the weeks to come I dialed the number more than once. There was never an answer. I also sent a letter expressing how much the book had meant to me as a child and asking if she knew where I could find a copy.

Several months later, I finally did get *The Lonely Doll* from the book searcher. Illustrated with black-and-white photographs, *The Lonely Doll* is the story of a doll named Edith, mired in loneliness, seemingly parentless, eating her cereal alone, going to bed alone, wishing for friends, begging some pigeons on the windowsill to be her friends and watching as they just fly away.

One morning, two teddy bears appear in her garden. They tell her they've come to be her friends and move right in.

One rainy day, Mr. Bear takes his big umbrella and sets off on some mission. Home alone, Edith and Little Bear despair of a way to entertain themselves. But as they explore the house, they discover, behind a set of louvered doors, a grown-up woman's closet and dressing room. The identity of the woman to whom all this belongs, and her absence, is never explained. It might be Edith's mother, but from all indications Edith has no mother.

A full-out, frenzied dress-up session follows, in which Edith and Little Bear adorn themselves with glamorous rhinestones and pearls, a petticoat and a hat with roses and ribbons, high-heeled shoes, a leopard handbag.

In their recklessness, they knock over a vase with one long-stemmed rose. The water spills into a jewelry box, but they are oblivious. Wielding a fully swiveled-out lipstick, Little Bear goads Edith to put it on. She says she wouldn't dare: "You know what Mr. Bear would say." With that, he uses the lipstick to scrawl "Mr. Bear is just a silly old thing" across the oval mirror, when who should appear, coming through the louvered doors, reflected in the mirror, but . . . Mr. Bear. Spankings ensue, but the deeper issue, striking terror in Edith, is that their being bad could jeopardize the whole arrangement—and that Edith would be, once again, abandoned and lonely. But when the little ones clean up the mess and promise never to do "it" again, Mr. Bear "solemnly" promises that he and Little Bear will stay with her "forever and ever."

About the time the book arrived, I received a phone call from a woman named Brook Ashley. She said my letter had been forwarded to her in Santa Barbara, California. She said she was Dare's unofficial god-daughter and legal guardian and that Dare, now eighty-four, was living in a hospital on life support. She said she was coming to New York to begin closing up Dare's apartinent. Did I want to meet her at 11 East Eightieth Street?

When I arrived, Winkie Donovan, Brook's childhood friend, was also there to help. And so, in some surreal way, was someone else. The living room was filled with portraits, some life size, of a beautiful blond woman. Spellbound, I circumnavigated this bizarre exhibition. "That's Dare," Brook said. "They were all painted by her mother." Dare, I was shocked to realize, looked very much like Edith.

One portrait was turned to the wall. On the back it read: "To my good and precious child, Alice Dare Wright." It was signed "Edith Stevenson Wright."

Edie, as Dare's mother was known, had been a portrait painter of some renown, whose subjects included Winston Churchill, Calvin Coolidge, and Greta Garbo (it was the only portrait for which the actress ever posed).

As I left, Brook said she might someday call on me to help arrange Dare's obituary. Later, Brook gave me Dare's fat leather-bound scrapbook containing the record of her publishing career, including jacket covers, reviews, and other articles relating to the first twelve of her nineteen books for children. The Lonely Doll had been her first book. I had never known of the rest.

Published by Doubleday in 1957, The Lonely Doll had received mountains of publicity and was serialized in Good Housekeeping. It climbed the children's bestseller list in the New York Times and was published in six foreign-language editions. (It would remain in print, in various formats, for thirty-five years.) Just in time for Christmas

1958, the Madame Alexander Doll Company brought out an Edith doll.

Very little of the coverage was biographical. What did exist often presented Dare in relation to her mother. *Mother's Artful Influence*, read one headline; *Model Daughter*, another.

When the *New York World-Telegram and Sun* asked Dare "Why the preference for dolls?" she replied: "Well, they'll stand still for two-three hours for one photo—with never a complaint about wages. And all that bending over keeps a girl trim."

Girl? I later realized Dare would have been forty-three in 1957, the year *The Lonely Doll* was published, and forty-eight when she gave her age as thirty-five to the *Saturday Evening Post* in a 1962 "People on the Way Up" feature. (Sales of her fifth book, *The Lonely Doll Learns a Lesson*, had just exceeded 200,000.) But Dare was completely honest when she was asked about Edith. "I don't think of Edith as a doll," she said. "She was my friend when I was a child. She's a personality in her own right."

At home I sorted through the piles of clippings and photographs I'd been given by Brook. There were photos of family and friends, but mostly they were photographs of Dare. There were magnificent photos of Dare playing dress-up in elaborate costumes, but the most startling were the ones depicting Dare across a spectrum of ages, in what could be described as undress, or partially so, and just as posed as those of her in costume. Posing, always posing, but for whom?

From my very first visit to Dare's apartment, it was clear to me that I would go the distance in my investigation into this mysterious life. But at the time I never knew in any conscious way what drove me, what I was really looking for, why I thought about the book after so many years, or even why I once cared about this book so much.

Now, I think I know.

Looking back, I realize that like Dare, I didn't think of Edith as a doll either. She, too, was my friend when I was a child. She was a little girl with a problem, and the identification couldn't have been stronger. I was so happy to find her.

My grandparents had given me *The Lonely Doll* during a difficult time in my family when I was five. My unconscious gave it back to me all these years later. It knew what I no longer did, that I once was a little girl who had thought well of herself and her world, and if I could travel back to find her, I could reclaim that part of myself. The book could show me the way back.

By the end of my journey, I would discover many, many women who spoke with great emotion of the powerful hold this book had on them as children. And some, artists and writers, who said they carry it with them in their thoughts as they work. Meg Wolitzer, who has written children's books as well as novels, told me, "As a writer, I've never not thought about that book."

When *The Lonely Doll* floated back up into my consciousness, my only intention had been to find the book. Now it had become my mission to rescue Dare Wright, who once told an interviewer that her idea of the "greatest luxury was to go out leaving all the electric lights burning."

Dare, I was to discover, had lived in her own version of a wonderland. And so I followed Dare's trail, spending two years talking to anyone I could find who knew her, trying to make sense of the world I had stumbled into.

In 1917, when Dare was three, Edie divorced her Canadian husband, Ivan Wright, leaving him the custody of their five-year-old son, Blaine. Ivan and Edie seemed to have made a pact that the brother and sister should never see each other again. Edie and Dare moved to Cleveland, Ohio. There Edie put an Italian Lenci doll on "will call" at Halle Brothers, a department store near their home, until she could make the full $11.50 payment. The two named the doll Edith.

In 1924, one of Edie's portrait subjects offered her the use of the penthouse of his office in the Hanna Building as her studio. For the next forty-five years, its fifteen hundred square feet, with a northern-exposure skylight, would be her home. That same year, she enrolled Dare, who was nine, in the fourth grade at the Laurel School. Perhaps because Edie's living arrangements were ill-suited to a young child, or because commissions were coming in from far-off places, necessitating travel, Dare was enrolled as a boarding student. When Edie was in town, Dare would spend weekends with her in the penthouse.

That following spring, Dare's first published effort, "The Little Green Door," appeared under the heading "An Imaginary Story" in Laurel's 1925 yearbook. A brother and sister, twins, live in a palace with their father, the king. In one of the highest towers is a little green door that the children have been forbidden to enter. They do anyway, and encounter an old woman who keeps them there to "hear [her] story." Meanwhile, after a long search for his children, the king finally finds them behind the green door. But the old woman refuses to relinquish them until her floor has been covered "with something that is the color of gold." The king does his best, but a small space is still left uncovered. His daughter fills it with a snipped-off lock of her golden hair. With that, all the gold and the old woman vanish, and "The king and his children went downstairs and lived together happily."

Did Dare worry her father, now regal in her estimation, might not be able to find her imprisoned in that "highest tower" of the Hanna Building? Did she feel she had somehow transgressed by going there in the first place? If this was an angry dig at her "old woman" mother for denying her her father and brother, it was one of the very few she ever allowed herself.

She had already internalized her mother's obsession with "golden hair." It might have perplexed Dare as a little girl that the many portraits her mother painted of her always depicted the brown-haired child as blond, although in every other way they were the striking likenesses of which Edie was so capable. By the time Dare was eighteen, she had lightened her hair. In the years to come, she dyed it blonder and blonder.

In fact, a slightly different version of that fairy tale describes what really happened. Dare entered that green door of her mother's world, a world that may have glittered but was only "the color of gold."

The old woman—her mother—who lived there put a spell on her so that she would stay a child forever, and would never be bad (sexual).

In return, she would never be abandoned and never be alone. They would live in that tall tower forever, each other's eternal companions.

In 1934, after graduating from high school, Dare moved to New York to attend drama and art school. She tried, with little success, to be an actress, and went on to work as a fashion model, including a stint as the Maidenform bra model in 1950. By the mid-forties she'd made her way to the other side of the camera, and her fashion photography appeared in *Vogue, Harper's Bazaar,* and *Town & Country.*

Her apartment was a glamorous and ever-changing stage set for which she made most of the furnishings. She held many of her photo shoots there and developed her film herself in a darkroom set up in her bathroom.

In the evenings, she would hold elegant cocktail parties dressed in gowns of her own creation. Her inner circle included Eugenia Rawls, Brook Ashley's mother and an actress, and her husband Donald Seawell, Brook Ashley's father, an entertainment lawyer, later publisher of the *Denver Post* and founder of the Denver Center for the Performing Arts; Tallulah Bankhead, Seawell's client, Rawls's best friend, and Brook's godmother; Gayelord Hauser, a health food guru with a Hollywood clientele whom Dare and her mother met on the beach at Cannes in 1930, and at whose villa in Sicily they were frequent houseguests; his friend Greta Garbo; and Vincent Youmans, whose father had written "Tea for Two" and "No, No, Nanette." Though tall, blond, and dazzlingly beautiful, she was strangely child-like, avoidant, and shy, and always somehow confused by her powers over men.

Unbeknownst to Dare, her brother, Blaine, was also living in New York. When her father's brother, Dare's uncle Austin Wright, learned of Dare's move, he convinced Edie and Ivan's second wife, now a widow (Ivan had died in 1927), to allow him to orchestrate a reunion. The 1934 reunion, in Central Park, of the twenty-two-year-old tall, dark, and handsome Blaine and the nineteen-year-old newly golden and always enchanting Dare was highly charged, recalled Austin's son, Meade Wright.

"They fell in love," he told me, as though this were usual. They had even wanted to marry, Meade said, thinking to conceal their brother-sister relationship. That idea, however, seems to have been dropped. Neither would ever marry.

After the war, in which he had served in the Royal Canadian Air Force and later the American Air Force, assigned to a Thunderbolt fighter group, Blaine bought a run-down fishing camp on Butternut Island near Walton, New York. He rechristened it "the Isle of Pot"— he loved the wordplay potential of "going to Pot"—and lived there for the rest of his life, subsisting on the revenues of a trout-fishing lure, "the Phoebe," that he invented. The lure, named, so he said, for an Englishwoman he had loved during the war who had been killed in the Blitz, is still manufactured today. Some twelve million have been sold to date.

But, in 1943, by all appearances, Dare's prince had come, and Blaine provided the introduction. Philip Sandeman, of the sherry-and-port-producing family, had been an RAF fighter pilot and Spitfire squadron leader during the war. As princes go, Philip was ideal, especially since he almost always remained at a safe distance. First there was the war, and afterward he lived across the ocean. (Brook said, "What happens next, i.e., sex, was never thought through.") The couple stayed in contact throughout the war, and the two were engaged in 1947. That fall Dare flew to England to meet Philip's family and to see the house in Slough, outside London, that he had picked out for them.

Upon her return to America, Dare told her friends she was having doubts about his commitment. Her mother, however, was not deterred. In February 1948, she placed a lengthy and hyperbolic wedding announcement in a Cleveland newspaper. Almost no detail was omitted but their ages. Dare was thirty-four; Phillip was twenty-seven.

Edie had also embarked on the long-distance interior decoration of the house, and planned every detail of the wedding: ordering the wedding dress from Worth in Paris, recruiting Donald Seawell to give Dare away and Eugenia Rawls to be matron of honor. Following Edie's timetable, Philip did fly to New York the week before the wedding. But sometime before the April 14 wedding date, he asked Blaine to accompany him to tell Dare the wedding was off.

"It was something very sad," said Philip's brother Brian. "Another woman got her talons into Philip, and set him against Dare." When I asked her name, he said: "We knew her as 'the Witch.'"

Philip had spurned the exquisite doll who was his fiancée. Brook and others have surmised that he wanted a "flesh and blood"—in other words, a sexually willing—woman.

For the next three years Dare seems to have hung on to the dream that Philip would come back to her. Edie no doubt fanned this fantasy. Dare sent Philip's mother, Marie Sandeman, photographs of alluring portraits Edie had painted of her in this period. In all of them, Dare had posed in low-cut white gowns. (Edie also did many portraits of Philip in absentia, painting from Dare's photographs of him. These paintings were signed by both mother and daughter.)

Dare also staged elaborate photographs of herself, seated at her dressing table, a sort of shrine to Philip, with a pencil drawing of him that she had sketched and a bottle of Sandeman sherry. Clutched in her hands is a letter he had sent to her. She is turned, glancing at the camera, wistfully, hopefully.

In May 1949, the tangled web of Dare's personal life spun out further when she was accused by the socially prominent Mary Amelia Veit Marsh of having an affair with her millionaire husband, "Castor Oil King" Fenimore Cooper Marsh. Following her suspicions, Mrs. Marsh, her two brothers, and a private detective had "raided" the Bristol Hotel room where Dare was living to find her there with Mr. Marsh. Mrs. Marsh took her case to the Supreme Court, where she sued Mr. Marsh for divorce, naming Dare corespondent. The case was reported in lurid stories in the New York tabloids in July, and the trial began in December. As it turned out, Mr. Marsh, an amateur photographer, was helping Dare set up a darkroom in the bathroom of her hotel room. If he had other intentions, he had picked the wrong woman.

By December 10, Mrs. Marsh withdrew her charge, and the case was settled. The judge ordered Mrs. Marsh to give Dare a letter clearing her of misconduct, but not before the *Daily Mirror* reported that Dare's lawyers (Donald Seawell and his partner) had "subpoenaed two gynecologists who were prepared to testify [their] client was a virgin."

Having extricated herself from the Marsh mess just as 1950 was beginning, Dare's thoughts were still on Philip.

But in 1951, at the age of thirty, Philip was killed flying in a demonstration air show, training reserve pilots for the Korean War.

In the years that followed, Donald Seawell said, "Men always did beat a path to her door." Dare wasn't interested. "She never seemed quite of this world," he said. "She was ethereal, somehow above normal courtship."

Even though Philip was gone, his image was captured eternally on canvas and photographic paper. For the rest of her life, Dare hung these portraits of Philip in her apartments, with one by the front door. And for the rest of her life, no man would ever get in the door to Dare's broken heart—or to her virginal body.

After Philip's death, Dare rented her first New York apartment, having lived until then in a series of hotel rooms. It was a twenty-five-hundred-square-foot ground-floor studio apartment at 29 West Fifty-eighth Street, with a dropped living room, high ceilings, a fireplace, and an adjoining terrace accessed through French doors in the back. She painted the wood floors in black and white squares, and echoed this motif on the concrete terrace out back. She made voluminous drapes for the windows and installed smoked-glass mirrors throughout. The glamorous all-white boudoir was fitted out with a taffeta-canopied princess bed, and next to that, set off by louvered doors, was a dressing room with a vanity table and an oval mirror, and a large closet.

Edie and Dare were virtually inseparable. Dare would make frequent visits to the penthouse in Cleveland, and for at least one week a month, Edie would come to New York, staying with Dare, and sleeping, as was their custom, in the same bed. They seemed to have no idea of the oddness of this arrangement. As Edie told Brook: "I reach over and pat her little bottom in the night."

Dare had left Edith behind in Edie's penthouse when she moved to New York, and now that Dare had her own apartment, Edie sent on her belongings, including her childhood dolls. After the first and biggest trauma of Dare's life, losing her father and brother, consolation had come in the form of Edith. Now, after the second, losing Philip, her doll was back again.

Edith was a mess, Dare later told interviewers. Her wig was yellowed and tangled and her clothes were in shreds. Dare quickly set about undertaking what she called Edith's "rejuvenation," but transformation would be the better term. Edith never again resembled her former self. Instead she was given a completely new look: long, straight blond hair, usually worn tied up in a high ponytail and bangs, and gold hoop earrings. It was a look that had everything in common with Edith's owner.

Dare also acquired some teddy bears in this period, after her brother went on a drunken shopping spree with Dorothy Tivis Pollock, a former model who headed the Figureheads modeling agency, where Dare was registered for a time.

"Blaine was drunk," Dorothy said, "and got weird as he always did when he drank. We passed FAO Schwarz and he saw a teddy bear in the window. He decided I had to have one. In we went, but when he saw all the bears, he said it would be terrible to buy just one because the bear would be lonely. With that he directed the saleswoman to pack up the entire lot, about a dozen Steiff bears, hundreds of dollars of bears. Since Dare's apartment was just around the corner, we went over there, carrying all these damn teddy bears."

Within minutes of their arrival, Dorothy recalled becoming the unwilling witness to the puerile spectacle of a grown-up brother and sister sitting on the floor with all the bears, telling bear stories in various bear voices. Soon, Dare added her childhood dolls to the party.

"Edith," Dare later told an interviewer, "looked so happy with the bears" that she decided to photograph them all together.

But it was a spurned suitor, Anthony Palermo, who encouraged Dare to make something of her photographs of her inanimate housemates. Palermo, who dubbed Edie "tag-along" for her intrusive presence on dates with Dare, and who was taken aback because Edie treated Dare "like a doll," found that he got no further even when Edie was not around, because Edith always was. One date began with Dare chiding him for his rudeness to Edith. "You didn't say hello to Edith," she told him angrily, as though he had rudely neglected to acknowledge a human presence. On another occasion, when he tried to kiss her, she held Edith out in front of her to block his advances.

Palermo, despite losing his battle to get Dare into bed, unwittingly made a magnanimous suggestion. "Since they're real," he said of her inanimate housemates, "why don't you write about them? Make a story, make a book."

Dare seems to have wasted no time in following Tony's directive. She thought up a story line, made Edith outfits, posed her cast in her apartment and around New York, and shot and developed the photographs. These she pasted onto board and made into a perfect replica of a bound book, impressively professional but for the handwritten text in black Magic Marker.

Donald Seawell, who also thought her work had book potential, did his part by bringing it to the attention of the publishers he knew at the Players' Club on Gramercy Park.

The next eighteen books followed at the rate of about one a year. The majority stuck with the original cast of characters, Edith and the bears, although three involved Lona and Persis, her other childhood dolls. She later added live animals into the mix, including kittens, dogs, ponies, and ducklings, and, following a Random House editor's suggestion, did a four-book *Look at . . .* nature series, chronicling a kitten, a colt, a calf, and a seagull from birth to maturity.

Apart from the straightforward *Look at . . .* books, the other story lines replayed the same set of themes: seeking love and approval, fearing abandonment, risking separation and autonomy. In other words, the issues—and trade-offs—inherent in growing up, issues with which their author struggled her entire life.

The story of *The Lonely Doll* was, in some measure, her own story. In the book, a tour de force of wish fulfillment, she found a way to make it right, removing a mother from the proceedings and providing her alter ego, Edith, with love and rescue in the form of two male teddy bears, an alter ego father and brother.

With the publication of *The Lonely Doll* came a recognition that Dare had never experienced and with which she seemed highly uncomfortable. Edie, however, was completely at home with Dare's success and all the attention. Letters from her file at the Butler Institute of American Art in Youngstown, Ohio, often make reference to Dare. "My daughter," she writes in but one example, "is a writer and illustrator of childrens [sic] books—with Doubleday and Random House. Mr. Bennet [sic] Cerf says she is the best out of their junior department." Dare did save several letters Bennett Cerf, C.E.O. of Random House, sent to her. From 1966: "You are one of our most brilliant and certainly most beautiful authors—and I only wish that droit de seigneur rules were still in effect!" And another from 1968: "You looked so pretty last night that Mayor Lindsay now thinks he wants to go into the publishing business."

Although Edie continued to paint until the week before she died, she was apparently happy to help Dare with her accidental new career. Based on the photographic record, the two became a sort of team, with Edie in the assistant's role. Adoring travel, they built it into the story lines of Dare's books, the most elaborate one being *Lona: A Fairy Tale*. For this, they traveled throughout Europe scouting out castles and scenery—and toads—for the story of the princess who must overcome the spell of an evil wizard who has changed her into a tiny doll. When Lona is in her full-size incarnation, before the spell and after it is lifted, Dare herself posed as the princess. She would set up the shot, focus the camera, don her princess gown, and have her mother trip the shutter.

Even on vacations they would lug along cameras, tripods, even movie cameras. I have still to make my way through all of the dozens of 16mm films. Without sound, they are as mute as the photographs—but so much more chilling. Edie is never without a lit cigarette, and always appears in a cloud of smoke. In one scene, she gesticulates in the air with a paintbrush, as though waving a magic wand. And how strange to see Dare, ever immobile in the photographs and portraits, move for the first time, with none of the grace I would have imagined. Her movements are awkward, jerky, as if she were crippled in some way. I think of Laura in *The Glass Menagerie* or the doll, Olympia, in *The Tales of Hoffmann*.

It was in the fifties that they discovered a new way to entertain themselves. Edie and Dare began photographing Dare naked. Like the dress-up sessions in which they engaged and always chronicled in photographs, these nude pictures had no professional purpose, and were never shown to others. The obsessive nature of this "game" is evidenced by the fact that the same pose would be photographed again and again using a variety of cameras and film.

Maybe this was the ideal meshing of Dare's closet exhibitionism and overt narcissism with Edie's voyeurism. Maybe it was also a kind of bloodletting. Dare's unwritten contract with her mother required that she remain a child; sexuality was in direct conflict with this. Maybe, if sexual desire overcame Dare despite the taboos, it was Edie's intention to let it out privately, and thereby silence it, in the controlled circumstances of a photo shoot.

Some of the nude photographs depict Dare, unadorned, in all sorts of poses. Others include props, such as one of Dare on the beach, holding a fish in one hand with Edith the doll sitting by her. Some are quite elaborately staged, like the one of a nude, crouching Dare caught in a gigantic net, done up as some sort of sea creature with a sea-flora headdress and exaggerated makeup.

The most extraordinary of this genre are a series of Dare on a beach, wearing nothing but a pearl necklace, her limp body tangled up in driftwood, shells, and seaweed. Whether faceup or facedown, in all of them she looks as though she were dead and had just washed up on shore with the tide.

No one I spoke to ever knew about these photos, but almost everyone knew of the extreme closeness of the mother-daughter relationship. Some said it was as though they were sisters; others saw it as pathological, or perhaps even incestuous.

"It was a very twisted relationship," said Brook. "Edie never let go, ever. She kept her in a world of fairy tales and managed to maintain her purity."

"Edie fanned all this fantasy," said Dorothy. "In a way Edie retarded her. She never allowed Dare to grow up."

Almost no one who saw them close up viewed Edie's influence as benign. Speaking to Dorothy of his mother, Blaine once said, "If I could tell you the wreckage she has wrought—and my sister is part of it." And Dorothy recalled shouting matches when she would arrive with Blaine to visit Dare and Edie. "Blaine would see Dare all dressed up like a fairy princess and scream at his mother, 'My sister's not a doll!' "

In July 1975, Edie, aged ninety-two, died in her sleep in her daughter's bed, with Dare, then sixty-one, by her side.

The next morning, a distraught Dare called her former drama teacher from Laurel, now a neighbor, to handle the arrangements, which amounted to Edie's cremation and the return of her ashes to Dare. There was no funeral. Dare seemed to be in some denial that Edie had even died. She never arranged an obituary for her publicity-adoring mother, and I was told she left unopened the condolence letters that poured in on word of mouth.

Edie's will left everything to Dare, with no mention of Blaine. Dare did go to Cleveland to bring Edie's belongings back to her already crammed apartment. It was then that she came to live surrounded by images of herself, the portraits Edie had painted of her, the fruits of a lifetime of posing.

Now, for the first time in her life, Dare had a chance to forge a self away from the one Edie had imposed. Instead, Dare seems to have taken over the job of further crippling herself. "She was under her mother's spell. When her mother died, she didn't know what to do," said Tony Palermo.

She did manage two more books. In 1978 she produced *Edith and Midnight*, in which Edith and Little Bear attempt to capture and bring home a wild pony, and in 1980, at the age of sixty-six, she published *Edith and the Duckling*, the story of Edith and the two bears caring for a duckling after its mother disappears. The photographs for both were shot in Walton, so that she could be near Blaine.

She tried to keep up with the more persistent of her fans, and with her appearance as well, to confused effect. She ate less and less. Her body, curvaceous although always slim in her prime, became more like a preadolescent's, and she wore clothing, makeup, and hairstyles suitable for a much younger woman.

She also began drinking excessively. But if in alcohol she sought a retreat from the real world, it betrayed her, too, lifting the lid on feelings long locked in or never experienced while her mother's spell was still potent.

One particularly difficult evening came in October 1980. At dinner with Tony, who was visiting New York, she became drunk and launched [on an angry tirade about] having ruined her life and said she wished she had married him.

Very late that same night, she called Jeanne Frank, an art dealer whom she'd met at the neighborhood bookstore. Frank recorded her thoughts in her journal the morning after the chilling phone call: "Is it a doll's house? Nora lived in a doll house. Dare never grew up to that and I see this at least 60-year-old woman, her long blond hair, 20-inch waist, dressed like a doll, an exquisite one, surrounded by her beautiful apartment, all of it a stage setting, and I don't want to see it crumble, it would be too cruel." For Dare, she concluded, it seemed only death could provide relief from the fears and anxieties that a world without Edie provoked in her.

But it was Blaine who died next, in 1985, at the age of seventy-three.

Dare's descent, triggered by Edie's death, gathered steam with Blaine's. "You know," she'd tell Jeanne Frank, "life is getting so real."

No bears were coming to care for her now that her mother and brother had disappeared. Maybe the bears would have understood. Her friends certainly didn't. Twice, they arranged her admission to Smithers, an alcoholic treatment center on East Ninety-third Street. Both times she escaped, running the thirteen blocks home, once barefoot and wearing only a white nightgown.

Dare withdrew. For a time, those who had known her the longest still tried to visit, but she made it difficult. When her mother's lawyer,

Allan Hull, in whose Cleveland law office still hangs a full-length portrait of Dare and a surreal painting of Dare's left eye, came to visit, she couldn't unlock the door. He had to borrow a screwdriver to take it off its hinges.

One of her last visitors was Vincent Youmans. She did let him in, but he was not sure she even recognized him. When he handed her a bunch of anemones, her favorite flower, she accepted the bouquet, smiled, and threw it in the trash can.

Having banned or been abandoned by her old friends, she was lonely, and would roam the streets and Central Park looking for new ones. Not surprisingly, the vagrants she found there played too rough, so she eventually retreated back home.

There, on her living-room couch, she neatly lined up photographs of Edith, Ivan, and Philip. Seating herself in an armchair opposite, she would talk to the "friends" who could no longer hurt—or really help—her.

"Sometimes she would talk to a photograph of Philip all day long," said the nurse Brook hired to care for her in 1987. To her mother's photograph she would say "Edie, Edie, Edie" over and over again. To one of her father she would say simply: "Why, why, why?"

In 1994, she suffered respiratory failure while undergoing medical tests. She would never again be able to breathe on her own and has been hospitalized at a long-term-care facility ever since.

I have visited her there, immobile, tucked tightly into bed, her waxen head propped up on pillows, her arms resting on her stomach. A tube comes out of her throat, hooked up to a network of clanking machines.

She is still beautiful even in this hideous circumstance. She is Edith, the horror-story version: the gold hoop earrings, the high ponytail gathered to one side, ending in a long, yellowing white braid, now under the spell of yet another evil wizard. If her former nurse has been there, a teddy bear is always placed in the crook of each arm. An ambulatory patient there proposed marriage.

When *The Lonely Doll* was reissued, I brought her a copy, which I read aloud to her on each visit, holding the book so she can see the photographs. What she actually hears, or sees, is impossible to know. But if I glance at her face while I read, a look of childlike wonderment has come over it. From the moment I hold up the book's cover, her mouth breaks open into her widest smile.

POSSUM LIVING
David Gates

I found Do l l y Freed's *Possum Living* (Universe Books, 1978) in the attic of the fixer-upper farmhouse I bought in 1985, along with a stack of Sunset books on such topics as building decks and preserving vegetables. The previous owners had been utopians, too. Its grocery-bag brown covers and faux-typewriter typeface fit the post-hippie, Carter-era gestalt suggested by the subtitle: "How to Live Well Without a Job and with [the next word almost careted in] No Money." It advocates a life of quasi-Beckettian simplicity: foraging in supermarket Dumpsters, burning scrap wood and dead branches in woodstoves homemade from oil drums, raising rabbits in the basement ("We take close to 300 pounds of meat out of that cellar per year"). What makes all this refreshing is Freed's utter lack of high-mindedness. "We live this way for a very simple reason: It's easier to learn to do without some of the things that money can buy than to earn the money to buy them. . . . So if you're thinking spiritual or sociological thoughts, don't waste your time with me."

Supposedly Freed was nineteen years old when she wrote this, living with her divorced father, a.k.a. the Old Fool, in a Philadelphia suburb. Here and there she gives glimpses of a rancorous, downwardly mobile, borderline-violent milieu like that of her contemporary Raymond Carver. "A friend of ours," she notes in passing, in a chapter on "everyday nitty-gritty law," "lost his cool and threatened his wife's lawyer in open court." She goes on to advise better methods of bringing an "adversary" to reason: "Visit his house late at night and do something to let him know he has an enemy who has no intention of playing the game by his rules." Among Freed's broad hints: cut his phone line, poison his dog. The dark stories she never quite tells and her evenhanded contempt both for the culture of acquisition and consumption and for ecopuritan ideology make *Possum Living* one of the out-of-control classics of American cantankerousness, like *Walden, ABC of Economics, Steal This Book!*, and *The Closing of the American Mind*. It directly inspired parts of my first novel, *Jernigan*: my protagonist's girlfriend raises bunnies and reads a magazine called *Suburban Survivalist*. I credited *Possum Living* in my acknowledgments, but never heard from Dolly Freed. That was back in 1991; both my dog and my phone line are still okay.

SEX AND THE SINGLE SQUIRREL
Elissa Schappell

I have been a lot of very different people in my life—a cheerleader and a coke fiend, a good daughter and a bad girl, an exhibitionist and a shut-in, a religious seeker and a nihilist. It is my sickness that I can imagine doing, or being, just about anything. This is complicated by the desire to infiltrate the lives of people much unlike myself, to see how they really live. How else to explain why I would willfully dress up in a raccoon suit and let strangers grope me?

Unlike a true "furrie," I don't feel that my best and truest self can be expressed only through an animal alter ego, through sexual or non-sexual role-playing online or in person, perhaps through the adoption of furry ears or a tail, or a full fur suit. I don't have to an intense spiritual connection to the animal world, and despite an erotic fondness in my girlhood for a sheepskin rug, I have never had a carnal urge to *possess* a stuffed animal—or, not yet.

For the Anthrocon Furries of Myth and Legend convention at the King of Prussia Hilton, located just miles from the scenic battlefields of Gettysburg, I have chosen to make my debut into the "furric fandom" as Miss Trixie, enchantress of the night. I am fabulous in my rented raccoon fur suit, which appears to have been crafted out of a 1970s midpile brown-and-black-striped shag carpet.

Furrie fans have come from all over the United States, as well as Canada and Australia, to rub shoulders and noses with other lovers of Sierra Club calendars and Sonic the Hedgehog video games, not to mention their online furrie sex partners and chat room confidantes. They've come for the furrie workshops like "fursuit dancing" and "fursuit sewing," roundtables on "furrie spirituality," furrie drawing classes, an erotic furrie art auction, and more. The furrie set is vast, encompassing many worlds: there are also sci-fi aficionados, computer wizards, Renaissance folk, gaylaxians, nerds, cat people, dog people, erotic-art fans, born-again Christians, lovers of parade balloons, shamans, healers, animal rights activists, bikers, and curiosity seekers.

I have chosen Trixie, or Trixie has chosen me, because we share certain personality quirks. Like the Kinko's employee I met who was a wolf—loyal, dangerous, a loner—or the substitute teacher who was a panther—sleek, brave, and feared—I, like raccoons, have a fondness for the dark and for dramatic eye makeup, plus a jones for spying on the neighbors, inciting the kind of commotion that causes people to throw on their robe and grab a flashlight. Trixie, masked and mysterious, like desire itself, plays to all my worst voyeuristic tendencies. Hidden behind her face I can move undetected, in the darkness of my suit, taking in all the action around me. It is hot in my head, and my breathing is heavy, echoing disconcertingly in my ears. It's the same sound you hear in slasher movies, the frantic panting of the stalked ingenue hiding in a closet watching the killer, chain saw slung across his back, sniff her panties. Or maybe it's the other way around. Indeed, aren't I the crazed maniac hidden in the shadows, just waiting for my moment to pounce?

Certainly I do not look scary. Sadly, I am not regulation human-raccoon size, so the suit hangs on my shoulders and bags around my ankles, giving me a kind of hip-hop rodent look. My head is a huge plaster cast, fitted inside with what looks like a welder's helmet. All breathing is done through a narrow slit scarcely big enough to accommodate a cocktail straw, and through my big, sexy, heavily lashed eyes, which are made of mesh. Trixie's wide-spaced eyes are cute, but render me walleyed. I keep bumping into people and furniture, paws out feeling for the walls, like a drunk in a Beatrix Potter book. I catch glimpses of people in bunny and tiger ears, and others wearing bear, iguana, and fox tails. But I have yet to see another fur suit.

The mood in the hotel lounge is that of a homecoming reunion. Clearly, judging from the all the snuggling and canoodling going on in the lounge, the delighted yips and coos of recognition, most haven't laid eyes or paws on one another in months. And, unlike at home, where no one suspects that the junior lawyer likes to dress up like a wolf and crash through the forests with other guys dressed as wolves, here they can be out. *We're here, we're deer, get used to it.*

For others, it's the first time they've met snout to snout, and so there is the requisite uneasiness at discovering Big Big Ben is a petite Jewish woman who wears glasses, and that Kitten with a Whip is not a bossy dominatrix but an obese and meek manager of a health-food store who rode twenty hours on a bus to be here. It intrigues me that there is so much psychic fallout when you find out that the online partner with whom you have been engaging in frisky fun isn't the gender you imagined them to be. That a person doesn't mind having virtual sex with another species, but doesn't want that person to *not* be of their gender, or to *be* of their gender, seems odd. Oh, the slippery machinations of lust.

In the lounge there is a bulletin board on which people leave messages searching for furrie friends, offering hugs, or noting who gives the best back rubs in Canada. Stuffed animals are in abundance. I recognize some men I saw in the lobby earlier, middle-aged, solid industrious types, buttoned-down Republicans, I'd guess. The Willie Lomans of the animal kingdom, here they are talking animatedly about hikes they've recently taken and books they've read, petting the stuffed badgers and otters they hold in their laps like children.

While many furries carry and love stuffed animals, most are quick to distance themselves from the "plushies," also referred to as "Gundies," "plushisexuals," or "stuffies," whom they consider a subspecies of furrie. Plushies are folks whose primary preference for sexual satisfaction is *boinking* stuffed animals. Their motto: *In Plush We Thrust.*

Not unlike other feared or misunderstood minorities, plushies have developed a vernacular all their own. See if you can follow: You're feeling *yiffy*, so you've lit musk-scented candles and put *The Chipmunks Do Barry White* on the stereo, because tonight is the night you and Paddington are finally going to *boink*. Tonight, Paddington gets *baptized*. Paddington is a *talented plushie*, meaning you won't have to open up a seam to create an *SPH (strategically placed hole)*, in which one could insert an *SPA (strategically placed appendage)*. Paddington can pose with its legs spread and its ass in the air, *begging*. All day at the office you can't stop fantasizing about Paddington's *boink-space*, the place on the plushie that is the most rewarding and enjoyable to *poke*. One of the great things about plush sex partners is you never have to send them flowers or call them the next day! Which is good, because this morning, walking past FAO, you got a *plush-rush* just seeing the new plump Gund bunnies— tomorrow after your lunch hour two saucy Flopsy bunnies will be yours. Can you say *plushgasm? Buy pairs for spares*. Did I mention *plush lovers* never get jealous? Your biggest concern is the carpet burns on your crotch.

Later that night, after Paddington is asleep, sweet dear, you feel *yiffy* again. It's only nine so you drag Piglet out of the closet. Piglet, the old whore, is *plushphile gray*. While *plushplunging* Piglet you grab his *handlebars*, meaning you are gripping his arms or legs in order to *give a meal* or a *gift* to Piglet. Soon Piglet will have to be *retired*, seeing as he's almost too worn and soiled with *spooge* to be a regular partner. Give me Gundies or Give Me Death!

Okay, weird, but is it any weirder than what "mundanes" (non-furries) do? What furries disdainfully refer to as *meat sex*?

A downside to wearing the fur suit is the fact that I have to keep drinking water to keep hydrated, and thus have to keep taking off my suit to go to the bathroom. Washing my hands in the sink, I happen to find myself sink to sink with a dominatrix skunk in fishnets, high heels, a black bodysuit provocatively pinned together with safety pins, and the coup de grace: a black thong *over* the bodysuit.

"Great outfit," I say, taking in her ensemble, the gloves, the whip.

"I have to have someone feed me my french fries," the sex skunk says, reapplying red lipstick. "Not that it's a problem."

"Of course," I say, drying my hands. She looked like a real pro. I'd read about a furrie convention in Los Angeles where they sold animal dildos, horses, cows, and best of all—the corkscrewed meat muscle of a pig. I wonder if she might know about such a thing. That would be something to see: I wonder what it would be called: *The Porker? The Happy Hambone?*

"Hey," I say, as off-handedly as possible. "You look like you might know the answer to a question—um, do you know where—*if*—they sell sex toys here?"

She looks annoyed. "I am a pissed-off skunk, low on money."

"Oh, I'm sorry," I say. Then, "See, what I am looking for is a kind of dildo." She stares at me like I am an idiot. "Um," I say, "a pig dildo—do you know if they even exist?"

The skunk just looks at me and shakes her head with disgust. "Here? I don't think so." *She* looks at *me*, Miss Trixie, with disdain. Her? The polecat slut! Then it occurs to me that she thinks I am one of those despised zoophiles, who actually engage in intercourse with animals. A minuscule and dark subculture of furries I hesitate to even mention.

Before I can explain or offer some obviously spurious excuse—*It's not for me, it's for a friend*—she bolts. I suppose I should be thankful the bitch can't spray.

Outside I walk slowly and gingerly. I could take off my head and see just fine, but I cannot. If the fur suits could be said to have a philosophy, it would be: *Don't take off your head.* Don't take off your head or you will scare the crap out of some kid. Mindful of the innocent, furrie is about fantasy, trust, and play. In truth, no one wants to see my face. *I* am not important, what matters is my animal other—my own best self, the most me part of me—*Trixie.* The fun-loving, happy-go-lucky little troublemaker. The furries want to *know* Trixie, they want to *play* with Trixie. But mostly, it seems, they want to *hug* Trixie.

I hear them before I see them. "Ohhh, how cute!" they cry, and then appear like a pack before me. "Do you like hugs?" someone says.

I freeze, as if in the headlights of a barreling school bus.

At first I can't tell how many there are. But I think I make out four, perhaps five, large, docile, flour-white strangers wearing soft-soled shoes, with plushy teddy bears snuggled inside their overalls. I panic as they move in for the hug, a giant squeeze. I can see polar bear key chains girdling a man's waist, pins that announce: I ♥ BEAR HUGS, and EVERY TIME A MUNDANE DIES A FURRY GETS ITS WINGS. Off balance, I'm overwhelmed by claustrophobia. My breathing echoes in my ears, like in *2001*. *Open the pod bay doors, HAL* . . . and my head rises up off my shoulders. I can't even run—my ankle is still tender from my slip in the garage last night. I am close to shrieking when, as quickly as they appeared, the gang of huggers tuck off with a kindly wave.

I rush to the "fursuit walking" class. My brothers in furs are lined up against the wall as if at an obedience school mixer. While I am grateful to see my fellow fur suits, I am also a little alarmed. It isn't the big red dog who earlier was posing for a drawing class, or the uncostumed French boy with winged-back hair chatting up a man who is a dead ringer for the guy who slices cheese in our deli. It's the hyenas.

Instead of wearing a huge plaster head like me, the hyenas (I think they are cousins) have affixed long latex snouts to their faces, wear fangs, and have painted their faces with red, orange, and black face paint. They've also glued realistic brown and orangey fur to their arms and legs. Their feet, in Birkenstocks, flaunt their black toenails. Their necks strain against their leather collars. They remind me of the ubiquitous tubby guy at football games who has painted his torso in his team's colors, the logo scrawled across his poochy man breasts.

They look me over hungrily; my heart beats fast. They are predators, right? The worst kind, they even eat dead things! In costume or out of costume, you can just tell.

I am thrilled and repulsed at the same time. I don't think I'd like to be ravaged by dogs, or at least not these dogs.

Our teacher, a tall lithe man in black ballet shoes, calls us into four lines and sends us across the floor in pairs. Our first walk is a rocking side-to-side march where we swing our arms like jolly teddy bears. I try not to look at my fellow furries, to just stay in my "Trixie head," but I can't help it. I'm embarrassed and uptight. I'm not a gamboling teddy bear, I am a spaz. My hands fly up to steady my rocking head at least once every pass. I must look as though I have a toothache, or am reeling in a state of perpetual shock. All these pups for me?!

Nevertheless, those in costume seem to do much better than those in their street clothes. The orthodontists and optometrists, Cub Scout leaders and college debate kings aren't as loose as those of us in character. Some blush, others actually duck out of class while we fur suits ham it up, wiggling our heinies and flapping our arms, giggling out of a mix of freedom and silly embarrassment.

After the regal walk, the hyenas converge on me, just as I feared they would. I press myself flat against the wall. What if they have rabies, or worse, herpes? I catch myself. I have to be cool, *think furrie*. They begin stroking me, petting my arms, and scratching my back. When one of them starts to enthusiastically massage my right breast—advertently or inadvertently—I yip, and sort of wave my paw menacingly at them, baring my teeth. Miraculously, they back away. Despite more than a decade of bumping hips on the New York subway, I find I am squeamish—no, scared—about being touched by strangers. My heart is beating in my mouth, and I can't breathe. They sniff at me curiously. I fight to stay still, reminding myself, *I am Trixie, Trixie, dammit. Trixie is fun loving, Trixie is playful.* The boys peer through my eye holes (truly the windows of the soul) to scope me out. Do they think I am a man or a woman? Does it matter? In desperation, I growl. They growl in return, and snarl, rubbing my ears and nuzzling at my neck with their snouts. I want to scream, but instead growl louder, and they stop and cock their heads with suspicion. My mother's admonition to never pet a strange dog runs through my head. Obviously animals have different personal-space issues—strange dogs pile up together and lick each other's balls; squirrels cram into hollow trees like frat boys in a telephone booth. I am just waiting for someone to actually bite me.

I have to confess, I have always been a biter. Always. Even now, I occasionally want to bite people, out of anger, desire, fondness. Sometimes I do. Years ago, when I heard that Sylvia Plath had, the first time she met Ted Hughes, bit him, I took it as evidence that biting was a sign of genius—not just lunacy. I saw a wolf in the lobby earlier. I think I'd like him to bite me. I know, though, that I do not wish to bite or be bitten by these foul hyenas.

The highlight of the "fursuit dancing" class comes when our teacher, Coco, the portly mascot of the Hershey, Pennsylvania, hockey team, announces, "A time may come when you want to go to a furrie dance, or a furrie rave, or at some time you might wish to slow-dance with your heart's desire."

Absolutely. While I've adopted the Pogo as the official dance of raccoons, if tonight at the furrie ball, the opportunity to get down with a sulky wolf-boy or a buff gargoyle arose, would I not want to be ready? Or what about my "fursuit walking" teacher, who has, for this class, slipped into his tiger suit?

"Everybody find a partner," Coco says.

Everyone pairs up quickly, leaving me, the only girl, alone. Spurned, I am forced to ask Le Tigre to dance with me. He nods his assent, though it is clear that dancing with a raccoon, and worse yet, a girl, is beneath his station. It's all so Jane Eyre!

Despite being a decent dancer, I plod all over Tiger's big, expensive padded feet. "Dip me," I whisper, "dip me"—after all, I *am* a lady. Reluctantly, halfheartedly, he does so, which is good, as I have to grab my head to keep it from rolling across the floor. For our last dance Coco calls us all into the middle of the floor and instructs us to hold hands in a circle around him. "Know your limits," he warns us. "It's hard to dance with big feet and get funky."

As the song "I'm Too Sexy" begins to shake the room, we set off in a manic ring-around-the-rosy around Coco as he spins, grinds his hips, does the Travolta point, and whirls, then he tags one of the boys. "This is your chance," he yells over the music, "to just go wild and crazy. No one is going to judge you here!"

Indeed, we cavort wildly. Like a bunch of schoolgirls hopped up on Baby Ruths and RC, we circle fast, fast, faster, while shrieking, *I'm too sexy for my shirt, too sexy!!!* When I am finally tagged for the solo (last of course) I don't care, I go wild in the center. I am the masked mistress in the cage. I am go-go coon.

The Furrie Ball is the highlight of the first day. By day's end I am starting to get used to people grinning at me, looking me up and down, and taking my picture. I pose like a Vargas girl and I wave coquettish as the calendar girl sexpot I once dreamed of being. I *am special*, after all; I am a living plush toy. Probably never in my whole life have so many people wanted to get into my pants and had no idea, or even cared particularly, who I was, literally, inside.

I spot a couple who'd taken my picture earlier. They seem to be furrie connoisseurs of some kind, although they don't wear costumes themselves. Instead, with their longish, frowsy hair, purple-and-turquoise natural-fiber scarves, and hemp clothing, they look like people who run a candle shoppe and make their own cheese.

"Hi," the man of the couple says.

"Mrow," I say. I go back and forth between making what I can only imagine to be raccoon noises and actually speaking.

"Ooh, what happened to your tail?" the man says, turning me around so he can ogle at my butchered bottom. I had hoped no one would notice that my tail was missing. But perhaps it's a turn-on.

All day long no one has mentioned it, and now, suddenly, right before the dance, it's all about the look. I knew it.

"Farmer cut it off with a shovel," I say. They seem nice enough. The man winces, then laughs. "Uh-huh," he says.

"Must have hurt," the woman says, moving her dark hair away from her face. She licks her lips and laughs.

"Terribly," I say. Not to flatter myself, but I think they're flirting with me. They're both looking at me in the way people do just before they kiss.

"Want to come sit with us?" the man says, gesturing at a recently vacated couch. I wonder how much animal hair is in that upholstery. The girlfriend leans in to me and begins caressing my shoulder. I let her.

"It'd be fun," the woman says, dropping her head on to my shoulder.

"Maybe later," I say, suddenly nervous. "I am looking for a friend, a mouse, or maybe he's more of a mole. Have you seen him?"

They both shrug, it's all casual. Why can't I be more casual?

"We'll look for you," the woman calls out as I scurry away. I'm embarrassed at how flustered I am, then later, am miffed that my first real invitation to join a threesome has come while I am in Trixie. After they leave, I think, *I could have a threesome in a raccoon suit, right?* It's a titillating idea. For me, the whole add-a-lover dynamic has seemed overwhelming and vaguely hilarious; an orgy is just one step away from hairy naked people building human pyramids. I know I would laugh, but in Trixie, as Trixie, wouldn't that all be okay?

When the ballroom doors open, eager furries pour through the doors. Inside it's dark and rainbows bounce off a large disco ball. A friendly coyote hands out Cyalume sticks, and I am thankful to have something to do with my hands. No one smokes. No one drinks, unless of course they've poured rum into the Coke cans. It's murder. Inside, a cheery, older, bland-looking British gentleman I imagine to be a podiatrist or a vicar nods to me. Poking out of the top of his Sansabelt trousers is an appallingly worn-looking Elmo doll. Elmo appears to be in either ecstasy or great distress, or both. I can see it now, the gotta-have Christmas gifts of 2003—*Come on My Face Elmo* and his pal *Bend Over Grover.*

I cannot tolerate the strobe lights, so I close my eyes to dance. I think perhaps this is a good thing, perhaps I will be more graceful undistracted by undulating furries. I enter the throng and manage a jaunty, lead-footed Rex Harrison sort of jig. I attempt the jolly Winnie-the-Pooh-style fanny shake we practiced in class today but lose my footing, staggering blindly into the crowd. I scan the crowd for Coco. *Oh, Coco where are you? Rescue me from Old MacDonald's mosh pit!*

Suddenly I am so tired I am staggering under the weight of my head and I have to go to bed.

I share the elevator upstairs with a guy who is wearing parachute pants engorged with Beanie Babies. In fact, his pants are so weighted down with Beanie Babies he is danger of losing them. I recall a chat board where people swapped stories of wearing Swampy and Mystic in their underwear like furry ben-wa balls when they went to work.

Back in my room I shuck off Trixie and lay her carefully across an armchair, her head facing me. I brush her fur and examine her for spills, stains, gum. I am starting to feel attached to her. I fall asleep that night counting Beanie Babies struggling over a fence. Good night, Cuddles, good night, Sparky.

I start my morning in the Dealer's Den, a treasure trove of furrie collectibles and goodies, comics, art, and toys. At first glance it looks like any convention, with your average-looking joes in Coke-bottle glasses hunched over cases of classic comics, the occasional dude in camouflage selling war medals and postcards. Upon closer inspection you notice that almost all the comics feature animals or stuffed animals—even the erotic art and porn. Whether it's *Oui* or *Blueboy*, whether one prepares for a date by gluing faux fur to one's body and slipping on a dog collar, or splashing on Canoe and slipping into a pin-striped suit, clearly humans are keyed to react to the same kind of stimuli. We are pretty consistent in what turns us on—the only real difference I see between furrie porn and human porn is that furrie porn has more of a sense of humor. Witness a *Gulliver's Travels* gang bang: a chained lion overwhelmed by an army of sadistic Beanie Babies wielding studded dildos. In another pictorial a teddy bear is exploded by the force of a fox's jism.

Of course, there is the traditional locker room fantasy featuring a huge killer whale with a killer hard-on, preparing to snap a towel at the ass of a smaller, but equally endowed, baby beluga whale fairly dripping with innocence. Then there are the ubiquitous soft-core spreads—the sort of layouts celebrities do in *Playboy*. There are rabbits in naughty negligees. There is a slinky, pink-nippled mouse bathing in a martini glass—very forties—and besotted squids and octopuses doing things only eight-armed creatures versed in the Kama Sutra can do. There's Rudolph in the midst of a seven-reindeer orgy; a wide-eyed reindeer lass in bells being taken from behind by a creature who appears part lion, part wolf, the gift tag around her neck reads

Don't Wait Until Christmas, while another reindeer, alone on a tropical beach, looks shocked as wild dogs go down on her. Don't you hate it when that happens? There are foxes with pierced nipples chained to walls, and a mouse engaging in autoerotic asphyxiation with a giant boa constrictor—a little something for everyone.

The implications of interspecies sex are amazing. Forget a utopian society where every human marries someone of another race—imagine dogs and cats living together in sin. In fact, not surprisingly, there are also domestic-bliss shots, drawings fit for a close-mated couple's Christmas card, such as the portrait of two middle-aged male huskies sharing a pizza and a six-pack. It might just as well read *Season's Greetings, Larry and Carl.*

I peek my head into the Diversity in Fandom meeting long enough to get the gist of the anti-mundane patter. The discussion is being led by Trickster, a twenty-something guy whose long dark hair hangs down to the middle of his back. I recognize him as the wolf boy I was lusting after earlier in the lobby. He's all in black, including, of course, a black dog collar.

"I see people in the fandom who are not dealing with mundanes," says a man in a tie-dyed T-shirt and a studded collar. Some people nod.

"Fuck that, we should isolate ourselves from the outside world," quips one of the men who earlier established himself as being particularly well versed in the human-genome-trans-humanism business; part of the fandom clings to the dream that one day the DNA of animals will be successfully grafted to that of humans, allowing the creation of a true race of lizardmen.

There are murmurs of agreement.

"Hey, on the whole we are more accepting than the general population," he reminds us. Which seems true, overall—maybe this is why I like them.

In closing, Trickster reminds everyone, "When you talk to mundanes, be nice. After all, mundanes are the future furries."

*   *   *

I am so hungry I could eat an entire can of garbage. On my way to the snack bar I stop into a meeting of "The Herd," which is being led by two cowboys, one outfitted with sinister-looking gold incisors. Some of the men in the group hold homemade or mail-order hooves in their laps, or stroke horse tails, silently nodding as the cowboy talks as if to a bunch of reluctant alcoholics at their first meeting.

"I don't wear tack and stuff," says the cowboy they call Whitehorse. "I'm not that tacky. I think it's a fetish. And, I get my manes from a hitching post. I don't want to think where it comes from," he says, "but isn't it better for the horse to be another new horse instead?"

The men nod.

"Listen, guys, this is all about building friendships," Whitehorse reminds the Herd. "After all, we're all horses."

I am getting better at walking and balancing my head. On my way to the lounge I can even lower my arms almost completely to my sides. I still can't turn my head, or really ascertain where my body is in space, but I can walk confidently in a straight line. I am forced to stop and turn my head, though, when I hear the loud, coarse peal of a woman's laughter nearby. Sitting at a table are three people. On one side is a nervous and emaciated little man with a sad frizz of coppery red hair and a lion T-shirt. Across the table is one of those classically cute nice guys whom girls only want to be friends with. Beside him, in his lap really, is a big-boned blonde in a white tiger suit. She nuzzles and nips at the guy beside her in a way that is unabashedly, desperately carnal. No one in the lounge can keep their eyes off her; it's like seeing someone hitting their children in public or watching a minor fender bender that could at any moment escalate into someone pulling a gun.

She is dangerous, and because I am not me I stride right over and say, "You are so beautiful, you could make Siegfried and Roy weep."

The tigress turns her attention away from the man and onto me.

"Well, hello," she says, sitting up straight. "I'm Tigress."

"You're gorgeous," I say. The red-haired man nods in agreement, beaming at Tigress, and then it dawns on me that in fact she is his wife.

"Sit down," she says, pointing to the spot beside her husband. I sit down carefully.

Both of them are wearing wedding bands, and while the lion husband is trying to seem nonchalant that his wife is nibbling this other man's ear, he fidgets, swallowing and stammering, and trying on occasion to get her attention by reaching out and stroking her arm—which she ignores.

"Male lions have sex like two hundred times," she says with a laugh. "Twice a month, and then nothing." She rolls her eyes. "Nothing." Her little lion husband attempts a faint smile and shrugs. "What do you expect?"

The taking of many sexual partners—having sex whenever you feel like it and with whomever you feel like it, regardless of species—is for some furries the most appealing feature of the furrie lifestyle. After all, most animals aren't monogamous. Sure, swans and scarlet macaws and some apes may mate for life, but as for remaining sexually true? Ha. Not to imply that all furries are horndogs—no, many are happily *close-mated*, but neither is necessarily the only one the other will mount.

Suddenly, I lock eyes with another raccoon. The first I've seen! And it's a boy! Ranger Rick is dark and pretty in a tight, striped top and black shorts, and he, he has a tail! A big long bushy one. I swoon. Instinctively my hand flies back to touch my stumpy rear, ashamed, thinking, for a moment, that I feel a tingle in the spot.

I excuse myself and stride right over to him and introduce myself. "Hello," I say in my most chipper Miss Trixie lilt, and lay a paw on his shoulder as though we'd been kits together, nestling in a log, not so very long ago.

"Hi," he says politely. "Can I take your picture?"

"Sure," I say and pose like Betty Page. I can suddenly imagine Polaroids of me as Miss Trixie at the center of a furrie circle jerk, and I shudder with a mix of horror and delight.

"So, you want to get together?" I ask. I am Miss Trixie, I am bewitched by her magic. I am one brazen raccoon.

Ranger Rick looks surprised. "I'm sorry?" he says.

"I mean, you want to go outside, run around," I say, "do some crimes? Maybe tip over some garbage cans? Play chicken on the highway . . ."

He laughs uncomfortably. "Maybe, uh, later."

I feel so ridiculous standing there in my little rented suit. Maybe if I had a nice suit, a good suit, he'd like me more. He just had to get to know me.

"Sure, later," I say, my face burning red. "Of course, okay."

As I walk away I think, Thank God he couldn't see my face! Then I start to feel aggrieved, for Trixie's sake. I wish I'd said, *Listen, pal, there are plenty of people here who'd kill for some Trixie loving! How many people have come on to you?*

Well, I suppose he could sort of count me.

I'm starting to feel depressed, and it's hot and stuffy in my head, so I head outside to get some air. It's clear and dark, but not too dark to spot a gang of previously meek-looking furries furiously beating a pile of beanbags with sticks, as though the beanbags had enraged them. Later I learn that these "beanbag rats" are created solely for this sort of abuse. I think I could do with a few of them, if only to defuse sexual energy.

When I return, the Costume Ball has begun. It isn't really a ball, in that there is no dancing, only a show and a photo op with the entertainers (furries love a photo op).

It quickly becomes clear that the appeal of most of the skits—dogs joyously, awkwardly rocking out to "Let's Hear It for the Boy"—is of spying on someone gleefully boogying down in their rec room. *Kick out the jams, Curious George!* The crowd erupts when the belly-dancing cats—about as exotic as hummus—begin their sweet gyrations, then grows silent when a dour warthog in green army fatigues skulks onstage, the scene darkens, and he goes into a creepy lip-synched rendition of the Doors' "The End." Afterward, I am actually happy to watch a pair of spunky foxes in spandex and headbands aerobicize to "Let's Get Physical."

Everyone in the audience is enjoying themselves, clapping or singing along, two-stepping with their stuffed animals, just living it up. The chemistry changes as soon as the cowboys from the Herd group appear onstage. The cowboy with the golden teeth leads out his buddy "Whitehorse" and chews out the horse for losing a race, calling him terrible things. When the cowboy turns his back, Whitehorse steals his lariat and lassos him, or rather attempts to lasso him—it must have worked in practice a hundred times, but this time the lariat has gotten caught on the cowboy's ear. After a terrible second, the crowd begins laughing, and you can just feel the man inside the suit seething. After he finally manages to disentangle the rope from his head, he attacks his buddy, knocks him down, and in ten seconds flat has him hog-tied. The room is silent, the rage and humiliation scarily acute.

For the finale, a drag queen, Lola Bunny, appears like a cartoon Venus. She is a vision in her purple microminiskirt, tight pink sweater (balloons pinned on for tits), and black fishnets. Lola would bring down the house regardless of who she followed, but the release of tension from the cowboys' masochistic miniplay makes her act the perfect climax for the conference. If I could remove my panties and fling them on the stage, I would happily surrender them.

As Lola begins to croon "Fever," her hips all aswivel, the crowd becomes unhinged, standing on their chairs, waving their stuffed animal pals, some screaming, "I love you!" I feel gleeful. After the show, people swarm around me taking pictures, and then the music comes on again, and we all start to dance. I dance the way you can only when no one you know is watching. I dance like I shall never dance again, for this is the last time I shall ever dance as Trixie.

This is what I remember when I am back at the costume shop with Trixie lying limp in my arms like a swooning lover. I have put off returning her for two weeks, and now have no choice but to either rent her again for a month or say goodbye. I don't completely understand my reaction. It isn't that I have a profound desire to zip her skin up over mine and become her: I don't. There is just something—the freedom the suit gives me, the idea that I will never be Trixie again— that strikes me as so sad, and I think, as I hand over her skin, that I just might cry.

ARACHNOPHILIA
Panagiotis Gianopoulos

During the year that I wore a Spider-Man mask—to kindergarten, to the movie theater, to climb our neighbor's red maple trees—there were only two photographs of me taken. I would blame this remarkably low number on shyness except that I've never been shy; instead the responsibility lies with my parents' longing to believe that they had a brighter, more normal child, a boy who didn't steal keys, or dance on the jukebox to Devo's "Whip It," or invite himself to strangers' tables and start eating their dinner—"It's okay, I brought my own fork."

The first photograph shows a standard pose: I'm standing beside my older sister, who is tall and rakish in a lime green Woodstock snow cap, and I'm glowering with a mix of heroic menace and a desire for ice cream. The second photograph, also with my sister, reveals us seated behind the wheel of my father's pickup truck. The picture should be titled "Luckily Spider-Man Isn't Driving"—not only because I was just five years old, but because I could barely see. The mask was huge, adult-sized, with roomy eyeholes that continually slipped down my cheeks and blinded me.

It wasn't a mask so much as a big red hood, crisscrossed with spidery black lines and cut straight across the bottom. It looked as if I'd emptied a bag of Doritos and placed my head inside. As childhood oddities go, this might not have been so terrible, considering the local competition: Jason Rouleau was eating beetles, Brad Farnier was grabbing electrical fences, and Doug Koombis claimed to be sleeping with his mother. And then there was Mark Ellis, who actually did stuff a bag of Doritos over his head once, but I don't think that counts, because he was making fun of me.

Like most boys I was something between eager and stupid, but unlike Jason and Brad—let's ignore Doug, as I hope his mother did when he snuggled with exceptional vigor—I didn't wear the mask to get attention. I wore it because I was Spider-Man. How I was both Spider-Man and a tiny unathletic Greek boy never challenged my upbeat brand of logic. It perplexed my parents, however, two kind baffled immigrants who loved me despite my personality, the only kind of love I trust. Routinely, they asked me to take the mask off for church.

"People will know my secret identity!" I screamed.

"Oh, they know who you are," my mother said.

"Our son." My father sighed.

"You'll be in danger!" I warned. "They'll use you to get at me. Like hostages."

"No one will hurt you," my father said, and squeezed my shoulder.

"Dad, the Vulture can *fly*. What are you gonna do against a flier?" Today I regret this lack of confidence in my father, not just because the Vulture is a fictional character, but even if he weren't, my father could defeat the Vulture simply by staying inside the house and watching television. Spider-Man was always dumb enough to venture outside when the Vulture was around, and so he always ended up dangling from the Vulture's ankle in midair and being slammed into a billboard. It was Spider-Man's magnificent lack of strategy that partly endeared him to me; he made the grossest, most ridiculous mistakes, and not only was he incapable of learning from them, but like me, it never occurred to him that perhaps he ought to. (Spider-Man isn't the only superhero unable to learn from his mistakes. Most superheroes suffer from this disability. What superheroes really need is a coach, someone who will review their past experiences and dispense valuable advice, like "Don't follow the Sandman to the beach" or "Any time you attend a black-tie charity function, expect trouble.")

It had been almost twenty years since I stopped picking up spiders in the hopes that they would bite me and pass on superpowers, since I had ceased wishing that my (as yet imaginary) girlfriend would call me Tiger the way Spider-Man's girlfriend Mary Jane did, nearly two decades after I had taken off my mask—the mask that might now finally fit my head—when I bought an adult-sized spandex Spider-Man costume. The excuse I gave myself was that I had a Halloween party to attend and I was tired of dressing as a vampire, or Indiana Jones, or Zorro, but the truth is that I had been longing to buy the costume for years, and I had resisted the urge out of a combination of good taste and the urge to protect my fragile psychological integrity.

As I unwrapped the clingy blue-and-red costume in my apartment, draping it against my chest and bare arms and posing in the full-length mirror, I deliberated whether to wear it to the party after all. The pros were many: I could climb fire escapes, do handstands, jump on couches, and shout "Thwip!" as I sprayed aerosol string in strangers' faces. And physically I was a perfect match; Spider-Man's alter ego, Peter Parker, and I were both five-ten, with short brown hair, brown eyes, and a slender to wiry build. (Spider-Man's musculature depends upon the whims of the illustrator, while mine depends upon working out, which is directly related to my romantic status and that rather unreliable commodity called will to live.)

The cons to wearing the costume were fewer but significant: it entailed acute genital exhibitionism, and it wouldn't impress women. Women like Batman. Batman is handsome, suave, and passionately driven. Batman is also a millionaire.

You'd be lucky to get a six-dollar bottle of wine from Spider-Man. He is continually behind on his rent. He has no health insurance—an important asset for a vigilante. His boss, a splenetic newspaper editor, pays Peter only for photographs of Spider-Man being beaten up or causing public damage, since he has a personal vendetta against Spider-Man (something to do with the newspaper editor's son, an astronaut, being turned into a werewolf or something . . . I forget). Thus if Spider-Man is triumphing, Peter is starving—a handsome formula for self-hatred. And the bad press Peter haplessly provides Spider-Man ensures that the police often shoot at him as he's handing them a captured criminal. (I used Spider-Man's eternal "It's not what it looks like!" cry to the police with equal inefficacy with my mother. To her credit, she never fired live rounds at me.)

Behaviorally self-destructive, impoverished, misunderstood, rooming for years in his aunt May's house, Spider-Man hardly seems worth admiring, let alone emulating at a Halloween party. Yet along with his peerless wit—sarcasm is an alarmingly rare commodity among people who stroll around in public dressed in colorful spandex and give themselves names like Electro and Molecule Man—his unassuming qualities are precisely what account for his relentless popularity: the millions of comic books, the multiple cartoon series, the upcoming movie release, his presence on everything from underwear to boxes of lowfat Cheez-Its.

Even the way in which Spider-Man acquired his powers is defiantly unimpressive: not by being adventurous (like the Fantastic Four, who voyaged into space), or by being heroic (like Daredevil, who pushed someone out of the way of a truck), or by being an alien (Superman is from Krypton, a planetary Westchester County where the residents dress like Abba), or even by any exciting birth defect (like the X-Men, mutants who discover they can shoot bolts out of their eyes or chew through steel while other teenagers are shoplifting Oxy-10), but by being a nerd. While attending a weekend science demonstration, Peter Parker is bitten by a dying spider that has accidentally wandered into a radioactive beam. As its radioactive saliva enters his bloodstream, Peter is imbued with the proportional speed, strength, and agility of a spider, as well as some vaguely related other powers, like sticking to walls, and the nonsensical "spider-sense." ("Spider-sense" warns Spider-Man of impending danger, telling him to duck if he is about to be shot, or to jump if the Hulk is going to do something wildly uncharacteristic like throw a tank. "Spider-sense" alone explains why Spider-Man is still alive after almost never evolving his problem-solving strategies to take into account past experience. "Spider-sense" is an absurd power: it's so fine-tuned that merely shaking the hand of a supervillain in disguise can set it off, but if the spider that gave him his powers possessed "spider-sense," why did it wander into the radioactive beam that killed it?)

Spider-Man's response to discovering his powers is in equally refreshing contrast to standard superhero myth: he tries to profit from them. Even at the age of five, this made more sense to me than Superman's unchallenged do-gooderism. Peter disguises his face (the prototypical Spider-Man mask looked like a convenience store robber's panty hose), accepts a wrestling challenge against a bruiser named Crusher Hogan, trounces him easily, and wins the hundred-dollar prize. A television producer in the audience invites him onto *The Ed Sullivan Show*, where his sensational appearance makes him an overnight star. While waiting backstage after the performance, Spider-Man watches a burglar race down the hall, pursued by a policeman shouting for help. Spider-Man lets the burglar run by. The policeman catches up to Spider-Man and asks, "What's with you, mister? All you hadda do was trip him, or hold him just for a minute!"

"Sorry, pal, that's your job. I'm thru being pushed around—by anyone. From now I just look out for Number One—that means—me!"

Unless you're an Ayn Rand enthusiast, you'll concede that this comment begs for dramatic retribution. Spider-Man gets it a week later, when his house is burglarized and his uncle Ben is killed. Spider-Man chases down the murdering burglar, corners him in an old warehouse at the waterfront, and discovers—you don't have to be Joseph Campbell to see this coming—it's the fugitive from the television studio!

Amazingly, Spider-Man doesn't kill the burglar. He doesn't even break his legs. (Spider-Man is middle class, with the middle-class aversion to brutality; he opts for restraining criminals over really hurting them—unlike Batman, an aristocrat, who enjoys driving lower-class faces into brick walls. In Batman's defense, he witnessed thugs murder his parents when he was a child; his behavior is less symbolic of class warfare than an expression of pure psychotic rage. As an adult, I find Spider-Man's light-hearted violence reassuring. He isn't furious, yet he has every right to be. The world is infuriating; you don't need superpowers to recognize this.) No, Spider-Man simply leaves the burglar trussed up in webbing for the cops to find. As he strides away he realizes, ruefully, that "with great power there must also come great responsibility," or more accurately: with great power comes great responsibility, a snug-fitting animal-based costume, and infrequent sex.

Because although Spider-Man can do extraordinary things—balance on one finger, backflip indefinitely, outsmart a Ph.D. with eight metallic arms—his love life is fiercely ordinary. He spends as much time wrestling with girlfriends' expectations as he does with Kraven the Hunter. Whenever shy but cute Peter Parker manages to secure a date, he invariably ruins it by sensing danger and then sprinting away to fight crime. Naturally, Peter's date is insulted by his disappearance, and when he apologizes the next day, it never works, chiefly because he can't come up with a decent excuse. Bulimia, alcoholism, compulsive masturbation, any of these would work better than "I just can't explain," which Peter will whimper as the interior monologue laments: "If only I could tell her that I'm Spider-Man, then she'd understand!" As I grew older, I sympathized more and more with Peter's tragic situation, since I too often vanished (emotionally) just as I was getting close to a girl, and when pressed to explain myself, I would long to blame it on an alter ego—"It's Spider-Man's fault!" Of course, it was always Peter's fault. It always will be.

Spider-Man did fall in love eventually, a few times; he even got married to his longtime redhead sweetheart, Mary Jane—a fact I flirtatiously passed along to a redhead dressed as a sunflower at the Halloween party. The redhead said she could barely hear me and asked me to remove the mask. I raised an eyebrow—uselessly, since facial expressions are invisible when you're wearing a mask—and then tugged it off. Before she had a chance to do more than paw it with her long green evening gloves, a man dressed as Brett Favre came over.

"Let me try on the mask," he said.

If I'd had spider-sense, I would have anticipated Brett's arrival and ducked away with the slim redheaded sunflower. Instead, I watched him place his drink on the fold-out table and reach to take the mask from her. She looked over at me expectantly. I wasn't sure what kind of confidence I was projecting dressed in my mercilessly slinky costume. All I knew was that this scenario was suddenly too familiar;

in my mojito-inspired bliss I'd forgotten the other side of wearing the mask, when every day on the school bus Evan Sweeney would yank the mask off of my head and crouch behind one of the seats, waiting for Charlie Cloud to board. Charlie was a terrified albino who made beeping noises like a truck backing up when he was nervous, which was most of the time. As Charlie walked down the aisle with hesitant, horrified steps, Evan would lunge from behind a seat wearing the mask, causing Charlie to shriek and collapse on the floor. Although the same scenario played itself out every day, Evan hid behind different seats so that Charlie could never predict where he would come from and thus mitigate the shock. Charlie sometimes looked over to me for help, but I had none to offer as I sat with my head down and quietly sang my theme song: "Spider-Man, Spider-Man, he's got radioactive blood. Is he big? Is he small? He's got radioactive blood."

When Evan returned my Spider-Man mask to me, I never once objected, or pointed out that the mask was superfluous, that Evan could scare Charlie with a potato chip. I just gratefully slipped it back on. Children, more than anyone, understand power. And it's Spider-Man's powerlessness that I empathized with at the age of five. He wasn't saving the world, he wasn't saving the country, he was barely saving himself. He was a small-time hero, a nuisance to criminals; his day job tortured him, his girlfriends found him exasperating, bullies laughed at him, the police hated him—and yet, despite all of this, he kept at it, cracking jokes while every supervillain in the universe easily shrugged free of his webbing. He was everything that Superman and Captain America, with their shiny rhetoric and untouchable beefcake bodies, were missing: He was weak. And because he was weak, he was loved. It's the way of the heart, that stupid bleeding creature that defies logic, to love the foolish, the reckless, the hopeful, to love ourselves.

I watched the football player try on the mask. He put it on backward. These are our small, vital rewards. We need them. The redhead had walked away.

COOKING AND STEALING
Amy Bloom

We danced so hard to the Chambers Brothers' psychedelic soul, I broke the heel off one black suede boot and threw the other one under the couch. Sally got blisters on her heels from dancing so long, without stockings, in Frye boots. When two police officers came to the front and the back doors, to break up the party, Sally and I limped into the park, smoked Marlboro Reds until everyone had drifted out of the girl's house, and doubled back so we could drive home in my parents' Dodge Dart. It had some dead animal stuck in the carburetor (my father was a city boy and believed that cars, like subways, ran reliably without intervention); we drove all winter with the windows down and our hands over our noses.

We were best friends from the moment we met. I thought her batik halter tops were sexy, as she hoped, that her wide hips and short white hands were beautiful, and that her motorcycle-riding boyfriend was glamorous (so glamorous, she locked me in the girls' room when he rode up, after school, because she thought I couldn't be trusted, and I don't say that she was wrong, then) until I found him out—as weak and vain and helplessly cruel as Vronsky. She couldn't leave him, she said (she did, of course; before the year was over, she was dating a boy who was all not glamour: tortoiseshell frames and big ears and no transportation at all, but he was sweet and yielding, incapable of standing her up or of holding a lighter so close, it singed the tiny blond hairs on her smooth hands), but my job was to help her stay away from Mr. Motorcycle until she could. My job, as the better-armored person, was to keep us out from under the people who made her feel bad: her peculiar parents, her smug and blank siblings, her conniving psychiatrists. Sally's job was to socialize me, to bring me in from the jungle, and when she got me tottering along socially, she taught me how to be a friend, through the usual approach of endless intimate conversation and the happy development of our mutual interests: stealing and cooking.

Sally was a great shoplifter and a great cook and when we weren't stealing stuff to wear, we stole stuff to cook. Sometimes, when she was intent on making something, we even bought the ingredients. When we became mothers and wives, she became an even better cook and an upright person, and when she told me how she made her little boy bring back the chocolate bar he'd taken from the store, she didn't even wink.

She stole a beautiful black bathing suit for me from under the noses of the discerning salesladies at Saks and she stole a James Beard cookbook because she admired him. In the midst of chaos (her psychiatrist father was as crazy in his way as her "artistic" mother was in hers), Sally cooked to create order and pleasure. We cooked as privately, as discreetly, as possible, as if we were engaging in the most shocking perversities. The wish not to be seen cooking by our mothers was enormous and pressing. Sally didn't want her mother, the love child of Edgar Allan Poe and Martha Stewart (if they had left the foundling to be raised by Iggy Pop), interfering and suggesting and turning our pleasure into some ghastly exercise in bonding that might end in our helping her make her astounding, Hieronymous Bosch hooked rugs. Sally didn't want her father complimenting us on our newfound femininity. Her parents scared the shit out of me, and since my relationship with them consisted of my screeching around the corner at midnight as Sally leapt into my car in her nightgown and her mother hurled crockery at her, and then at us, I tried to get in and out of her house invisibly. (This once required me to hide under Sally's bed for an hour and a half while her mother talked to her about birth control.) I didn't want my mother to see me doing anything, ever, and since cooking in our house was largely a matter of defrosting the Stouffer's, the whole enterprise would have excited a lot of unwanted attention. But we cooked when no one was home—in particular, we fried, and when all that hot oil was too much and the spring leaves had started to unfurl, we made light and creamy things. I have not included among the recipes here her amazing chicken salad, nor our six different versions of Pimm's cup, which we drank in our backyards while putting iodine and baby oil on our legs for a quicker tan.

Sally was already sick, even when we were dancing to the Chambers Brothers, even when we wore our bathing suits to Jones Beach and let boys buy us french fries. By the time she was in college, and out and then back in, and waitressing, and clerking in bookstores, she had a brain tumor. Not trouble concentrating, as her mother said; not a hysterical symptom, as her father said; but a benign brain tumor that she would have removed many times and that grew back each time, even more resilient, even more tenacious than Sally was. She married a good man, and had surgery. She had her beautiful baby boy, and had surgery. She became a master teacher, and had a couple of brain surgeries along the way. She cooked anyway; she cooked even when it became a high-wire act and even when her sense of smell deserted her. I carried mint leaves and coffee beans into the ICU because their scent reached her. Everything reached her and she never stopped grabbing it, sniffing it, running her tongue over it, even in memory. As she was dying, nurses and doctors crowded into her room just to be with her funny, kind, insistent self. (She made me mind my manners with nurses who were not what I thought they should be, and she made me be generous with her time, as she was.) She made jokes with her keyboard when she couldn't speak. She critiqued my work and dictated the most loving letters to her friends and family, key by key.

Before her final surgery, we took our children out to Sardi's, which we had hoped would be nostalgic and glorious and which was neither. Unhappy waiters served us terrible food. Sally, who hated to waste money and hated to make a scene, gathered everybody up and—the effects of her last three strokes notwithstanding—flung her coat on as best she could, shook her head in reproach at the maître d', and led us out.

We came out on the street in front of two food carts, and after Hebrew National hot dogs for lunch, we walked uptown, slowly, for hot fudge sundaes.

"Never eat bad food," she said. "It's not just bad, it's wrong."

RECIPES

Every few days, we got together at someone's house, someone whose parents were both at work, and people who liked to get stoned got stoned, and the two guys who liked to take acid took acid, and Sally and I, who got sleepy when we smoked pot and were terrified of acid, made apple or peach or tropical fritters. It probably takes forty-five minutes to make these and we sometimes did it in half that time, when people were desperate, and sometimes in twice that time, depending on how many people were helping and what condition they were in. Back in the day, Sally and I sometimes chased these with shots of rum. Later, when the acidheads had become a beekeeper and a stockbroker (respectively) and all the potheads had become what you'd expect—ophthalmologists, journalists, judges, mothers, and fathers—Sally and I still cooked these for ourselves, for neighborhood brunches, and for our little kids, who loved them if you managed to remind them in time not to burn the roofs of their mouths on the hot fruit.

TROPICAL FRITTERS
Makes about 22 fritters

1⅓ cups all-purpose flour
1½ teaspoons double-acting baking powder
3 tablespoons granulated sugar
1 teaspoon ground ginger
salt
¾ cup canned chopped pineapple, drained
2 smooshed bananas
½ cup milk

1 large egg, beaten lightly
vegetable oil for deep-frying
confectioners' sugar for dusting

In a small bowl mix together the flour, the baking powder, the granulated sugar, the ginger, and a pinch of salt. (You can sift, if you're so inclined.)

In another bowl, mix the pineapple, the banana, the milk, and the egg, then add the dry stuff and stir the batter until it is combined. In a pot, heat 1½ inches of oil until it shimmers (or until it registers 375 degrees F. on a deep-fat thermometer, if you have one). Drop the batter by tablespoonfuls into the oil in batches of six, and fry the fritters, turning them once, for 1 to 1½ minutes, or until they are golden. Pick up the fritters with a slotted spoon, place on paper towels to drain, and sift the confectioners' sugar over them.

BETTER-THAN-GRANDMA'S CHEESE BLINTZES
Makes 14 blintzes

For blintz batter:
3 large eggs
¼ cup water
¼ cup milk
½ teaspoon baking powder
½ cup all-purpose flour
1½ teaspoons sugar
unsalted butter

For filling:
1½ cups farmer cheese
2 cups cottage cheese or ricotta
¼ cup sugar
1½ teaspoons cinnamon
½ teaspoon vanilla

To make outsides:

In a blender, blend all batter ingredients except butter and let stand 30 minutes. In a cast-iron skillet, melt a little butter over moderately high heat. Pour in enough batter to just coat the bottom of the skillet, swirling, and cook, undisturbed, until top is set and bottom is golden (do not turn wrapper over). Transfer wrapper to a paper towel, golden side down, and cover with another paper towel. Make more wrappers with remaining batter and layer with paper towels.

To make insides:

Blend cheeses, sugar, and cinnamon until smooth. Preheat oven to 250 degrees F. Lightly butter baking sheet.

Put 3 tablespoons of filling in center of each wrapper and fold opposite sides of wrapper over filling until sides barely touch. Fold in ends to completely enclose filling, and place, seam side down, on a baking sheet. Make more blintzes with remaining filling and wrappers. Find your cast-iron skillet again, throw in a lump of sweet butter, and fry the blintzes, starting seam side down and then flipping, until golden brown and slightly crisped on both sides.

Someone more health-conscious would say: bake blintzes, covered loosely with foil, until heated through, 5 to 10 minutes.

TRUE TIRAMISU

8 to 10 shots of espresso or very strong coffee (1 cup)

3 egg yolks and 2 egg whites (throw out one white)

⅓ cup sugar

1½ cups mascarpone (note from Sally to me, 1983: don't use cream cheese, for Christ's sake!)

2 tablespoons marsala (or amaretto or good brandy)

lots of ladyfingers—the hard Italian kind (note from Sally: the ones you don't use, you can eat or give to the kids instead of zwieback)

bittersweet chocolate curls or shavings (depending on your skill level) for garnish

Beat the egg whites with 1 tablespoon sugar until peaking softly. Beat the egg yolks with the rest of the sugar until pale yellow. (We never thought about salmonella, so if it worries you, cook eggs and sugar slightly in double boiler.) Add mascarpone and marsala to egg yolk mixture and blend well; add egg whites to mixture.

Brush espresso on one side of ladyfingers (Sally had several pastry brushes, one for egg, one for sweet, one for spicy, and one, I think, just for tiramisu, so that she did not have to use her BBQ sauce brush for desserts—as I do).

Line a 1-quart bowl or serving dish with the ladyfingers, dipped side up. Cover with ⅓ of the mascarpone. Continue alternating fingers with mascarpone. You should wind up with the mascarpone on top, obviously, then dust with bittersweet chocolate. Refrigerate 4 hours.

FRACTAL LOVE OF BRIAN ENO
Rick Moody

My maternal grandmother was ill most of my early childhood. She died of cirrhosis when I was five. I didn't know her really. She had huge closets for her gowns and blouses and shoes and night-dresses, mirrored closets that ran on opposite walls in the corridor between her bedroom and her bath. I think the extremity of her demise, her sadness and loneliness, her alcoholism, her frequent threats of self-slaughter, were implicit in the fact of my sister and brother and I spending a lot of time in that corridor, trying to catch glimpses of the endless, regressive doubles of ourselves in those facing mirrors. The silence in a house of difficulties is often caught up and stored in mirrors. We summoned it forth, this silence, surviving to flee afterward into the warmth and light of the living room.

There's a bell buoy in the harbor I particularly like. Haven't figured out why some days the foghorns perform their marine service even when the sky is clear. The interval between tollings of the buoy is unfixed, according to wave and tide; the interval between the bellowings of foghorns is fixed, according to the Coast Guard; yet the precise interval is different in the case of each foghorn, so that you might locate your position, with the help of charts spread wide on the surfaces of your navigating table. All these sounds in and out of phase. Sometimes it's like the unisons of Phil Spector records, bass flute and glockenspiel and electric guitar. Then, when these signals go out of phase, it's more like the inexplicable spontaneity of, say, Stockhausen or Brian Eno. On foggy nights, it's choral. Other days, there's just a bell buoy out there.

*   *   *

Not Enough Africa. Eno's response to the lockstep of much sequenced electronic music of the nineties (acid house, techno, breakbeat, drum and bass). What *Africa* means in this observation, I'd argue, is polyrhythms, and the tendency in African music for rhythms and meters to come and go in a flexible way in a piece of music. Or maybe *Africa* suggests the importance of improvisation, or maybe both of these things. One tends to overlook, in Eno's music—which often feels very European, very indebted to ideas of Western music, at least in terms of melodies and harmonies—the debt to non-European sources: jazz, world music, indigenous music, sound constructions. *Not Enough Africa* is also a political perception, therefore, and as with much of what Eno has said, it is applicable to American cultural debates. Which is to say that I find myself thinking *Not Enough Africa*, sometimes, when listening to Strom Thurmond talk on C-SPAN. In literature this is the case, as well; wherein realism (an artificial construction, a syntactical iteration, rather than a apprehension of truth) is the dominant articulation of narrative in American fiction. *Not Enough Africa* might therefore mean not enough *myth*, not enough spontaneity in voice, too much attention to *workshop style*, too much clarity, not enough collective unconsciousness, not enough attention to the imperatives of intertextuality. On the other hand, any debate about what Africa means is essentialist, in the old-fashioned sense, because *Africa* might mean different things at different times, according to the way ideas get refracted. Essentialism itself, after all, *doesn't have enough Africa in it.*

The Dalai Lama came to meditate in Central Park. In Strawberry Fields. At dawn. And we came up the East Side subway, from Brooklyn. Suddenly, at 4:45 A.M., the IRT was crowded with people, not *crowded* exactly, not like when you get on the number seven after a Mets game, but crowded enough with people that you weren't worried about getting *rolled* if you slipped in and out of consciousness, as most of us seemed to be doing, napping, and we didn't really have any idea exactly *where Strawberry Fields was*, because who pays attention to these things exactly, and we were violating ancient parental injunctions against being *in the park at night*, or at least it looked to be night when we got off the train at Hunter College and crossed town toward the park, it was dark, and we paraded in the middle of the road, down the center of Sixty-ninth, as you get to do only during the infrequent snowstorm, unless you are the sort who still comes home from clubs at that hour, as the sun is trucked out of its warehouse in Queens. Much fog that morning in June, and we went over the wall and into the park, and we didn't know where *Strawberry Fields was*, although we knew where the band shell was, and then we heard this unearthly lowing, from some obscure quarter, and all the assembled, the faithful, the kids, the believers, the indigents, the night crawlers of the park moved through night toward this lamentation, following sound, knowing nothing more than that this sound sug-gested the culmination of pilgrimage. Tibet had sprung up like an alien culture in Central Park, monks on the rocks above us with their ancient wind instruments, their ceremonial horns, and so unearthly was it that all of us assumed a certain posture, unavoidably, and a black Lincoln Town Car pulled up, out climbed a distant, balding guy in an orange monk's garb, and he sat among us.

The hydraulic brakes of New York City buses. The way dogs bark at sirens. Skips and pops and scratches on long playing records. The answering machine messages of strangers. Save on membership *today*. The price of this admission ticket may be applied toward a new membership, if purchased today or in the nest week. Dry cleaner, $9.75. Metrocard, $15.00. Taxi, $25.00. Dinner at Dok Sum's, $34.00. News, $1.10. Limit one ticket. Inquire at Lobby Membership Desk. Join now. Other Music: Black Box Recorder, *England Made Me*; Stockhausen, *Kontakte*; Ulmer, James Blood, *Harmelodic Guitar & Strings*; Throwing Muses, *In A Doghouse*; CD, *Misc Used*; Eno, Brian, *Shutov Assembly*. Retain portion for reentry.

I toured for five or six weeks to support one of my books and I was lucky to do so, and though it was not terribly long by the standards of the Danielle Steels and Stephen Kings of the world, or by the standards of rock and roll personalities or professional sports figures, it was long for me, as I don't like to travel and am not good at small talk. By the middle of the tour I was exhausted and anxious in a way I'd rarely felt before, and I was changing planes in O'Hare, changing puddle jumpers, which required going under the main landing strip over to the smaller terminal on the far side of the airport. *Am I certain this happened at all?* Under the strip they had a moving sidewalk, *a people mover*, a horizontal escalator, a quarter-mile long, perhaps even longer, and this corridor was lit only with strange neon fixtures in the brighter tonalities. The music there, in that windowless space, was distinctly different from your standard airport diet of classics and Muzak adaptations of Motown hits. It was electronic, digital, arbitrary, ambient. It wasn't Eno's *Music for Airports*, which I bought in 1979, when it was first released, and which I have played since more or less continuously, sometimes for days at a time. It wasn't this, but it was the same idea. Without Eno's model, that corridor itself would not have existed in the way it did, nor would we have come to see airports as an opportunity for a dignified and sober space, but merely as conduits, places to be gotten through, across.

Thursday, and the heron out in the cove is scrapping with some local gulls. Territorial, I figure. Hard to believe that a bird as beautiful as the heron (*tri-colored heron* is the only one I can find in my *Simon and Schuster Guide to Birds of the World*, though everyone here refers to them as *great blues*) could be saddled with a call as raw and unpleasant as the heron's. It's something like the righteous indignation of a season ticketholder in the thin air of the stands. I'm awake at 5:30 A.M., first light, and the heron sounds prehistoric, reptilian, so primitive is its wail during the altercation at dawn. Later in the day I go to see if I can get a look and I scare him (or her) up, off a piling on the end of a dock. The heron lifts off slowly, its reedy legs skimming the water. Then, tickling its belly on the tops of a couple of shrubs, it wheels to one side and alights on the desolate beach at the mouth of the harbor.

*   *   *

I heard *Roxy Music* in 1975, when I worked at the radio station where I went to school in New Hampshire. The strange synthesizer part on "Virginia Plain" was what I loved right away, the weird noisy droning of the one-four progression that serves as a bridge in that piece. These rumblings weren't like anything else I was listening to at the time. When I figured out that these and other conceptual interludes on the Roxy album were the work of a musician with one name only (it wasn't until later that he reverted to his full name), and that he had released records of his own, I acquired them all within a short time. By the late seventies, I would buy anything he was associated with, all of the film music, any record he produced, live collaborations (*801 Live*), fully detachable records made by musicians he used in his recordings (Brand X, Material, et al.). I was the only person I knew listening to this music. Or very close to it. Later in 1981, on a wall between Penn Station and the 34th Street subway station, I first saw that graffito of that period, *Eno is God.*

I got to talk to him. Twenty years after first hearing his work. I was writing a piece about David Bowie for the *Times*. Eno's *people* were hard to pin down as to his whereabouts, his availability, etc. He was heading off *on holiday* and didn't want to be interrupted. Through some prodding by my editor, I was connected by telephone. I was nervous. I had spent much of my life parsing Eno's output wondering about his next move, about the meaning of certain collaborations. Why "The Paw Paw Negro Blowtorch"? Why "King's Lead Hat"? (Because it's an anagram of "Talking Heads.") Why agree to produce the first Devo album? Because I was using the tape recorder on the fax machine in the dusty corridor of my apartment, I had to sit in there, in the hall, on the floor, with my list of questions. Perspiring. I imagined this discomfort was an influence upon Eno's answers, according to his own theory that what is of interest in a musical composition is what happens outside of the range of the microphone, the unrecordable facts of a certain production. To some of my questions, Eno was clipped and uninterested, as when I asked if he had felt any pressure to create a hit on Bowie's record *Outside* (which he produced), or when I asked if he ever read the postings about his work on the Web. On other matters, he was remarkably articulate. But as in his terrific piece for *Details* magazine on perfume ("The point for me is not to expect perfumery to take its place in some nice, reliable, rational world order, but to expect everything else to become like perfume"), Eno was always evasive *as an entity*, and later I was grateful for this, for the possibility that the meaning of Eno and Eno's output as an artist and musician was in no way consonant with Brian Eno himself, the guy on holiday who didn't want to be interrupted; the possibility existed that the process of Eno's work reflected other forces, forces that an individual called Brian Eno couldn't control or even fully describe, except perhaps laterally, as when describing perfume. Eno, then, in my encounter with him, had very little to do with Eno. I presume the same is true in the disjunction that afflicts all who are, to whatever degree, public figures. But in Eno's case, the possibility that personality and work might occasionally be confluent and occasionally not according to factors like chance—this seemed closer to his work by virtue of being, somehow, further away from it.

Once, during my high school years, during an assembly, a guy named Will gave a performance of John Cage's *4'33"*. He arrived in the chapel, sat down at the piano, raised the lid, and didn't play a note. We were used to recitals of Purcell or sermons about *tolerance or excellence*, or perhaps the school chorus would sing. This guy Will was an actor, a Thespian, an expert at the judicious prank, and so we watched him carefully, as the minutes unwound, we watched his face go through these gyrations—he was peaceful, he was fierce, he was amused—and the silence, which seemed arbitrary and accidental, began to acquire a gravity. It was the longest organized silence I'd ever experienced. You could hear a parochial controversy brewing. You could hear certain masters of Latin and math and science *wondering what the hell was going on*, while others knew, and still others knew and disapproved. It was for *our* benefit, though; it was for the benefit of the kids, and I would like to say I understood immediately, but I confess I thought it was a sham, a goof, until years later, when that silence seduced me.

Eno designed, at some point in the early seventies, a set of cards to be used as aids in creative endeavors: "These cards evolved from our separate observations of the principles underlying what we are doing." Entitled *Oblique Strategies,* some of these were very direct—*Use fewer notes*—and some really were oblique: *Go slowly all the way round the outside.* Some were very much of their time: *You are an engineer.* Some were timeless pieces of advice: *Honor thy error as a hidden intention.* The *Oblique Strategies* were never technical, as I hope these responses to Eno are not. Perhaps this is a good time to suggest that the essential works of Eno from the late seventies and early eighties were not only about process, but also about tenderness, gentleness, and attention. These qualities were at a considerable remove from most of the music I listened to during the period, which tended to be aggressive, cynical, and sloppy. But I thought then and think now that tenderness, though unfashionable, often makes for great art, for art that lasts, and that *what is neglected,* as Roland Barthes says—and the human emotions are neglected these days—often becomes the site of an affirmation. *Don't be afraid of things because they're easy to do.*

UNDERTAKER PLEASE DRIVE SLOW
Jo Ann Beard

*I*n *December 1997, Cheri Tremble committed suicide with the assistance of Dr. Jack Kevorkian. What follows is a merging of fact with fiction: the external details of Cheri's life and illness are as accurate as possible, gleaned from interviews with her friends and family, while the internal details—her thoughts, her memories, and what occurred after her loved ones saw her for the last time—are imagined.*

They come slowly down the street, two boys on bicycles, riding side by side through the glare of a summer afternoon. She's on the curb and the sun is so bright and hot it feels like her hair is on fire. If she glances down she can just see the rubber toes of her sneakers and the skirt of her sundress, the color of root beer. The boys are playing tug-of-war, leaning away from one another, front wheels wobbling, each grasping one end of a long black snake. They have pale matching hair that stands up like the bristles of a brush and their mouths are open in silent, gleeful shouts. The snake is dusty and limp, but as they sweep past she sees its eye, wide awake, and the sudden flat ribbon of tongue, scarlet against the boy's white wrist.

This is the way Cheri's life is passing in front of her eyes, in random unrelated glimpses, one or two a day. They come from nowhere, the bottom of her brain, and are suddenly projected, intense and silent as the Zapruder film, while she watches. This morning as she was eating her oatmeal what passed in front of her eyes was her first husband, shirtless against a blue sky, tying up tomato plants. And now tonight, climbing into bed, the Riley boys with a river snake, circa 1955.

The bed feels like a boat on choppy water. She pulls her foot out from the covers and rests it on the floor for ballast. That's what they used to say to do if you were drunk and had the whirlies. The phone rings in the living room and she hears Sarah's voice against the sound of the television. In those old TV shows and movies, way back when, the husband and wife had to keep one foot on the floor during the bed scenes. It meant everything was friendly instead of passionate. Well, it's working here tonight, the nausea is receding.

A wand of light appears and then widens; Bone's head is framed in the doorway. He pads across the room on velvet cat paws and freezes when he sees her bare foot on the floor. He stares at it in the dark with wide terrified eyes, then takes his place next to Nimbus at the foot of the bed. The girls were helping her burn leaves all afternoon and now the cats smell like marijuana smoke. In this morning's vision, her first husband was standing waist-deep in some unkempt garden of theirs, hair in a ponytail, a small frown on his face, and a joint behind his ear. Back in New York one of her chemo doctors had discreetly mentioned marijuana for nausea, and some kind soul had given her a plate of pot brownies which she had taken like medicine, eating one each morning for breakfast. She had wandered her Brooklyn apartment in a state of muffled calm, straightening bedspreads and dish towels and staring slack-jawed out the window until the monster awoke, nudged her back into the bathroom, pushed her face in the toilet.

Cheri stretches her toes reflexively under the covers, making sure they still work. She's seen pictures of her spine, ghostly negatives resting against a light box, and the cancer looks tiny, like a baby's grasping fingers. The doctor used a pencil with bite marks on it to show her the metastasis: here, here, and a tiny bit here. Her relaxation is so complete that the bed now has the soothing, side-to-side rocking motion of a sleeping car. Scenery floods past, mostly clumps of rocks and little hillocks scattered with dark green trees. *Here, here, and a tiny bit here.* A farm, a collie dog loping next to the tracks, and then the sudden startling face of a long-dead uncle. It seemed like he had shouted something but she couldn't catch it.

"What?" she says into the dark.

"Nothing," Sarah whispers from the doorway. "I was just standing here for a second."

How had she done it, raised these exotic wild-haired daughters? They were back in Iowa City temporarily, crowding their personalities into her little house, blearily eating bowls of cereal each morning before raking the leaves into bright piles or spading the flower beds. The rest of the time they lounged on the front porch where they kept their packs of cigarettes, smoking and having long murmured squabbles, going from flannel shirts to tank tops and back to flannel shirts again as the fall afternoons waxed and waned. Every evening one of them would ease out of the house and clunk away in motorcycle boots and vivid lipstick, down the street and into the neighborhood tavern. They mostly took turns, one of them swigging beers, shooting pool, and punching up embarrassing, elderly jukebox songs, the other at home sprawled in front of the television, pale as a widow, drinking cups of fragrant tea and eating malted milk balls by the handful.

Tonight it's Sarah, standing silent against the door frame, staring intently at the floor, hands gripping elbows, listening to her mother breathe. Cheri feels the stirrings of a cough deep inside her lungs. It's the monster, locked in the basement, and eventually it will storm up the stairs and burst forth, attacking her in her own home, swinging a mallet at her chest over and over. Once she can breathe again, she makes a joke out of it: I'm Buddy Hackett, I'm Gene Hackman. Nobody even pretends to laugh at this anymore; they're too tired.

"I thought you were sleeping," Sarah says. "The phone was for you."

Cheri nudges a cat away from her hip, making room, and Sarah climbs in beside her. It's a slumber party minus the fun. She was awake, she could have taken the call.

"He said you should rest," Sarah answers.

Who said?

Besides *terminal* and *cancer*, there are no more final sounding words in the English language. Jack Kevorkian. That's who.

And then, despite themselves, they are starstruck for a moment at the idea of this spry ghoul from the evening news picking up his phone in Michigan and dialing Cheri's own little house in Iowa, with its polished floors and eccentric armchairs. Backlit from the hallway, the cats' ears are almost transparent, like parchment lampshades. They watch the humans in their giddiness, faces sharp and impassive.

They'll be wide-awake alive and I'll be dead, Cheri thinks suddenly. Not just the cats, but everyone. Sarah, Katy, her best friends Linda and Wayne. Linda and Wayne's children, the lady at the pharmacy who calls her Churry instead of Cheri, the man covered in dirt and desperation who sometimes slept on her stoop back in Brooklyn. Her first husband, her second husband, *her own mother*, all those medical professionals.

His nickname is Doctor Death, and yet when it's over, he'll still be alive.

The lump was discovered during a routine mammogram two and a half years earlier. She spent the last normal afternoon of her life on the train, Baltimore to Penn Station, taking tickets and trying not to notice that an elderly passenger had a dog in her pocketbook. Amtrak had a rule against animals riding its trains but unless someone complained, Cheri didn't intend to notice. She planned to frown at the lady when they got to Penn, but she didn't even do that, since it was quitting time and she felt cheerful. The Chihuahua's tiny face was poked all the way out of the bag by then, smugly gazing about.

Before her appointment, she went to the gym, ran and sweated, saunaed, showered, and tried to fluff her hair up a little. She needed a haircut more than a mammogram, but what she really needed more than either was to find her MasterCard, which had better be home on her dresser, otherwise she had no idea. She walked to the lab in her running shoes, going over the last three days, mentally taking her credit card out at various moments—grocery store, dinner at Ollie's, a weak moment with an L.L. Bean catalog—and putting it back in her wallet. The waiting room was disappointingly full and so she looked at fashion models in a magazine and watched the other customers until she was called.

The X-ray technician was a young woman with cat-eye glasses and an unprofessional sense of humor. She wore bright yellow clogs. Here comes the S&M part, she said as the machine closed its jaws. Click, flash, other side. She collected the trays and went off to develop the films and show them to the doctor. Be right back, she said as she left the room. And didn't return.

Cheri sat waiting, searching her mind until she thought she might have located the credit card in the back pocket of her black jeans, which were probably stuffed in the hamper. As the minutes wore on, and then on, her hearing became heightened and her hands turned damp and cold. She rubbed them on her paper shirt. There was activity up and down the hall, doors opening and closing, voices leaking out. By the time twenty-six minutes had passed she no longer wanted the technician to return. Every time she heard footsteps in the hall she willed them in the other direction. *Get lost, get lost,* she said under her breath, and they did get lost, until once they didn't and then the knob turned and the room was filled with the starched air of courteous detachment.

"Doctor wants more films."

And that's how everything changes, not with the pronouncement even, but with a woman's disengaged expression. The room was engulfed in a tinny silence as she worked, arranging Cheri like a mannequin, folding her against the stainless steel, placing an arm up here, a breast in there, sending her home. Once, a long time later, when Cheri's life was passing in front of her eyes, she caught a glimpse of it again—saw the bright yellow cartoon feet of the technician and then saw her own naked left arm, in slow muted motion, rising obediently to embrace the machine.

The lump was a dreamy smear on the X ray, barely there, unfeelable except in her throat when she tried to talk. Linda spoke to her late at night, each of them standing in a dark kitchen, one in Brooklyn and one in Iowa City. Lump, lumpectomy, chemo, Cheri said. Yes, Linda said, that's what they do. A silence in which both of them wished they were seven-year-old hellions again instead of what they were—a train conductor and a nurse, mothers, women who wore uniforms and looked sexy in them. Best friends since age five. It seems to be happening to both of them, although it isn't. For the duration of the phone call, they manage to remain calm.

And the illness proceeds on its trajectory, a knife, a scar, a plant-filled atrium where people sit in cubicles getting their treatments. One of the things she learns is how to vomit from a prone position, into a curved plastic trough. After six months another pale lump is photographed, no bigger but resolute, like a schoolyard bully who comes back even after a terrible pummeling. Linda waits for the phone call and when it comes she sits down. Lump, mastectomy, more chemo, Cheri says. Okay, Linda says, and she covers her face with one hand.

This time there's a tray of knives, she sees them right before the anesthesia erases her. When she awakens her breast is gone, melted into a long weeping scar across her chest. The first time she sees it she feels a strange numbness, a smooth blank where her shock should be. A day later the mortification is so profound and clamorous that she has to disconnect, like hanging up the receiver when someone is shouting into your ear. Her daughters fold gauze and tear tape and change her bandages without flinching. They seem larger to her in her new whittled-down state, like giantesses come to bathe and swaddle her. I'm okay, she says forty times a day, until she comes to believe it, and then they relax, Katy returning to school and Sarah finding a job down the street at a Starbucks instead of going back like she planned. They decided it between themselves, Cheri in the dark, under the looming, purple shadow of follow-up chemo.

It comes at her with talons and beak—she recovers from the first treatment in the emergency room, dosed up with Compazine and tethered to a glucose IV in a curtained cubicle, listening to the audio portion of what sounds like a television drama but isn't: an elderly woman calling out for help, a doctor speaking loudly and testily to an underling, a man relentlessly berating his wife in Spanish while a baby cries at regular intervals, like a chorus. At 5.00 A.M. she and Sarah crawl back into a cab and ride home with their eyes closed as the sun comes up.

And it gets progressively worse, the exhaustion and illness so wretched that she feels like a dying animal. There is something of the barnyard about all of it—the earthiness, the smells, the sheer bovine physicality of being in such a body, plodding from bed to bathroom on tottering legs. Once, during a particularly bad afternoon when Sarah is at work, she hears herself as if from a great distance. The sound she's making is resonant and sustained, like the lowing of a frightened steer.

And then gradually she's well, the monster scoured clean with a wire brush, slinking off to watch her from a distance. She doesn't care. Fuck the monster. She takes up running again, and sits in the sauna breathing steam into her cells, a towel discreetly knotted over the hollow spot on her chest. Eventually the stares get to her and she decides to undergo reconstructive surgery. This is routine, a process by which tissue from the groin is fashioned into a breast, like building Eve from Adam. Only it isn't God running the construction crew, it's Sloan-Kettering.

Something goes wrong on the operating table. She comes out of the surgery shaped like a woman again but unable to walk, one leg slack and rubbery, refusing to hold her weight. Eventually she leaves the hospital on crutches and calls Linda from a chair in the center of her living room, staring into the kitchen at her cup of tea on the counter. They're going to waive my bill, she tells her friend. Nerve damage, Linda replies. Positioned wrong on the operating table, probably. Get them to help you.

But they remain thin-lipped and silent, unwilling even to diagnose the problem, let alone treat it. She tries everything from the crutches to a walker to a leg brace, hobbling, learning to carry her tea without spilling it but never figuring out how to ride the train without standing or walking. Disability runs out and Amtrak lets her go. She loses not only her paycheck but her pension and her benefits. She drags her leg up and down the street each day like a zombie, crutch nestled against her new breast, while pedestrians eddy around her and joggers sweat in the July heat.

It's night of the living leg, she tells Linda.

Come home, Linda says.

So her friends visit her in pairs, bearing bubble wrap and boxes and small, meaningful gifts that have to be packed along with the dishes and books. Nobody can believe this is happening, although they felt the same away about the lump, the chemo, the mastectomy, the other chemo. But crippled isn't cancer, and for that they're all grateful. They've heard that Iowa is beautiful. One of her former co-workers, a man from the Bronx, asks if she will have neighbors out there. She visits the clinic one last time, stumping past the waiting room filled with women in various states of deconstruction. The medical staff seems very pleased with how the breast turned out, and mildly surprised that she's leaving, but they know that cancer changes people, turns them around in significant ways.

I can't *walk*, she says tersely. I lost my job and my pension.

And Iowa truly is beautiful in September when she arrives. She moves into Linda and Wayne's spare room and sets to work getting back on her feet, literally. She undergoes physical therapy for numbness and foot drop, and the local doctors install something called a transcutaneous nerve stimulator which works, slowly and miraculously.

She feels bionic and hopeful in her leg brace and dungarees, restored to her former Iowa self, sitting on the dark porch at night with Linda and Wayne and one or two of their children, cats wafting around their ankles while they talk and talk. During the days she works on her leg, walking and stretching and balancing herself, practicing with the cane until she's almost like a regular person. They rake leaves right before a windstorm and wake the next morning to find them evenly distributed over the lawn again. They have barbecues and card games. She and Linda house-hunt with fervor, horrified at what they see until one day a little house on Davenport Street goes on the market and they get wild with excitement. Wayne looks it over and they scheme; Cheri calls her mother and arranges a loan, then lands a job in an optometrist's office where she doesn't have to stand or walk but can sit all day on a stool, her cane against the wall behind her. Within three months of arriving in Iowa, she has a house, a job, and a life.

This is her town now, bathed in pale January light, populated with students and bright, vivid women, the occasional interesting man. She hangs a string of white lights around her kitchen window and buys a tall, leafy schefflera tree for the living room which she replants into an orange-glazed pot. She talks on the phone and watches television in the evenings, drunk on coziness and midwestern domesticity. At some point she begins to sweat during the nights, waking up to a damp nightgown and clammy sheets. It develops into an Iowa head cold; she can barely breathe but it's nothing to her, a sniffle with a headache. Herbal tinctures from the health-food store, fruits, vegetables and good, heavy bread, lots of soup. The cold recedes eventually and she's left with chapped nostrils and a large lump on the right side of her neck.

Fear moves into the little house with her, taking up residence in the back of her closet, along with the down comforter that she can no longer use. The night sweats get worse, forcing her up and into the living room, where she knits to keep from touching the lump. She can't tell if it's sore or if she's just prodding it too much. It's definitely big. Linda is worried, although she's also reasonable: it could be a residual effect from the cold.

The doctor is circumspect, steepling her hands and furrowing her brow. Aspiration is called for, a long needle into the neck like something out of a Boris Karloff movie. She's the bride of Frankenstein, she's the girl in the thin nightie, cowering as the monster peers through her window. Mostly she's Katy and Sarah's mother, and they rally again, Katy on the telephone, talking of boys and clothes, her voice alive with fear, and then Sarah, who's been living in the general vicinity, on her doorstep.

She walks with Sarah in Hickory Hill Park after the procedure is done. The trees are denuded still and the sky is like milk, their faces raked by the damp wind but there's nowhere else to go and so they walk and think, not speaking. It's two years exactly since this all began. On the way back to the house, they hold hands like schoolchildren. Before the kettle can boil the telephone rings; the doctor wants to see Cheri in her office.

Cancer in the lymph system, metastasized from the breast. Statistically speaking, two years at the outside, with aggressive treatment. Without it, much less.

They are sitting in upholstered armchairs in front of the doctor's desk, like applicants denied a bank loan. Sarah leans forward from the waist and sobs uncontrollably, her face on her knees, hands clutching her ankles. This is how she cried as a toddler, when it was bedtime and the party was still going on. *This is my daughter*, Cheri thinks. *My other daughter is Kate.*

The doctor hands a tissue across the desk and watches Cheri intently. When finally she looks away, Cheri turns to Sarah and touches her arm. Sarah sits up, takes the tissue, and presses it into her face.

Don't cry, it's okay, Cheri hears herself saying. I had to go sometime.

The doctor doesn't disagree, which seems heartless, but also doesn't hurry them along, which seems kind. They collect referrals and then make their way through the waiting room and to the door, Sarah crying still, gently leading her mother. When they step outside into the dull afternoon light, Cheri is overcome with a feeling of weightlessness and vertigo. She's Fay Wray, nestled in the monster's palm as he scales the skyscraper.

Fifth-grade skating party at Ames Pond. She can see Billy Mayfield's bare hand holding her mittened one as he pulls her along, and her own feet in their pom-pommed ice skates, scissoring beneath her as she keeps up. Crack the whip with a line of sweaty kids and Cheri's at the end of it. Scenery whirls past—trash barrels, sparse evergreens, snow hut with faces grouped around a heater, the striped tail of her own stocking cap—and then the whip cracks and she's flung, hurtling across the ice on her back, turning once in slow motion as the clouds revolve, and then a sickening crunch. Through the ice and under, she plunges down in the dark water, skates sticking in the muddy bottom for an instant, and then rises slowly, spinning, until her head bumps on the underside of the ice. For one long surreal moment, before an arm reaches in and grasps the hood of her coat, hauling her out, she is suspended under the warped ceiling of ice. Inside the roaring silence of the water, she looks up and sees the skates of the excited children, congregating above her.

The flashbacks have begun now, coming to her when she's distracted in her kitchen, washing cups or staring into the fridge. Yesterday she was placing a flower in a vase—a lone iris, the color of grape soda—and suddenly saw a row of people yelling and shaking their fists at her. It bothered her for hours, until she finally figured out it was from back in her cheerleading days. The Ames Pond memory had been suppressed for thirty-six years, until tonight. It rose unbidden, like a genie, as she eased the cork from a bottle of wine. What she had chosen to remember all those years was actually an addendum to the memory: Billy Mayfield returning her blue mitten the next day at school, the one she was wearing when she rocketed out of his grasp. He handed it to her in a brown paper lunch sack, with Cheri's name written on it in blue ballpoint, a mother's spidery script.

They're drinking wine, waiting for Wayne to show up so they can get some dinner. It's cold but they put on jackets and head to the patio. Another volunteer iris, this one a strange pale yellow, grows near the garage. Cheri's garden is a tangle still but she's sorting it out; the air is fragrant with compost and lilacs.

Aggressive treatment at this stage would mean a bone marrow transplant. One thug beating another thug, with her in the middle. She's not going to do it.

People get through this, Linda says. We'll help you.

Never again, Cheri tells her. I said so the last time.

The bridal wreath bushes along the back fence are buried under tiers of ruffles. Each blossom is a small bouquet. They were married in the 1970s, Linda to Wayne and Cheri to Dave. Hippie intellectuals with garlands in their hair, intense frivolity, et cetera. Floating in and out of each other's front doors, macramé projects, and funky baby showers that included the men. Linda had two girls, then later, a boy. Cheri had firstborn Sarah, dreamy and social, then baby Kate with her black hair and shy grin.

In her spare time, Cheri immersed herself in the tenets of the

Socialist Party—which they all sort of agreed with in theory, if not in practice—and moved from political idealist to political activist. She spoke her mind more and more: *I believe an injury to one is an injury to all . . . the concept of classlessness gets to the heart of the matter— why it's so important to try and live it, put it into action, fight for it if need be. Without that you accept less, only your individuality.* Should have been a warning, but they were all taken by surprise when she left them, absorbed into another life that had more meaning for her. First to Chicago and then to the South, where she worked in factories and mills putting her principles into practice, shaping her life like wet clay until it hardened, leaving her in New York City years later, punching tickets on a train and liking it. She was always the type to do her ruminating alone, in the privacy of her own head, and back then, when she made the decision to leave her marriage and Iowa, she simply announced it and then set about getting it done, ears stubbornly turned off to pleas and reason. A few weeks later she had driven away with Katy in the backseat, wide-eyed and silent, while Sarah, arms outstretched toward the disappearing car, sobbed in her father's arms.

No chemo, she said so before and she's sticking with it. Her face is resolute in the narrowing light, unfaltering. Linda has seen this look before; right behind all that beauty and grief are the steel girders of pragmatism.

Of course, she didn't stick with the other decision, the one to let Dave keep Sarah. Bereft without her daughter, Cheri eventually got her back, paying penance then and for years after. This won't work that way; the penance for refusing chemo is most likely death.

They sit quietly, watching Wayne as he approaches up the back walk. One look at their faces and he knows what the decision is.

"Smells like shit," he remarks as he passes the freshly fertilized garden.

Now there are three of them drinking wine under the darkening sky, although one is already, imperceptibly, being erased from the tableau. They speak of restaurants, and narrow it down to Indian or Chinese. Wayne can go either way, although he's up for spicy. Linda is thinking good, healthy vegetables and brown rice. She stands and collects wineglasses, tucking the bottle under her arm. As Linda moves toward the house, Cheri reaches out and touches her sleeve in a silent, sideways gesture of gratitude. In this withering light, they could all be twenty again, in worn jean jackets and sneakers, Wayne's baseball cap.

An injury to one is an injury to all. She's made her decision, then, and they'll all live with it. Or rather, two of them will.

One month later, another night sky, this time over Mexico. There are clouds adrift and now the big yellow moon has a dent in its head. She doesn't care, it's all beautiful, the Aztec-tiled motel courtyard, palm trees in huge terra-cotta urns, their fronds rustling like corn. Katy is out walking in the night air with the daughter of another patient, and Cheri is reclining poolside, watching satellites blink overhead and sipping a concoction they gave her at the clinic. It tastes quite good, actually, if you don't think about it. Sort of like a piña colada boosted with iron shavings.

They can say what they will about alternative therapy, but it's doing as much for her as the chemo ever did and there's no throwing up involved. Mornings at the clinic are spent getting laetrile treatments, administered intravenously by smiling Mexican women who wear traditional nurse's caps and an assortment of ankle bracelets. After-noons are given over to consultations with staff members who take her history and offer advice on ways to coax the monster back into its cage. Lion tamers, holding out spindly chairs.

She spends hours knitting in the waiting room, surrounded by the shining, hopeful faces of the truly desperate. Today a gaunt and yet somehow baggy-looking man in a slogan T-shirt—the words LOVE ME LOVE MY HOG over a picture of a Harley-Davidson motorcycle—confided to Cheri that six months ago he weighed over three hundred pounds and was still hitting the booze.

"First my liver give out for a while," he said, hollow-eyed and shivering, "and then this cancer set in." His daughter, a plain Pente-costal-looking girl in a sundress and tennis shoes, reached over and pressed the back of her hand against his forehead.

"You're dropping again," she told him quietly, and left to wander the halls of the clinic, coming back with a wheelchair and an orderly. The motorcycle man waved to Cheri ruefully as they loaded him up.

"She don't let me suffer if she can help it," he said, staring up at the girl.

Les, a man Cheri knew from a seminar on purgatives, leaned forward after they were gone. "He might as well drink his coffee from a cup," he said. "Because no enema in the world will cure *that*." He was small and hairless, an elderly melanomic golfer in powder-blue pants. His son roamed the peripheries of waiting rooms and corridors in a suit and tie, snapping his briefcase open and shut, holding flowcharts up to the light like X rays, one-finger-typing on a laptop.

"He has to work wherever he goes," his father told Cheri. She made a polite gesture of commiseration but he shook his head. "He has to, he's the top over there. Nobody above him, from what I can tell." He ran a hand purposefully over his head and then looked at his palm. Nothing there, clean as a whistle.

"Wow," Cheri told him, and after a respectful pause turned to back to her knitting. Stitch, drop-stitch, stitch, cast off. In the waiting room, hours recede like a glacier, leaving bottles and wrappers in their wake. She is strangely moved by all of it, the sick people and their companions, the clean antiseptic smell, the inspirational messages calligraphed and framed on every wall. The sheik character who moves from treatment room to seminar with an entourage of mournful draped women. The elderly lady in a copper wig who sat down next to her in the Body, Mind, and Spirit lecture, reached for Cheri's hand, and held it for an hour, both of them staring ahead, holding on to the speaker's words like the bar of a trapeze.

That seminar closed with a quotation: *Worship the Lord your God, and His blessing will be on your food and water. I will take away sickness from among you.* Not exactly *The Communist Manifesto*, but who's to judge. Her friend listened intently and then extricated her hand, took out a small battered notebook and wrote *Exodus 23:25* at the bottom of a to-do list.

"You don't look a bit sick," she said to Cheri. Her eyes were wide and stark and her teeth didn't fit right. Cheri looked down at her own feet, brown in their sandals, Katy's red nail polish giving each toe its own personality.

"I am, though," she replied.

"I have bust cancer," the woman told her, whispering.

Today they ran into each other in the corridor and embraced spontaneously, Cheri taking care not to set the wig askew. The woman's husband stood quietly at a distance, staring over their shoulders, holding a straw purse.

This afternoon she came upon Les's son, the businessman, right here in this courtyard. Huddled on a stone ledge, half inside an over-wrought bougainvillea bush, he wore a suit with the tie loosened sideways, his usually smooth hair adrift and spiky from running his hands through it. A parody of a drunk man, only it wasn't alcohol, it was grief. Surrounded by giant blank-faced purple blossoms, he sobbed into a cell phone, eyes shut, mouth wrenched wide open in a child's grimace.

Now the courtyard is empty and dark, lit only by the muted lamps hidden amid the fronds and ferns. At the very center, the pool shimmers in its own light, like Aqua Velva. Cheri drops her robe and slides into the water, cool and bracing. She does a slow backstroke until it tires her and then turns over, dives, and comes up with her hair slicked away from her face, like a seal, or a woman who knows she's beautiful.

Courtesy of her mother, it all is. All Cheri had to do was ask. Fifteen thousand dollars, just like that, for palm trees and exotic blooming flowers, the muggy Amazonian gladelike feel of this courtyard. All from her mother and her mother's husband, who wrote the check without flinching, buying her, if not an actual future, then the promise of a future. And the miracle is that she now feels healthy, her insides rinsed and wrung out, her exterior massaged and polished, the very blood in her veins carbonated. And it isn't better living through chemo, it's simple and organic. Fruit, coffee, oxygen, and words. *You are loved, we love you, you can live, others have lived.*

The water now feels warmer than the air, amniotic. A familial sound drifts over the stone wall, subdued and infectious. Katy's laughter. They've returned from their walk, chatting just outside the gate, oblivious to the open shutters and the acoustic properties of the narrow street. Cheri lets herself drift backward until she's floating again, the sound of indistinct voices overcome by the water lapping against her ears. Eyes closed, she summons an image of Katy, with her wide grin and flat Brooklyn accent, hoop earrings, raucous hair; when she was in the room you couldn't look anywhere else, nobody could. Then Sarah, she of the beautiful, deceptively serene face, hair knotted behind her head in a careless bun, choosing her words thoughtfully, then speaking them in the broad cadences of the Midwest. They're interesting, Cheri thinks. Compelling. She imagines the two of them huddled inside the rhododendron bush in her front yard, like Les's son in the arms of the bougainvillea, weeping.

The moon is high in the sky now, looking smaller and less certain. Tiny, long-legged lizards run along the sidewalks. In just a few days she'll be back home, tending her garden with its sturdy, quintessential-Iowa flowers—morning glories, zinnias, black-eyed Susans, and the tall lavender cone flowers, with their rusty hearts lifted up toward the sun, petals flung backward like arms. *You can live.* For one prolonged, irrational moment, hope circles the courtyard like a great winged heron, banking slowly over the pool and the lawn chairs, the dark foliage, and then wheeling out into the night. Gone.

Others have lived. She won't be one of them. She feels it in her bones, quite literally.

The summer that follows is long and luminous. They canoe down the Wapsipinicon River, a rowdy cavalcade of humans and their coolers, and camp along the reedy banks, faces sunburned and firelit, marshmallows melting and blackening on sticks, the green nylon glow of flashlights inside tents. They climb into the car—Linda, Wayne, Cheri, and a pan of brownies—and take a road trip, fourteen hours of stupefying knee-high corn, and then the mind-blowing Rockies, in all their vertical splendor. An outdoor music festival in Telluride: bands they've heard of and bands they've never heard of, old tie-dyed dudes in stretched-out T-shirts and slender gray ponytails, and the new generation of hippies with radiant, stoned faces, hair dreadlocked into felt. They forgo the brownies and hike a steep mountain trail, Cheri faltering only once, Wayne trying to haul her up onto a boulder so she can see the vista. It's her mind, not her body—the vertigo of seeing it all fall away in front of her, leaving nothing but bright air and the strange shadows of clouds far below.

The house turns out to be hotter than expected, and the snow peas don't take off the way she thought they would, but who can complain about sun-drenched rooms and vines that produce flowers instead of food? She drives out into the Amish countryside one afternoon, returning with a black bear cub of a puppy that she names Ursa. They take long surreal walks together through the cemetery down the street, the puppy dragging her leash among the tombstones and Cheri ambling along behind, reading the inscriptions and doing the math. Forty-six years is a long time, if you look at it a certain way. Ursa is her seventh dog.

The glimpses from her past are benign and interesting—the sullen face of a beautiful girl, framed in a Dairy Queen window, the chrome-and-tan dashboard of an old Beetle, rearview mirror draped with Mardi Gras beads, a gnarled and mossy live oak, standing in the middle of a chicken-scratched, red-dirt yard, and once, amazingly, what had to be her own tiny feet, grasped and lifted into the air in the classic pose of a diaper-change. Weird. And she keeps them to herself, these unportentous images, as she does the gradual onset of pain. By September the cancer has divided itself like an emigrating clan, dispersing to her lymph nodes, lungs, and spine.

She takes the news stoically, nodding. It's fall, she could make it to spring, and they might be able to shrink the spinal tumor with radiation, enough to delay paralysis, keep her mobile for a while. They show her the films, and she stares transfixed at the perfect curve of her own spine caught and held by the shadowy fingers of the monster. *Here, here, and a tiny bit here.* The doctor sets his pencil down on the desk and she stares at it, composing herself, willing away the claustrophobic images of last summer, the botched surgery, her leg dragging behind her in the swirling Brooklyn heat, numb foot scraping along the sidewalk. A zombie, a reanimated corpse. All that for this.

It might not happen, the doctor tells her. Other things might happen first.

She takes that to mean death. In the context of paralysis, it seems comforting.

We can keep you comfortable, he says reassuringly. If it comes to that.

But I can't tolerate pain medication, she says. They never found anything that didn't make me vomit.

He writes something on her chart and closes it, holds out his hand.

And this, of course, is when the world turns glamorous. Her daughters look like movie stars in their low-slung pants and pale autumn complexions. The trees on her street vibrate in the afternoon sunlight, the dying leaves so brilliant that she somehow feels she's never seen any of this before—fall, and the way the landscape can levitate with color, or even her simple cup of green tea in the afternoons, with milk and honey in a thick white mug. Warm. Her hand curled around it, or the newspaper folded beside it, or a halved orange on a blue plate sitting next to it. It's all lovely beyond words, really.

Even the pain has a sharp, glittering realness to it, like a diamond lodged in her hip. She ignores it, gardening, pruning the dead foliage, sorting out the pumpkin vines; and still she walks each day, abandoning the stone cemetery for the dazzling woods at Hickory Hill. Troops of shiny-headed Cub Scouts move through the park, picking up gum wrappers and cigarette butts, stopping to pet Ursa, jostling each other, asking if she bites. They never heard of the name Ursa, but there's so much they haven't heard of that they take it in stride.

"Our dog got put to sleep from a brain tumor," a little boy tells Cheri. "His name was Pete and it might have been from eating grass with pesticide on it." He examines Ursa's head, lifting her ears and looking inside, and then stands up. "This one seems okay," he says with an air of mild disappointment. He's smaller than the rest, compact and green-eyed, with a tumultuous stand of dark hair. An early version of all the men she's ever loved.

When he lopes away, Cheri feels strangely alone, but not unpleasantly so. Today the sky feels like company, and this winding orange-and-yellow trail. The diamond glints suddenly, causing her to gasp and squint her eyes. The pain sometimes is raucous, frightening, other times a dull glow in her chest, like inhaling embers. It's her spine she can't stop thinking about; the recurring, disquieting image of being alive inside a dead body. Ursa turns toward home and Cheri follows at a distance, noticing how her knees bend and straighten with each step.

The girls are burning leaves next to the curb, great crackling piles of them. She sits on the front steps with her afternoon tea and watches, not speaking even when spoken to. She just wants to rest everything, her body, her mind. Unbidden, as she brings the white cup to her lips, a memory appears: her refrigerator in an apartment down south, from the time when she worked in an airplane factory, cleaning parts, up to her elbows in toxic gunk all day, despising it. A Suzuki quote, sent to her by a sympathetic friend, pinned to the scarred door of the fridge where she could see it each evening.

When you do something, you should burn yourself up completely, like a good bonfire, leaving no trace of yourself.

The girls pause to lean on their rakes, Sarah talking, Katy shaking out her hair, retying it. The fire has reduced itself to a thin meandering plume, like cigarette smoke, while leaves continue drifting down from the sky. *Burn yourself up completely.* That's it, then. She stands and looks at her daughters, raking coals in the waning light.

"I'm done," she tells them.

She doesn't think of it as killing herself, she thinks of it as killing the monster. That's why a gun would be so satisfying. But impossible, of course, given her circumstances. With window-leaping you have a crowd, and in Iowa City, that could mean one or two acquaintances. Drowning isn't possible, she tried it. In the bathtub, just as an experiment, to see if she'd have the nerve.

No one tells her not to do it. She isn't the kind of person you say that sort of thing to. Instead, they grow silent and wary, both daughters vacating the house for long hours, coming home for meals, steamed vegetables and instant rice, or carryout from a downtown restaurant. Burritos dumped on a platter, refried beans shoveled into a bowl. Katy serving it up, Sarah pushing it around her plate. Cheri sipping ice water, lost in the pros and cons of her afternoon's research.

"Did you know a person of my weight would have to fall fifteen feet to break her neck?" she asks suddenly. That's why people like to hang themselves in barns, where they can step off a rafter. Works better that way, otherwise you've got the problem of dangling there until suffocation occurs. No barns in the vicinity, unfortunately, but there is a garage. She's still going back and forth on asphyxiation.

Katy and Sarah stare at her, unblinking, forks suspended.

"No, I didn't," Sarah says finally.

So much for dinner. The girls clear the table without a word, and adjourn to the living room and the evening news. Cheri stays in her spot, chewing ice cubes and waiting for Linda, who has taken to stopping over each evening. Pills would probably be the best, but whenever you hear *suicide attempt*, it's pills, and whenever you hear *suicide*, it's something more decisive—a bullet, a rope, a long sparkling plunge from a bridge.

The cough begins its slow ascent, giving her time to brace for it. Rattling and chaotic, it sounds like a paint can filled with gravel and rolled across the floor. By the time it's over—the gravel slowly diminishing to sand, shifting, allowing her to breathe again—Linda is beside her and the girls are in the doorway. Ursa moves from one to the next, offering a rawhide bone.

"You eat?" Linda asks, eyeing the dishes in the sink.

"I'm eating water," Cheri tells her, holding up the glass of ice.

In the living room, Vanna White prowls the row of letters in a dress as gauzy and form-fitting as a shroud. The television is always on now, one show melding into another, nobody really watching and nobody able to turn it off. As the evening progresses, they stare into the muted flickering light, first Sarah and Katy, then Sarah and Cheri, then just Sarah. At eleven o'clock the phone rings, a man asking for Cheri Tremble.

"She's in bed," Sarah tells him, "but she might still be awake."

"No, no," he says. "Let her rest if she can."

Cheri had written the letter only a few days before, outlining her situation, her intention, and asking for his help. He plucked it out of his stack of appeals and responded immediately—the impending paralysis and the fact that she couldn't tolerate painkillers were the deciding factors. If the medical records support her account of what's going on, Kevorkian is willing to help.

It's all true, Sarah whispers.

The living room is dim, lit only by the moonglow of the television. It all looks unfamiliar suddenly, and temporary, like a movie set. Kevorkian sounds just like a regular doctor, only sympathetic. He asks Sarah several questions—about Cheri's support system, how much care she needs, what the pain levels are like right now. Before hanging up, he explains that his patients have to come to him, he can't go to them.

He laughs at this, ruefully, and Sarah laughs too. She has no idea why.

In the dark bedroom at the end of the hall, Cheri is floating, unaware. The sleep train is just leaving the station, tracks unspooling behind like grosgrain ribbon. The familiar Amtrak scenery rocks past: sparse woods, long brilliant flashes of water, the ass-end of a Delaware town, row houses with garbage bags taped over the windows. A neighbor from her childhood hangs sheets on a line, wearing a housedress and men's shoes; as the sleeping car passes, the neighbor turns, watching its progress, shielding her eyes from the sun. A farm dog, running too close to the tracks, and then the face of someone she may have known once, an uncle perhaps, gaunt and shadowed, telling her something she can't quite hear.

"What?" she says into the dark.

It is left up to her to set the date; Kevorkian is flexible. It's October now, and Cheri explains that she wants to make it through Christmas.

"Oh, I hope much longer," he says.

This touches her deeply for some reason, his empathetic response, his hope that she can remain alive as long as possible. He doesn't even know her! His voice is soothing over the telephone, and kind. More like a pastor than a doctor, really, although the medical questions he asks are sharply intelligent. For the first time Cheri is able to describe the pain in unminimizing terms. The relief of this causes tears to course down her cheeks, although her voice remains steady and businesslike.

She's to contact Neal, his assistant, when she has a date. Neal will give her directions on what to do then. For now, just try to be comfortable, get what she can out of her days, settle her affairs. And tell only the people who must know.

Kate, Sarah, Linda, Wayne.

She goes as herself for Halloween—starkly thin, the extraneous flesh chiseled from her face, neck, wrists—and doles out chocolate bars to a sporadic procession of Disney characters and unraveling mummies. One boy with fangs and a plunging widow's peak hauls his sister up onto the porch, a tiny blond in a Pocahontas outfit. She holds her bag open distractedly, mask atop her head, peering past Cheri into the living room.

"The lady who lived here before died," she says. "And we've got her parakeet."

Her brother glances up at Cheri, and then quickly away. "She's lying," he says apologetically, dragging the little girl off the porch and into the darkness. The dog follows them for a moment and then materializes again in the porch light, wagging her tail at the bowl of candy.

Ursa will go with Sarah, and the cats probably with Linda, unless Katy speaks up. The house, back to her mother. She spends the next week sorting through her belongings, musing, then composes a will and places it in the top drawer of her dresser. To the Petersons she writes:

Linda, please take my gardening hat, the one I wore at Telluride. Wayne, you could use a good corkscrew. I'm fond of my brass one, made in Italy (at least I think it's brass). I've had it about seventeen years. Brandice, help yourself to your favorite sweater and Kailee to your favorite piece of jewelry. Schuyler, take my

fishing pole and catch some big ones for me ok? TJ, you can have
my Assistant Conductor hat pin from when I worked on the
trains in New York City. It should be where this will is.

Her daughters, of course, are more difficult. The lists have to be
weighed, items shifted back and forth until a precarious balance is
achieved:

Sarah, I'd like for you to have my jade necklace, silver tea set,
darkroom equipment, camping stuff, crystal vase, my books and
exercise bike. Also the family heirloom silver and brass curios
and the picture of McGregor and the blanket from Mexico.
  Kate, I'd like for you to have my silver chain necklace, ruby
ring (which gramma has), camera and accessories, rocking chair,
bike, round mirror, word processor, stereo and political books,
and pottery from Mexico.

By early November her yard is done. If there were going to be a next
year, she would have moved some of the plantings, the peonies closer
to the house, the little yew farther away. But it's set for now, everything mulched and orderly, her tools cleaned and stored in the basement. By the time she has her household in order the exhaustion has
become so acute it feels like sandbags are hanging from her limbs;
sometimes just pushing the hair back from her face takes more than
she can summon.

The lady who lived here before died. The body devolves into
compost, but we live on in our parakeets. She dreams of them,
fluorescent feathers glimpsed through dark foliage. Her naps have
become restless, sweaty affairs, the pain now unceasing, surrounding
her and fading, like the Doppler wail of an air-raid siren. She half
imagines it will get better, like a fractured bone or the stomach flu, but
of course it can only get worse. Worse than this!

She has Thanksgiving with Linda, Wayne, their family, and her
daughters. They linger at the table for a long time, telling stories and
drinking coffee, Cheri so exhausted by the effort of sitting upright that

she mostly listens, watching their familiar faces in the warm light, attuned to the murmur of daughters in the kitchen, the comforting sound of dishwater running. By the time she leaves—supported on either side, Linda following behind with leftovers to stow in the trunk—Cheri is so depleted that she can't keep the querulous thoughts at bay. She's nauseous with envy and rage, the unfairness of it all.

And of course nobody truly understands, but she can't see where it would matter if they did. The sandbags, the diminished lung capacity, the clangorous pain. It's all so intensely personal and claustrophobic, the heightened present mixed up with the banal past—this morning she nearly swooned from the vertiginous sight of her old maple dresser rising and falling, a pistoning bedpost, and the striped-shirted body of her brother Sean flinging himself up and down as they jumped on her bed. And last night she only catnapped, moving from bed to armchair and back to bed, dreaming random images of turkey farms, of rickrack on the neckline of a blouse, of the Beatles walking single-file across a road. Once, right before dawn, she looked down in her dream and saw phosphorescent insects alight on her hands and arms.

I can't make it to Christmas, she tells them. I thought I could but I can't.

The news is devastating; she supposes it's possible none of them really believed it before now. The girls collapse against her and then grow strangely calm, wandering shell-shocked through the house, speaking to each other in thin, echoing voices. Linda flinches when she's told, then breaks into tears, hands over her face.

They have three weeks to get used to it. After some consideration, Cheri chooses a Tuesday, the most nondescript day of the week. She calls Kevorkian's assistant, Neal, then books a flight to Detroit for December sixteenth, and a night's lodging in a Bloomfield motel. According to the plan, that's where the suicide will occur. Her body will be taken from the motel to the hospital and then to the morgue, where somebody—the coroner?—will perform an autopsy.

She wants cremation, a small service, no flowers. Katy goes with her to make the arrangements and they try not to be too surreal about it but have to keep consulting their list.

The funeral director is a young man with intensely sincere eyes and pure, palpable compassion. Cheri grows sleepy in his presence, forgetting some of the things she meant to bring up.

"What about transporting my body if I should die elsewhere?" she asks.

"If you're choosing cremation," he says carefully, "then that can be done at a facility near where the death occurs." He pauses, thinks. "And we'll work directly with them to receive the, uh, from there." He stares at the backs of his hands for a moment, turning his wedding ring one way and then the other, an absentminded gesture that gives her time to fill in the blank. Her body, reduced to a mound of kitty litter in a biscuit tin.

"Okay then," she says, and they all stand, formally, and stare at one another. Katy is wearing the miserable look of someone waiting for a tetanus shot, determined to be brave for the nurse's sake. The funeral director touches Cheri's arm and looks into her eyes; his own are red-rimmed, which takes her by surprise.

People are so kind! She reels from it sometimes, the mute commiseration, the gestures of support and assistance so subtle she barely recognizes them as such. Kate, the first time she helped her mother take a bath, had seemed merely to be idling, recounting an anecdote, sitting on the closed toilet seat with her legs crossed, eyes roaming around the edges of the room. When Cheri had finished bathing, Katy lifted her out of the water—casually, still talking—and wrapped her in a towel. Never in the whole process (holding out the underwear to be stepped into, retrieving the sweatpants warm from the dryer, tugging a pair of thick cotton socks onto the feet) did either of them let on that they'd performed a transposed version of this twenty years before.

Linda makes telephone calls to their circle, urging people to visit now if they want the chance. A few friends stop by during the afternoons and evenings, bearing casserole dishes or loaves of bread. Putting the food away in the kitchen gives them time to compose themselves—they were warned, of course, but nevertheless it takes a moment. The deterioration has accelerated in the last days, ravaging her body but leaving her face as translucent and still as frosted glass.

They kneel next to her rocking chair as they leave, keeping it together, promising to call in a few days, see how it's going.

Her breathing is labored after these visits, either from the exertion of talking and smiling, or from suppressing the panic that rises up when she tells them goodbye, unable to confess her plan, to take proper leave of her friends. She retreats to her bedroom and lies on top of the covers, arms folded around a pillow to keep from coughing, tethered to an oxygen tank by a length of clear tubing. The cancer has taken over completely now, crowding her out of her own body. When she touches her chest it's the monster she feels.

In eleven days it will all be over. Eleven! Alone in her room, she whimpers with the terrible grief of it, of being forced to abandon herself like a smoldering ship. It's impossible to imagine not existing, she discovers, because in order to imagine you must exist. The best she can do is picture the world as it is now, without her in it. But even then, she's the one picturing.

On the morning of day nine, she rests on the sofa and watches, absorbed, as a man climbs a telephone pole, his belt weighted with tools and an oversized red telephone receiver. He stabilizes himself with a safety harness and then gets busy, untangling a skein of multicolored wires, holding the red handset to his ear, possibility even speaking into it, although she can't imagine to whom. Once he takes pliers off his belt, gives something a good twist, and a sprig of snipped wire falls through the air to the grass below. Something about that scene, framed behind the glass of her living room window, embodies what she's been struggling to understand. It's momentary, a flash of insight so brief it can't be seen, but must be remembered, like the glimpse of a shooting star. The man with his cleats thrust into the pole, his weight tangible in the leather harness, the dark red of the telephone against the bright yellow of his hard hat, and then the tendril of wire falling away from his pliers—this is the world without her in it.

On the eighth day, she imagines dying with her eyes open, the naked vulnerability of it. She's got to remember to close her eyes and keep them closed, no matter what. And if Kevorkian approaches her and she should panic or start bawling, will he give her a chance to calm down or will he take it as a sign that she is conflicted, not ready, and refuse to go through with it? She forces herself to visualize the final scene over and over until it loses its meaning and becomes as ritualized as taking communion. No last-minute change of mind, no hysteria; she will simply greet him, explain herself in measured tones, express her gratitude, offer her arm for the needle, close her eyes.

By day seven, she understands air travel will be impossible, unendurable, because of her weakened state. A new plan is made for Wayne to rent a van and drive all of them to Detroit—Cheri, Linda, Sarah, and Kate. None of them can be present at her actual death, of course, since it's illegal, but still they'll be taking her there, nine hours away. Cheri feels momentarily frantic at the idea of this, her loved ones having to participate in her fate, but can't hold on to it for long. Too sick, too busy grasping her own thin hand, pulling herself along. Almost overnight, she feels herself beginning to detach from them; not because she wants to, but because she needs her own full attention. This is simply part of what happens.

Linda comes over in the evenings to wait with them, a little blast of refreshing cold entering the house with her. She brings food as well, and leans against the kitchen counter as they eat, chatting, then busies herself as best she can by sweeping up the fallen leaves from the schefflera tree, folding clean towels, petting Ursa. When she goes home they resume the vigil, tiptoeing around the house in their sock feet, staring for long moments at the television, or at their own spectral faces reflected in the dark windows.

Wayne shows up a few days before they are to leave and sits with Cheri awhile, making quiet small talk until she tires and then saying goodbye, squeezing her hand momentarily before he stands. Sarah and Katy call to him from the backyard, where Ursa has chased one of the cats up a tree. They are near tears, both of them walking in circles, coaxing the cat in high urgent voices. Wayne climbs a few feet up the tree and lifts the cat off a branch, manually detaching each claw, and hands it down to Sarah. When he glances behind, Cheri is standing at the kitchen window, waving thank you.

On the last night, Linda makes sandwiches for the trip, egg salad with lettuce, while Wayne plots the route using a road map and his computer; Sarah and Katy, after a dinner of yogurt and leftover soup, place the cats in bed with their mother and watch as she pets them and they purr, as Ursa puts her nose up on the covers and gets her ears combed and her face kissed; they listen as she reminds them: I love you, my *chicas*, never forget.

And Cheri, on her last night, weeps with relief when she's finally alone, suffers about five minutes of teeth-chattering fear, calms herself by imagining the faces and whispering the names of all her past dogs, then lies quietly with the pillow pressed to her chest, watching the interior images that click on and off like slides.

Near dawn she sleeps for a while and dreams of gathering Easter eggs: a violet one nestled between the white pickets of a porch railing, a pink-and-green one camouflaged in the grass next to a wire fence, an azure one balanced perfectly and precariously on a water spigot.

They leave under cover of darkness, like duck hunters or criminals, barely whispering. They settle Cheri on the bench seat in the middle of the van, oxygen canister next to her, daughters behind her. The van door glides closed with a soft thud, and while Wayne climbs in and situates his coffee, Linda stares out the windows at the neighborhood emerging in the grainy light. Straight-edged prairie bungalows surrounded by sugar maples and oaks. Cheri's little corner house painted a curious shade of dark vanilla with bright white trim; a thatch of low evergreens pressed against the porch. It all seems so calm and unadorned, as full of hidden promise as the bulbs planted beneath the kitchen window.

Cheri refuses herself even one last look. That was then, this is now.

Already she needs more oxygen, just from the effort of getting this far. Linda turns on the dome light and adjusts the dial; Cheri breathes deeply, head down to combat the nausea. Sarah begins crying silently in the back, and Katy leans forward to touch her mother's shoulder. The town flattens into countryside and they drive due east, straight into the sunrise, pillowy December clouds edged in apricot. Linda passes the thermos to Katy and Cheri lifts her head briefly, asks to have the oxygen turned up again.

Halfway through Illinois, she begins to panic over possibly having to go to the hospital if the tank runs out and can't be refilled. She had made all the plans for the trip, including how much oxygen to bring, but her needs have increased sharply just over the last few days. If she has to go to the hospital, they'll call her doctor, and her doctor will put two and two together. Inside the tight black place behind her eyelids, she watches herself clench her fists and hold them up against the sky.

Wayne tracks down a pharmacy in Joliet and Linda somehow gets the tank refilled. All they know is she walked in with it empty and walked out with it full. Determination and twenty-five bucks, she tells them. Cheri keeps her head in her hands through the next two states, trying not to vomit. Sarah and Kate take turns comforting her and resting their foreheads on the back of her seat, dazed and leaden. Car crazy, longing for a cigarette.

Cheri lifts her head briefly and seeks out Wayne in the rearview mirror. "I need to stop at a bathroom," she tells him.

He finds a funky, old-fashioned Clark station, where he can pull right up to the washroom door. Two of them help her use the facilities while the other two lean against the van and smoke. Cheri has never been this freaked out in her life, and that's saying something. One thing she's learning is that it's important to stay in the moment, not to leap ahead even fifteen minutes. Right now she's staring at herself in a shadowed washroom mirror, now she's in the cold wind next to the van, trying to get her gloves on. Now they slide the door open and she steps back, looks at her daughter's face. Now getting settled, taking the oxygen tube, returning the stare of the guy pumping gas. Frozen cornfields, a deflated barn, looming underpass, and then the interstate. She drops her head back into the cool damp shell of her hands. Now the buffet and roar of semis, now a quavering sigh from somebody inside the van. The tires begin making a rhythmic clocking noise, passing over seams in the concrete.

Cheri opens her eyes intermittently and stares at her knees, just to stabilize and remember where she is. Lying down isn't possible, although that's why they got the van. Her lungs are full, and the nausea is overwhelming. Breathless and gasping, she runs down a twisting white corridor inside her head, the blat of a siren bouncing off the walls; suddenly the narrow hallway opens out onto a suburban backyard, the floor becomes grass, and she's on a swing, knobby knees pumping, reaching toward the sky with her Keds. The chains go slack for a long instant each time the swing reaches its apex. She's panting with reckless exhilaration.

"Do you need it turned up?" Linda's voice, disembodied, and the monster inches away, Cheri's breathing calms.

"Thank you," she whispers into her hands.

The swing now has stopped, and still seated, she walks herself around in a circle, twisting the chains, then lifts her feet and spins, body canted so far back that her hair brushes the dirt. She's breathless and dizzy under the limp August sky until someone reaches out, turns up a radio, and cold invigorating oxygen flows into her nose. Another someone gently stabilizes her as the van banks onto an exit, takes a left turn, glides over a bump, ascends, descends, and stops. When she looks up from her cupped hands they are idling under the canopy of the Quality Inn.

Thank God. She retreats into her hands again.

Behind the registration desk is a holiday wreath and a mirror; in the mirror is the face of a crazy person who looks only marginally like Sarah. She pulls it together as best she can—tucking in the migrating strands of hair, straightening her jacket, clearing her throat—before meeting the eyes of the clerk. He's a man in his fifties, white-haired, wearing glasses.

"My mother reserved a room," she tells him. "Cheri Tremble?"

He stares at her, assessing. "Where is she?" he asks.

"I'm getting the room," Sarah answers slowly. "She's in the car, with a headache."

He continues staring at her for a moment, then steps into an office to call someone, speaking low but keeping an eye on the desk and the young woman shifting from foot to foot, zipping and unzipping her coat.

Sarah deliberately turns her back on him. The lobby is awash in a franchised gloom—couches arranged here and there, glass coffee table with an extravagant arrangement of silk flowers, and a breakfast station with a do-it-yourself waffle iron and plastic bins that dispense cornflakes. The clerk steps up once again to the desk; the wreath behind his head is decorated with spray-on snow and sparkling plastic fruit made to look like marzipan. He knows what's going on.

"I'm sorry, I can't give you a room," he tells her.

"Why not?" she asks, incredulous.

"We've had some problems with Dr. Kevorkian," he says. He looks pleased, which frightens Sarah. She thought he just called his boss, but it could have been the police. He has the excited and pious expression of a man capable of making a citizen's arrest.

"This is crazy," she answers, backing away. "We have a reservation."

"Hunh-uh," he says loudly. "Nope."

And then Sarah's back in the van, telling Wayne to drive, get out of there, Cheri's struggling to breathe, unable to make a decision, all of them thrown into a panic that propels them out of the parking lot and back into the early-evening traffic. They drive around in circles for a few minutes until they find a pay phone at a gas station, and Linda leaves a message for Kevorkian's assistant, Neal Nicol. They wait as long as they can, motor idling in the cold, rainy twilight, oxygen tank dwindling, Cheri suffering wave after wave of anxiety. The fear of dying tonight is nothing, she realizes, compared to the fear of still being alive tomorrow morning. She leans forward and then back, rocking herself slowly, trying to calm down. When no one calls them back they pull away reluctantly and drive a few blocks more, to an Office Depot.

Linda, Katy, and Sarah go inside and compose a fax to Kevorkian, explaining their predicament in all caps:

TO: DOCTOR

CHERI TREMBLE IS IN THE DETROIT AREA. SHE WAS NOT PERMITTED TO REGISTER AT THE QUALITY INN . . . WE HAVE TRIED TO REACH NEAL A NUMBER OF

TIMES WITHOUT SUCCESS AND WE ONLY HAVE ONE
SMALL TANK OF O$_2$ LEFT . . . WE ARE FAXING THIS
FROM OFFICE DEPOT IN BLOOMFIELD.

FROM: CHERI'S FRIEND

The store is warm and well lit, a man stands in line near them
holding a wastebasket and a package of Bic pens. The boy at the copy
counter takes their fax and sends it without comment, then lingers
nearby, casting sidelong glances at Katy. A few feet away, down the
office-equipment aisle, a young couple in matching ski jackets feed a
piece of paper into a shredder and watch as it emerges in long, graceful
strands.

The phone rings and a fax begins chugging through.

Thank God, Linda whispers.

Sarah and Kate stand next to the van in the twilight, smoking and
waiting for Neal, who is on his way. The drizzle stops momentarily
and one by one the parking lot floodlights buzz to life, turning
everything green. Inside the van, just visible through the smoked
glass, Cheri is sitting once again with head in hands.

"This is fun," Katy says.

"Yeah," Sarah answers.

They can hardly look at one another, faces bathed in the alien light.
Each knows what the other is feeling, being so urgently compelled
toward something they are profoundly and instinctively opposed to.
Not Kevorkian, exactly, but the simple fact of Cheri's death. Neither
of them has fully absorbed the fact that if all goes as planned she will
cease to exist *this evening*. This evening! They scan the faces in the cars
that glide past, easing into and out of parking spaces, people on their
way to buy envelopes. Before anyone has a chance to get worried, a car
pulls up, and a large man jumps out and hugs them. Neal. They're to
follow him to Kevorkian's house.

They wind through an affluent neighborhood, past suburban castles
with iron gates and leafless, glowering trees; inside the van the only

sound in the long interval between the windshield wipers is the wheeze of oxygen moving through the tubing. It's trash day in this neighborhood, garbage cans materializing and dematerializing in the thin steam that rises from the streets. They follow Neal up the driveway of an unassuming ranch house tucked among the sprawling mansions. Suddenly, a man is framed in their headlights, peeking out from the attached garage. Gaunt and sunken-eyed, with a military crew cut and an animated expression, he gestures for them to pull inside, and then hops nimbly out of their way.

Jack Kevorkian, as seen on TV.

Relieved and terrified, everyone bursts out laughing, even Cheri.

The burden is shifted somehow, with that momentary release of hysteria. In his cardigan sweater and open-collared shirt, Kevorkian has the amiable and authoritarian air of a retired general. He is clearly the center of the group, in control, his voice resonant and welcoming as he introduces himself and Dr. Georges Reding—a psychiatrist who, along with Neal, will remain in the background as witness and assistant.

Wayne half carries Cheri into the living room, where plastic chairs have been arranged in a semicircle, one of them draped with a blanket to make it more comfortable. Katy sits next to her mother and Sarah at their feet. Whatever numbness had gotten them all through the long ride from Iowa is wearing off. The house feels temporary, like an office set up in a trailer, and the men seem both hearty and furtive, like Bible salesmen.

Cheri is awake now, unintimidated. These men are familiar to her; she understands the dynamics of idealism, the personality traits of a certain kind of fanaticism. She rallies, giving a coherent accounting of her medical condition. They want to ascertain that this is her decision.

"Yes, mine," she says clearly. She holds her oxygen tube out like the stem of a wine glass and gathers herself before speaking again. "I only have forty-five minutes of oxygen left."

"We have time," Dr. Kevorkian says kindly. "Don't worry."

Katy and Sarah stare at each other, wide-eyed and trembling. Forty-five minutes is fifteen times three. Everything is welling up, faster than they can absorb it.

Dr. Kevorkian speaks to all of them, describing what he calls a patholytic procedure, the intravenous injection of a combination of drugs that will make her go to sleep, relax her respiration, and stop her heart. Cheri listens carefully, nodding, and then signs her name over and over, Cheri Tremble, until she's hearing it inside her head like a chant.

Linda and Wayne must sign papers as well, and are told to leave the state via the most direct route possible. It's all printed out for them: the coroner, the funeral home, what to do and when.

Cheri hands her driver's license to Kevorkian, for identification of the body, then gives her billfold, address book, and glasses to Sarah. It's time.

And now the girls are dissolving, wailing, saying their goodbyes in a chaos of hands, mouths, faces, hair, tears. At one point or another, both are in Cheri's lap, holding onto her, crying so violently and so desperately that everyone is trying to shush them. They're inconsolable; every time they pull themselves away and start toward the door, they turn back to their mother. Cheri is trying to soothe them, kissing foreheads, whispering. Her tank now says thirty-two minutes.

She says a hurried goodbye to Linda and Wayne, reaching up to embrace them weakly, then watching as they gather her daughters and try to lead them from the house, each one breaking away briefly, running back to kneel at Cheri's feet, sobbing.

Cheri calls out to Linda, "Take care of them!"

"I will," Linda promises, her face haggard and despairing. It's all a jagged blur of grief: the careening house, Katy's heaving shoulders and Sarah's stricken face, Wayne's jacket-clad arm as he tries to usher them from the room, Linda's own unspoken words of farewell fluttering inside her chest like snared birds.

At the door, Sarah turns and starts back toward her mother. *You can't just leave a person like this*, she thinks. *You can't.*

"Sarah!" Cheri says sharply.

Sarah stops. Her mother is sitting in the draped chair, the three men standing in the shadows behind her. *You can't leave a person like this.* But she sees from her mother's expression that it's too late.

Cheri has left them.

When they're gone the house is filled with a beautiful, queer silence. It's like the airy, suspended moment that follows the last reverberating note on a pipe organ. *I'm alone*, she thinks, her heart suddenly clopping inside her chest like hooves, her head too heavy for the fragile stem of her neck. No family, no friends, no way out except through. She slumps forward in a swoon and then immediately rights herself, overcompensating like a drunk. *Please*, she thinks, picturing herself erect and composed. *I'm sorry.*

When the men first touch her she flinches and cries out, but then grows calm as they minister to her. Two of them help her down the hall to a small bedroom, propping her with pillows to ease her breathing, tucking a rolled-up blanket under her knees, covering her with a thin blue chenille bedspread.

Dr. Kevorkian takes a seat next to her. The tank is at eighteen minutes, he explains. When it's at ten, if she's ready, he will start the procedure. Cheri half closes her eyes and reaches out, entwines her fingers with this stranger's. She's beyond words now, transfixed by the images flickering inside her head, left hand gripping the folds of chenille.

At first it's meaningless, frantic electrical impulses taking the form of memories—a Mexican lizard on an adobe wall, panting like a dog; a pair of dusty ankles; her father in a sport coat, nuzzling a kitten; her brother Sean with a sparkler, framed against a night sky, spelling out her name with big cursive flourishes, the letters disappearing even as they are written. And then the pain is gone, leached out of her so completely that she feels hollow and weightless, borne aloft, the back of her head tucked into the crook of an elbow, legs bent as they were in the womb, flannel feet cupped in the palm of a hand. Spellbound, she uses her last minutes to gaze up at her mother's young face.

Cheri?

She nods, still watching her mother, and someone takes her arm. The needle is cold, and in a moment she's numb, separated from the men by a thick layer of ice. She breathes slowly in the narrow pocket of air and the children in their bright skates congregate above her head. She lingers there for a moment, her cheek pressed against the underside of the ice, until a hand reaches down and pushes her under.

NIT-PICKERS
Kathryn Harrison

Late on the Saturday afternoon following Thanksgiving. I'm standing in the supermarket checkout line with my nine-year-old daughter. Cereal, juice, milk, pasta. Bananas, yogurt, cookies. My daughter's pullover is dirty, her long brown hair tangled, only half of it left in the ponytail holder. I watch her scratch her head.

"Stop it," I say.

"I can't."

"But you know how itching is. Scratching makes it worse."

She sighs. "Can I have a quarter?" she asks.

"If I have one." My pockets are filled with receipts, dirty tissues, an apple core, sandwich rinds, and even Milkbone crumbs, detritus from the day spent on the road, all of us—two parents, two children, the dog—returning from a holiday spent at the kids' grandparents'.

My daughter turns the handle of the vending machine and retrieves the gum ball with her left hand, continuing to scratch with her right. Children do scratch, of course, and they slouch; they sneeze and yawn without covering their mouths; they worry their loose teeth with dirty fingers. I make it a point to resist unnecessary censure, but this scratching—dedicated, passionate—for some reason it bothers me. Suddenly I remember a letter from the school nurse two weeks prior, the one that informed parents of fourth graders of a case of head lice in their child's class. I stare as my daughter's ponytail holder slides off and onto the floor, dislodged by the force of her scratching.

"Didn't go through," the checkout girl says. "Maybe you should watch while you punch in your PIN number," she suggests, sarcasm sharpening her tone.

I run my debit card back through the slot. *Not head lice, please not head lice*, I pray, and yet I know it must be lice that's causing the itching. For wouldn't their arrival be that of a long-expected blight? The consummation of a dread fueled by conversations with other mothers, anecdotes traded over the phone as we preside over our respective kitchens, overlooking homework and saucepans, pencil in one hand, slotted spoon in the other. We navigate the small panic of the working mothers' dinner hour with telephone receivers cradled between ear and shoulder, glasses of wine we'd rather share in person, but where would we find the time? It was just the previous month that I adjusted the receiver to whisper, *You forgot to carry over into the tens*, a drip of olive oil staining my daughter's homework, then asked, "But what happened, really? Not an actual breakdown."

"Well, you know, she ended up having her daughter's head shaved."

"Not *shaved*."

"Okay, a crew cut. And she broke up with the guy she was seeing. And she went back into therapy."

"Yeah," I'd conceded. Head lice could do that.

I hurry my daughter out of the market, hustle her across streets, hissing, as though a passerby might care to eavesdrop, "I think you might have lice."

She stops scratching. "Really?" she says, and she pauses midstep, looking more interested than alarmed.

I pull her along the sidewalk, hand tight around her biceps, remembering how I resented that same businesslike grasp and yet unable, under the circumstances, to be gentle. "I have to look," I pant. "With a good light. A magnifying glass."

At home, I sit my daughter under a halogen reading lamp. I can't find the magnifier, but under the bulb's glare I don't need one to see that, yes, a tiny something is crawling on my daughter's scalp. Against her dark brown hair the louse looks slyly translucent, its minute gray legs moving with fugitive industry through her hair. I drop the hank I've separated, left with an impression not unlike a *National Geographic* cutaway of life in the grasslands—a menacing, miniature forest blown up for the purpose of edification, of exposing the clandestine life at root level. I smile at my daughter, I give her a hug, and try not to do what I want to do, which is scream, weep, run. After all, I don't want her to feel unclean or stigmatized.

My husband, however, is not so often spared the fallout of my neuroses. "Something's happened!" I tell him, interrupting as he triages the mail that arrived during our absence. He doesn't answer, and I step dramatically between him and the pile of bills on his desk. "Lice!" I announce.

He looks up. "Oh," he says, and then he pushes the phone bill toward me. "What are these 956 numbers? Is someone calling for horoscopes or something?"

"Head lice! Lice! Lice all over her head!"

My husband looks at me. In fact, I've only seen the one louse, but its image—so fleeting, so furtive—has seized hold of my imagination in a way that a more explicit encounter might not have. Already one has multiplied into legions of vermin.

"What does that mean?" my husband asks carefully, his eyes straying back to the bill.

"It means that—that I have to go to pharmacy, right now, before it closes! That we all have to wash our hair with lice-killers. That I have to do the sheets and the towels and—"

"You want me to go to the pharmacy?" he offers, less out of generosity, I suspect, than out of a desire to avoid the first maneuvers in a campaign of bed-stripping and late-into-the-night laundry. By virtue of the mothers' dinner-hour network of rumor and information, I know what's required to rid a household of head lice: stuffed animals must be confiscated and sealed in bags; clothing and all personal effects subjected to hours in a hot dryer; heads bowed under chemical rinses; hair raked with a nit comb until tears flow.

I look at my husband who, like most husbands, lacks the ability to come back from the store with the right brand of detergent, the unbruised apple, the size of diaper that corresponds to the size of the person to be diapered. "I'll go," I say. "You'll get the wrong stuff."

"There's nothing I can do?" he asks, hopefully.

"You can put them in the bath. Start with her, and make sure her clothes go into a garbage bag, not the hamper. I'll be back in ten minutes."

Galvanized out of my post-holiday-six-months-pregnant-and-spent-the-day-on-the-turnpike exhaustion, I slam out of the house and arrive breathless and prickling with anxiety at the pharmacy, where I spend more than fifty dollars on one of each pediculicide the store carries. I hunch over the counter as I sign the credit card receipt, sure that all the people in line behind me with their suddenly not-so-embarrassing armloads of douches and ear wax dissolvers and hemorrhoid creams are watching me with disgust, stepping back to avoid even tangential contact with a person who is buying *the family-size pack of NIX lice-killing shampoo.*

A tear, one I recognize as worthy of a schoolchild, slides down my nose. My fifth-grade homeroom teacher, Mrs. Knowles, was tall and thin, with meticulously combed silver hair. Perhaps teaching was more vocation than economic necessity, because when the southern California temperature dipped into the low fifties she wore a very un-schoolteacher-like black mink jacket that set off her hair in a manner that even children could appreciate. A fastidious person whose long, manicured fingers remained magically untouched by chalk dust or red ink, Mrs. Knowles was given to spontaneous lectures on personal hygiene. Routinely, she sent boys to the principal's office for the commonplace vulgarities of belching or nose-picking. Girls were warned of the dangers of sharing hairbrushes, combs, scarves.

Head lice, she announced, were a *deserved affliction* that visited the slovenly; and when her black eyes rested briefly on my own head I knew that I must be infested. Clumsy, with unkempt nails, tousled hair, wrinkled blouse: I was a person whom lice would savor, and for weeks after school I sat on the tiled bathroom counter with a magnifying glass in one hand, a flashlight in the other, determined to catch one. That I never saw any evidence of lice did not convince me I wasn't a host, and I spent the remainder of fifth grade unable to meet Mrs. Knowles's penetrating gaze. As I was ashamed to raise my hand to produce answers I knew but was unworthy to utter, my grades fell. Surreptitiously, I spent my allowance and birthday money on medicated dandruff shampoo, thinking it might effect a cure. Behind the locked bathroom door I applied it full strength and left it on until my scalp tingled.

When I come home from the pharmacy, my husband is eating a peanut butter and jelly sandwich, his plate balanced on the bills.

"You were supposed to be putting her in the bath!" I cry.

He smiles. "I thought if I got myself something to eat you wouldn't have to worry about my dinner," he counters, still seeming calm, clearly unable to understand that we're embarking on a dire war.

The first night of the first campaign against lice is not, in retrospect, so bad. There are tears, yes. And, yes, the shampoo smells and burns, the combing hurts (nits, or louse eggs, are cemented to hair shafts with a seemingly bionic adhesive), and yes, the favorite stuffed toys are smothered in bags. But when at last we are all in bed, scrubbed and smarting, sister, brother, father, and even pregnant mother who failed to see any fine print cautioning people in her condition to avoid contact with pediculicides, I feel briefly optimistic. I've worked hard for hours. I'm going to win.

On Monday morning, I send a note to the school nurse, admitting, like a good citizen, that my daughter has had lice and that she and her brother were treated. My communication has a shrill quality and makes it clear that I hold the school responsible for our suffering. When I call the nurse later that day I try to sound friendly, but a querulous tone takes over.

The nurse sighs. She is patient. "People always hold the school responsible," she concedes, and then she tells me about a child whose persistent case of head lice was finally cured when the vector was identified not as a classmate but as the child's grandmother. The nurse offers to send a packet of information home with my daughter: alternative treatments, protocols of hygiene taken from *The Lice Buster Book*, a pamphlet from a professional nit-picking service that will, if needed, come to one's house to end an infestation. I hang up feeling both rebuked and a little self-righteous. Haven't I devoted days to this already? How can she imply that the scourge is not yet over?

By the time I get the packet, another week has passed, during which I have continued to launder and scrub and—uselessly, according to the Xeroxes—send out carpets to be steam-cleaned. Alone in the house, aided by the unnatural strength granted by adrenaline, and ignoring the wisdom that dictates against pregnant women lifting heavy objects, I've heaved up beds, desks, and filled bookcases to pull out rugs, which I've then rolled and carried down flights of stairs.

For two weeks we live on chilly floorboards, and then, just hours after the carpets have been returned—sanitized, deodorized, pet-guarded: I say yes to every potentially louse-unfriendly option—my son starts to scratch his head.

"It is true, is it not, that this isn't a medical emergency?" Over the breakfast dishes, my husband tries, quixotically, to combat hysteria with reason, "That lice can't really hurt the children?"

I nod, lick tears from over my lip. Exhausted after another night of chemical shampoos and three-hundred-watt nit combing, I've slept only a few hours, tormented by nightmares of every imaginable dermatological blight, from baldness to leprosy.

"Lice don't carry diseases?" my husband presses.

I shake my head,

"So it's only pneumonia that might kill them?" He tries, uselessly, to get me to laugh. Subfreezing weather has arrived, and yet there's never a hat or a scarf to be found, all of them being gradually, day by day, reduced to dryer fluff.

What will end this scourge? According to the pamphlet from the lice eradicating service, in the last several years a subgroup of the vermin has developed resistance to killing agents like NIX, a fact of which I am well aware, having watched lice swim with energetic defiance through tides of supposedly poisonous shampoos and creme rinses. And the products don't even claim to kill nits, an adult female laying as many as ten a day for thirty days . . . *each louse with three hundred potential children and*—I do the simple math over and over, the product seems impossible—*ninety thousand grandchildren* . . .

"There's this service," I offer. "They'll come to the house and—"

"How much does it cost?" My husband stands from the table. "Sixty dollars."

He looks at me with suspicion. "Only sixty?"

"An hour," I add, apologetic.

"That's outrageous." My husband shakes his head, gathering papers into his briefcase. And he doesn't even know how much it cost to send the rugs out to be boiled.

I follow him through the front door, deafening myself to complaints about his missing hat, all his missing hats, and thinking dark thoughts about his handsome beard, his general hairiness, his affection for knit watch caps. It's probably him, *the vector*, why not? He claimed to have left the NIX on for fifteen minutes, but did he? He never reads package directions, considers weekends an excuse to forgo bathing, doesn't floss. Lies to his dentist about not flossing. At night I listen for sounds of him scratching; I make sure there's a wide moat between his pillow and mine.

On the street we head in opposite directions. Today I'm one of the class parents who will accompany my daughter's class to a children's theater production of C. S. Lewis's *The Lion, the Witch, and the Wardrobe*, adapted from one of my favorite novels. Still, sitting among rows of elementary school students, all fidgeting, stretching, and scratching in their familiar and probably benign way, I can't watch the play, surrounded, as I feel I am, by happily squirming vermin carriers.

For Christmas we return to my husband's parents, this time to their Virginia cabin, driving through the pretty Shenandoah mountains in our minivan, the vehicle that my father-in-law politely suggested might have been the original, Pandoral source of our infestation. Strewn with fast food bags, dog hair, candy wrappers, smelling of fertilizer, mildew, indelible-even-if-long-past episodes of motion sickness, ours is a car that would fall under suspicion whenever health or hygiene was the issue.

But no, my husband tells his father, the car spends days locked up and unoccupied, and head lice are obligatory parasites, they need fresh blood every twelve hours.

This Christmas is, in most respects, one of the best we've had. The children are transported by their first skiing lessons, and Santa has been astonishingly extravagant: two new iMacs, purple for him, blue for her. Sitting among torn wrapping paper, my seams splitting with the promise of new life, my face shining in the festive glow of the tree, I feel cold with dread. Both sister and brother are scratching their heads, and what if the itch isn't dry skin brought on by so many caustic shampooings? Having reached the point where the children duck and run from examination and, worried as I am that they might give lice to their cousins, having been asked by my husband's mother not to reveal our unsavory blight, what can I do?

Toast crumbs. Pollen. Salt spilled from a shaker. Sawdust. Stray bits from a chemistry set: for me every surface of the cabin crawls with lice. To keep anxiety at bay, I police the headgear situation, forbidding anyone to share hats, and each night sizzling everything in the dryer.

In bed, under an immaculate winter sky, stars glittering in fiery immunity to human torment, I'm host to a wild nervous itching that targets my pubic region. Though I well know that head lice and pubic lice are not the same creature, it seems in the dark that these lice, *our lice*, might lack discrimination; and I succumb to the indignity of midnight searches, using a hand mirror and flashlight to see what my pregnant belly obscures from direct observation.

By the time we return home, I'm not only fretful but pessimistic. Still, I surprise myself with the storm of desperate tears occasioned by the third discovery of head lice, these, on both son and daughter, seeming to saunter insolently down the pathway made by the comb. "I'm calling them," I say, and my husband doesn't need to ask who. I advance on him with comb in hand. "I'm not kidding. I can't take any more."

My husband's eyes crinkle in conjugal been-there-don't-go-there apprehension. "Call," he agrees, and then he says the one thing that tells me how desperate I must seem: "I don't care how much it costs."

It's 8:30 on a Wednesday morning when I dial the lice service and get a recorded message from a doctor, whose voice asks my name and number, in return offering a cell phone number in case of emergency. I write this down and consider dialing it—certainly the presence of parasites on my children is a crisis. But is it an emergency? I can't imagine the conversation the faceless doctor and I might have, were he to answer. Would it begin with my predawn nightmare? *Together my children and I are falling down a long chute, like a laundry chute, at the bottom of which is a vat of something that's supposed to cure lice, except it doesn't—instead they're crawling through our tear ducts and* . . . It seemed unlikely that a reliable professional would invite the kind of hysteria overwrought mothers are capable of delivering.

I manage to wait until nine, when the doctor's assistant returns my message.

"Can you send someone today?" I plead.

"I'll try. But I have to tell you," she cautions, "it's our busy season." I hang up, reduced, until ten, to those petitionary prayers it's embarrassing to make, even silently, to oneself. Then the phone rings.

"Twelve-thirty," the assistant says.

"Do you take checks, credit cards? Should I get cash from the bank?" I picture myself with a suitcase crammed with a cartoon ransom of banded bills. Any amount to return my children to me unharmed and deloused.

"Checks are fine." She warns me that it might require many hours to one-by-one hand-remove the nits from both my children's heads—the only true method for eradicating lice—and that the sixty-dollar-per-hour fee will not include the cost of shampoos, oils, travel expenses, tips.

"Of course," I say, the banded bills shifting from twenties to fifties. "I understand."

The doorbell rings at the appointed hour, and yet, when I see two soberly dressed women on my front step, one carrying a dark folder and what appears to be a briefcase, their missionary aspect and expressions of dire intervention deceive me. They must be Jehovah's Witnesses, who frequently proselytize in my neighborhood. I open the door, and they both nod in a curt, businesslike way and step inside, out of the cold, before I can politely refuse any tracts.

"Do you have a table where I can set up?" the one with the briefcase asks.

"Oh." I look from one face to the other, confused. "You're from— you're the lice people?"

The woman who inquired about the table smiles with faint condescension. "You are Mrs. Harrison?" she counters.

In reply I step back and out of their way, inviting them further into the hall. "The kitchen?" I suggest. Another curt nod, and the two follow me and watch as I peel back the holly print tablecloth to expose an edge to which they can clamp the base of a folding lamp produced from the black bag.

"Christmas," I offer in unnecessary explanation for the gaudy cloth, an old favorite of my grandmother's.

"Plug?" the woman asks, shedding her overcoat and gloves. The other continues to silently unpack equipment.

Apparently we are under way, having forgone any pleasantries of introduction. I call the children from their rooms and they creep reluctantly downstairs, for once stepping carefully on the creaking old treads.

The lamp is the kind I associate with the watchmaker's trade: a circular fluorescent bulb mounted around a large magnifying lens. Switched on, the bright eye illuminates a Mary Poppins–like production of items from the one deceptively small case: several gallon-capacity Ziploc bags each holding four plastic applicator-tip bottles of amber liquids, a selection of fine-toothed combs and slender wooden sticks, a dozen large plastic hair clips, a bottle of rubbing alcohol and a shallow bowl in which to pour it, a roll of white paper towels, and a large, felt-backed, plastic table cloth to unfold and spread on the floor.

Set-up is efficient, accomplished without conversation. I and my two children watch in uncharacteristic silence, nodding submissively as the taller woman, who never offers her name and whose terse manner inhibits my asking it, explains that she will be doing today's job, her companion is here only as an apprentice, to observe. She hands me a form, one that includes questions about possible allergies, and as I complete it I understand that the emergencies to which the doctor's message alluded must be those of anaphylactic shock, some dangerously dire reaction to his formulas. I hesitate, briefly, before signing.

The first order of business is to check all our heads. My daughter sits in a chair placed under the circular bulb, and the nit-picker begins to examine her scalp, using one of the wooden sticks to part her thick hair. For the purpose of inspection she has donned intimidating headgear: glasses like those for welders, the heavy, square magnifying lenses set in a visor so cumbersome it requires additional bracing in the form of a band that goes over the top of her meticulously cornrowed hair. "See how I open the head," she says to her apprentice, and I shudder, helplessly, her words evoking playground accidents, split skulls. A few minutes later, after my son has had his turn and I am sitting with the light pouring over my shoulders, she repeats the phrase, and I hear "open" as I would "unpack," as though it pertained to a text, the content of my head easily readable under so many watts and powers of magnification.

When I stand up from the examination chair, the expensive nit-picker looks pointedly at my swollen midriff and asks, "Did you tell the office about this?" Having reached that point in pregnancy where people often address remarks to my middle rather than to my face, I'm used to people asking if I'm well while inquiring, really, about the progress of gestation; but how we're doing isn't what the nit-picker wants to know.

"Did I tell them I was pregnant?" I ask, feeling myself blush under her fixed stare, apologetic as an unwed teen.

She nods, lips pursed, conveying exasperation. With no evidence of lice and only one nit—"loose on the shaft," as the nit-picker describes it—I present a complication: I cannot be treated with the same shampoo as that indicated for use on my children.

I shake my head. "I didn't think—" *I had any*, I was going to add. "Where's the phone? I have to call."

I show her to the desk. "Is it necessary?" I ask. "For just one? If it was loose, not really stuck to the hair . . . Maybe it was dead?" I suggest, hopefully. What I don't dare articulate is my suspicion that she was mistaken, maybe it wasn't even a nit—for how can a person have a single egg, and that in the absence of its parent? How likely is it that a solitary unwed louse would have so quickly traversed the forest of my hair, leaving one lone offspring in her wake? But the nit-picker, already in consultation with the office that dispatched her, doesn't answer my questions.

Standing over my daughter, working up a pungent lather, the nit-picker conveys the tenacious, the steadfast if weary quality of our own convent-trained Belizean nanny. The doctor who owns this service must be quite rich—as prosperous as the agent through whom we found our nanny—having intelligently capitalized on the squeamishness of women like me: mothers who have tried and failed, who have enough money and not enough patience to forgo the expertise of one of his employees, women perhaps all like the one standing in my kitchen, smoothly dark and industrious, with a melodious island accent, a disdainful mien, and a youth that prepared her for the possibility of relentlessly tedious tasks. Our nanny has worked for us for ten years now, cleaning up spills and tears, arranging play dates and walking the blocks between them, flinching at the casual profanities that sometimes issue from the largely secular mass of predominantly white and affluent children in whose company she finds herself. Our nanny, I know, loves and disapproves of us in equal measure. The nit-picker only disapproves.

"Do I have to be treated?" I ask her. It's now a half hour after she has hung up with her office, time during which I've waited for her to reveal whatever verdict proceeded from the exchange, monosyllabic on our end.

"Ask the doctor. Only he know," she says. This is, I discover, a standard response. Though I never meet or speak with the calm voice that has masterminded this war against lice, it is his hidden wisdom that will dictate the precaution of treating my head's micro-infestation with a special solution formulated for pregnant and nursing mothers (and delivered, hours after a second phone consultation, to my door), his wisdom that mandates the follow-up applications of shampoos and oils and vermin-repellent drops.

"What's in it?" I ask of the golden, thick-as-honey liquid the nit-picker has worked into my daughter's hair.

She takes her time answering questions. "Ask the doctor," she says, finally, when she leads my daughter to the sink.

As for my repeated question of the significance of the nit being "loose" on my hair shaft, she tells me that she believes this to mean the egg is "no good," but concedes that this may be one of the many "mits about nits," her accent biting the end of the word *myth* down to a hard T.

With a wooden skewer about half the length of those used for shish kebob, the nit-picker parts my daughter's hair into sections, clipping back all but one at the nape of the neck. Then, again with the skewer, she separates perhaps ten or twenty hairs from the section and scrutinizes them under the lamp and through the headgear.

Although I can't read the expression in the nit-picker's eyes, every so often I catch a glimpse of one, huge and Cyclopean, behind the magnifying lens. Spiked with lashes of Betty Boop–like proportions, it reveals a margin of white sclera all the way around the iris and gives her an aspect of preternatural sensitivity that I associate with certain photographs of Marcel Proust, reports of his rooms baffled with cork to protect their famously neurasthenic inhabitant. Below the visor, the disdainful nostrils, I watch the nit-picker's mouth, learning to read the small movements that accompany her task. When she finds nothing, her pretty lips are closed and immobile, but upon the discovery of a nit, she purses them a little more tightly and maintains their rigor as she grasps the egg with her fingers and slides it down the ten or twelve inches of the hair shaft. Holding the tiny thing tightly between index finger and thumb, she rinses it from their tips in the waiting bowl of alcohol and wipes them on a paper towel. Then, having made this much progress, she relaxes her mouth into its former, not quite so stern attitude, and moves on to the next afflicted hair.

The process by which each nit is detected, grasped, and eradicated has the smooth elegance of any set of motions that has been practiced countless times, motions, like those of spinning, for example, that a novice performs with seemingly palsied clumsiness. The methodical concentration I witness teaches me how laughably inadequate my efforts have been. Of course I knew, somewhere I knew, that I wasn't getting all the eggs by combing, but how quickly I succumbed to the pressure of tears. How quickly, in retrospect, I gave up. I find myself fantasizing about turning any number of ill-completed tasks over to a professional. What if someone like this paragon of quiet industry were to apply a comparable thoroughness to alphabetizing our library, cleaning out closets, updating the address files?

As she works, the nit-picker murmurs homilies to her apprentice about patience, diligence, the value of a job well done, and in each instance I find myself lacking. This is the kind of work that progress has not altered, an unpleasant task to which I applied the wishful new world alchemy of science, money, and convenience: a box from the drug store costing $22.99 and containing two bottles of NIX, a plastic comb, a printed page of instructions, and, of course, an 800 number. What is required is old–world tenacity, hands that glean the grain, card the wool, weed the acres.

Under such hands, my daughter behaves with exemplary self-control. Not yet ten years old, she is no more patient nor docile than anyone would expect of a child her age. But on this afternoon she will sit, still and quiet, for more than five hours of hair-pulling, a book in her lap, eyes trained on its pages, sometimes overbright with tears but never once flashing with the wild anger occasioned by my own attempts at this chore. Unexpectedly, there is a peace to this wan winter tableau—a calm both demanded of us by the nit-picker and proceeding from our humble recognition that a stubborn problem is being eradicated through sheer perseverance.

I sit, my own work before me, in an effort at redemption: if I cannot myself delouse my child, at least I can keep her company while the job is done, I can apply myself to earning the money that I'll hand over to the lice removal agency: more than five hunderd dollars for the seven hours the nit-picker will spend in my home. But the women's raptness, as if they were engrossed in a fascinating rather than monotonous occupation, distracts me. Again and again I find my eyes straying from my own work back to the three faces held in the halo of light.

My daughter bears a pout reminiscent of her toddler years. Her cheeks are flushed, a dark lock hides her forehead, and she's cracked the spine of her book, opening it wide to see a photograph more clearly. It's the *Guinness* (Guy-ness, as she calls it) *Book of World Records*, a cheap paperback version bought in an airport to while away a layover, and it strikes me as almost the obligatory companion for this trial. Even its title is one I associate with tedium, with sifting through the relentlessness of human experience, searching for the amusing exception. This edition (its twenty-fourth, published in 1988) contains the same photographs that fascinated me as a child: Ethel Granger's grotesque thirteen-inch waist; Shridhar Chillal's curling fingernails, totaling 158 inches in length and painted in stripes of alternating colors; the morbidly obese, motorcycle-riding twins. The illustrations, small and underexposed, render their subjects all the more mysterious, unknowable, and I watch as my daughter scrutinizes each. Freaks are few, and most of life consists—like nit-picking—of unrelieved repetition. Head lice are a commonplace affliction, unlike that of Charles Osborne of Anthon, Iowa, who hiccuped for sixty-five years straight.

The nit-picker stands from her chair, perhaps to relieve her back more than to get a better perspective on my daughter's head, and exhales a long, tension-filled sigh. Two hours have passed, a long time to examine not even one half of one head, and a very long time for a child to sit with forbearance while a stranger pulls her hair. I catch my daughter's eye, and at my expression of sympathy her chin wobbles, she picks the book up from her lap and shields her face from compassion: too proud to cry in front of these women she does not know.

"Maybe a little break?" I suggest, timidly. "A glass of orange juice? A chance to go to her room for a new book?"

The nit-picker nods, a brief dip of her head that conveys less acquiescence than indulgence. She is made of tougher stuff than we, it says.

In the bathroom, my daughter and I hug and she deliberately smears my bulging middle with tears and mucus. "It's boring!" she says. "It hurts!" She stamps her feet. "This is ruining a whole day! A whole day will be gone!"

"I know, I know," I say, and I placate, I bribe. Why is that, like an old woman, my daughter counts her days and even her hours? Is she already the child of her parents, always conscious of mortality, begrudging each misspent minute?

"As soon as it's over," I promise, "we'll go to J&R Computer World." We'll look for a game to play on her new iMac. "Maybe the one where you can build a better Rome, or—"

"I want the whole store!" she says, a measure not of greed but of torment. "That's what it will take to make up for this!" She forgets to cry quietly, forgets the women on the other side of the bathroom door; and I'm reassured by her anger, relieved to see that the unnervingly stoic child I've been watching is, after all, my little girl, capable of great self-control, and of temper tantrums. "Why did this have to happen?" she wails. "Why did it happen to me?"

I give my standard response to tribulation, which always recalls a snippet of Indian television I saw more than eleven years ago, in a hotel in New Delhi. Tired, dirty, jet-lagged, my husband and I sat dully before an old black-and-white set that offered one channel, one program. A dusky talk-show host, looking like a subcontinental Mike Douglas, interviewed a turbaned ascetic who sat cross-legged, emaciated under his robes, on a sectional couch. "Human destiny," the ascetic said, "it is as a field sown with misfortune." As he spoke, the ascetic swept the air with his bony hand and smiled benignly. His words lilted with the cheerful inflections of a British Indian accent. Admittedly, the idea of Fate seems freighted for a trial such as head lice, but if God is in the details then so, assuredly, is the devil. How else to explain the ingenious small torture of a misplaced eyelash? A paper cut? The amount of damage to the foot's naked sole wrought by a single piece of Lego?

Upstairs, my daughter dries her eyes and gets a new book while I check on my son in his room, blond head bent over a box of football cards.

"It's not my turn," he says, not looking up.

"Not yet," I agree.

Back at the kitchen table, I find myself trying to penetrate the mysterious superiority of these two women who refuse tea, water, Christmas cookies, an invitation to use the bathroom.

"Have you ever caught lice?" I ask, groping for small talk rather than the faux pas I end up making. Though I hurry to qualify the question—"From your work, I mean?"—neither woman answers. The apprentice is silent, as she has been all afternoon; and the nit-picker returns to my daughter's head.

"No," she says, several minutes later, and she says no more.

Although I know myself to be a person who can sit at a quiet task for long periods, by the third hour I, too, feel ready to whine and stamp my feet, and when the mail arrives I jump up to retrieve it, grateful for any diversion. After perusing the pile of catalogs and holiday cards, I pass them on to my daughter, who seizes a photo greeting and Xeroxed newsletter from a family we dislike. With delighted malice she reads aloud the litany of the siblings' accomplishments. Black-belted chess champions, they study Sanskrit on Monday, harpsichord on Tuesday, underwater yoga on Wednesday. For Christmas vacation, the same that we've devoted to scratching, weeping and surreptitiously examining our private parts, they traveled to the third world to rebuild the governments and sewer systems of all the islands of the Malay Archipelago. My daughter and I make catty remarks about each boast, the disapproving expression of the nit-picker encouraging my guilty laughter. Still, when my daughter shreds the photograph and wishes a headful of nits on the sister she particularly dislikes, I catch an unsuppressed and quite un-Christian twitch of amusement that momentarily rumples the nit-picker's purse of concentration. The fourth hour devolves into a gleeful recitation of the names of all the unlikable children we know, as we distort their juvenile failings into Roald Dahl–like extremes and punish them with amounts of nits calibrated to their crimes.

When my daughter is at last deloused and de-nitted, her hair is thoroughly oiled with a product that smells like citronella. I ask its ingredients, and the nitpicker sighs so gustily that I relieve her of the obligation to answer. "I know," I say. "Only the doctor knows."

Now that it's her bother's turn, my daughter sits beside me, eager to witness an equal measure of suffering. But, alas, his hair is short, his tribulations disappointingly brief. Worse, his golden hair commands grudging admiration from the two women, who smile and sigh with pleasure as it parts under the skewer.

Within an hour, he is released and it's my turn to sit in the chair under the bright bulb. The special pregnant women's solution is a sticky gel rather than a soap, and its properties do not make for smooth combing. How many years has it been since I've been handled with such rough maternal authority? I find the shampoo both extreme and humiliating in its aggression, the rinse in the kitchen sink similarly punitive, stinging suds washing into my eyes. Here is another instance that proves how routinely adults require children to soldier through discomforts they themselves rarely tolerate. One CD-ROM for each hour my daughter endured, I determine, cringing under the nit-picker's attentions—but we have to postpone our trip to J&R until tomorrow, I tell her.

"No!" she says. "Please!"

"Sweetie, the store closes at seven."

"Please," she begs one last time, but her tone is resigned. How can she hope to triumph over the combined authority of clock and nit-picker, both hanging over her mother's head? She sits down, allows herself to be mollified by the extravagant winces of pain I make in response to the nit-picker's attentions.

When my husband arrives home from work—punctual, as he promised in response to these blighted circumstances—he is the last of our family to submit to a head check, sitting under the light with good-humored tolerance, tilting his head agreeably and posing the kind of disarming questions I never think to ask.

"Let's see—have you ever had to delouse a man with a toupee?" he asks, and the dour woman laughs. No, but she has discovered lice on a man with a hair piece sewn into his scalp.

"What did you do?"

"I called the office. I told the doctor I'm not—I won't handle this." And ditto for the man with recent hair implants. She laughs harder, perhaps at the idea of thousands of dollars' worth of the little plugs yielding to the head-jerking comb, popping out with juicy abandon.

How sensibly my husband seems to navigate life, how naturally he puts people at their ease. Had he been home with us today, perhaps the nit-picker would have laughed all along. She pronounces my husband's own enviably thick hair vermin-free and, catching my incredulous look—not that I've looked forward to his being subjected to this costly punishment, not *exactly*—she smiles. "The fathers," she says, "they never get them."

"But why?" I ask. Why should they escape? She shrugs, continuing to smile mysteriously, almost conspiratorially, as she and her apprentice pack up the bottles, the lamp, the cloth. With enchanted speed, the room is restored.

She looks up, mischievous, as she slips my check into her folder. "Ask the lice," she says. "Only he know."

THE LAUGHING FISH
Eliot Weinberger

I n *The Ocean Made of Streams of Story*, the eleventh-century
Kashmiri precursor to *The Thousand and One Nights* as a vast
compendium of nested tales, there is an image that reappears in
insomnia. The king sees one of his wives leaning over a balcony
and talking to a Brahman. In a fit of jealousy, he orders the Brahman
to be put to death. As the man is being led through the town to his
execution, a fish, lying in a stall in the market, bursts out laughing. The
king stops the execution to find out why the fish laughed. (The reason
is that the Brahman is completely innocent, while the harem of the
king's dissolute wives is full of men disguised as women . . . but that's
another story.)

In a footnote, the annotator of the 1923 edition of the C. H. Tawney
translation, the seemingly omniscient N. M. Penzer, M.A., F.R.G.S.,
F.G.S., cites an article in the 1916 volume of the *Journal of the
American Oriental Society* on "Psychic Motifs in Hindu Fiction,
and the Laugh and Cry Motif." Its author, identified only as "Professor Bloomfield," classifies the various kinds of laughter found in
that literature: "There is the cry and laugh together, and each sepa-
rately. Of laughter by itself, there is the laugh of joy, of irony, malice,
trickery, and triumph. Then there is the sardonic laugh, the enigmatic,
fateful laugh (sometimes with ironic humor in it), and finally there is
the laugh of mystery, as in the case of the fish that laughed." The
taxonomy seems more human than Hindu, but in any event, the
category of mere mystery for the laughing fish is weak. With the
exception of the shark, fish have never been given any human
attributes. No fish is as contented as a cow, sly as a fox, wise as
an elephant or an owl, industrious as a bee, faithful as a turtledove,

self-sacrificing as a pelican, or even as lowly as a worm. Aesop, though he came from a maritime culture, has only one talking fish in his hundreds of fables: an undersized pickerel who tries to persuade the fisherman to throw him back. Without any particular personality, it merely argues for its survival.

Adam doesn't know their names. He is shown all the beasts of the field and the fowls of the air and—the theological questions are unresolvable—either names them (by what process and in what language?) or calls them by the names they already have (which assumes a divine language, now lost, where the signifier was not random). But no fish are hauled up before him in Eden. His ignorance continues on as a blank area in the human brain: the otherwise multilingual often struggle to translate the fish on a menu.

D. H. Lawrence, in a celebrated poem in *Birds, Beasts and Flowers*, writes: "Fish, oh Fish, / So little matters! / . . . To be a fish! // So utterly without misgiving / . . . / Loveless and so lively / . . . / . . . soundless, and out of contact. / They exchange no word, no spasm, not even anger. / Not one touch. / Many suspended together, forever apart, / Each one alone with the waters . . ." The poem takes six pages to say: "They are beyond me, are fishes."

The beyond of the fishes may be why watching them is the most peaceful activity on earth, floating above them with a mask and snorkel. (A public aquarium is contaminated by the presence of the sounds of the other people; an aquarium at home always remains in the context of the other objects of one's life; scuba is inextricable from its respiratory anxiety.) More than merely watching bright-colored creatures dart around, its tranquillity comes from its total lack of human association. Fish have no connection to our emotional life: unlike the other creatures, they do not mate (as Lawrence, naturally, keeps repeating), they hardly squabble, they do not care for their young. Even insects work. A fish swims and eats, is pure movement and beauty. It inhabits a world we can only watch weightlessly, soundlessly, and behind glass. To watch fish is to not be oneself. Even in a magnificent landscape, we inhabit that landscape; it is full of smells and sounds and imagery that connect to countless thoughts, feelings, memories, artworks. Standing under a night sky inevitably leads to thoughts of one's significance in the universe. But a fish neither reflects nor questions our existence. A fish is and we are: to become engrossed in watching fish is to forget that we are, but without, as mystics experience, becoming part of what we observe. The world is everything that is not the case. A laughing fish would not only be like us, it would care enough to laugh at us, a terrifying thing.

A TRAIN OF POWDER
Francine Prose

I f Rebecca West's masterpiece, *Black Lamb and Grey Falcon*, is required reading for anyone wishing to understand the Balkans, *A Train of Powder* should be given to every juror in every capital case to supplement the judge's instructions. Written between 1946 and 1954, these reportorial accounts of four controversial trials consider crime and punishment, innocence and guilt, retribution and forgiveness. As compelling as Court TV but without the frisson of voyeurism (and with the compensatory satisfactions of West's breathtakingly lucid prose style), these elegant narratives remind us of the preciousness and fragility of our right to trial by jury. The exercise of that right depends on impartiality, intelligence, empathy, respect for our fellow humans, and, above all, on the concept—the rule of law— that some of our politicians have lately labored so hard to degrade.

The book's centerpiece is "Greenhouse with Cyclamens," a lengthy three-part essay on the Nuremberg Trials. West was sent to Germany by the *Daily Telegraph* in time to cover the closing arguments and the sentencing of the Nazi leaders; she was encouraged by a lawyer who pointed out that, because of the prevailing shortage of newsprint at the time, most newspapers hadn't provided much coverage of the trials. The precision and clarity of West's observations animate her crisp sketches of the defendants:

> Hess was noticeable because he was so plainly mad; so plainly mad that it seemed shameful that he should be tried. His skin was ashen and he had the odd faculty, peculiar to lunatics, of falling into strained positions which no normal person could maintain for more than a few minutes, and staying fixed in contortion for

hours. He had the classless air characteristic of asylum inmates; evidently his distracted personality had torn up all clues to his past . . . Baldur von Schirach, the Youth Leader, startled because he was like a woman in a way not common among men who looked like women. It was as if a neat and mousy governess sat there, not pretty, but never with a hair out of place, and always to be trusted never to intrude when there were visitors: as it might be Jane Eyre. And though one had read surprising news of Goering for years, he still surprised. He was so very soft.

West portrays Nuremberg as a "citadel of boredom" from which, in the trial's eleventh month, everyone longs to escape—everyone but the accused. To make us see the Nazis as eager to prolong the trial (just as we would be in their situation, if we could imagine being in their situation) she forges a daring, imaginative link between our humanity and that of men we consider morally subhuman. Similar leaps are made in the book's other essays, one of which concerns a lynching case and two others which provide accounts of British trials, one for murder, another for espionage. Though the structures of the essays often suggest the cagey withholdings and revelations of the murder mystery, the real source of narrative tension is their author's determination to get under the skins and into the psyches of everyone in the courtroom, from the French judges at Nuremberg to the South Carolinian jurors.

Characteristically, West seems to be looking everywhere at once, gazing past the quotidian rituals of the trials to observe the larger communities from which the participants come. But always her attention keeps tracking back to the accused.

West's obsession with the criminal psyche is partly metaphysical, for she is one of those writers who believe that concrete details can be piled up like a ladder to bring us closer to some higher mystery, or truth. Ultimately, however, West's fascination with those on trial has less to do with philosophy than with morality and compassion. Always her effort is to see (and make us see) that these demons are men, and that whatever we might learn from them and their crimes will be lost to us if we insist on assigning them to some other species.

She reminds us that "if a trial for murder lasts too long, more than the murder will out. The man in the murderer will out; it becomes horrible to think of destroying him." She describes the Nazi war criminals as they are about to be sentenced:

> Their pale, lined faces looked alike, their bodies sagged inside their clothes, which seemed more alive than they were. They were gone. They were finished. It seemed strange that they could ever have excited loyalty, it was plainly impossible that they could ever attract it again . . . They were not abject. These ghosts gathered about them the rags of what had been good in them during their lives. They listened with decent composure to the reading of the judgements, and, as on any other day, they found amusement in the judges' pronunciation of the German names. That is something pitiable which those who do not attend trials never see: the eagerness with which people in the dock snatch at any occasion for laughter.

West is present in the courtroom when the men are told they are going be hanged. "No wise person," she asserts, "will write an unnecessary word about hanging, for fear of straying into the field of pornography." Yet she concludes the first part of "Greenhouse with Cyclamens" with a bloodcurdling disquisition on the history of this form of execution, a description of the eleven condemned men slowly choking to death and of Ribbentrop struggling in the air for twenty minutes before finally expiring. Of course she believes that the Nazis, those "abcesses of cruelty," deserved to be punished—though she feels the act of execution further extends the long trajectory of cruelty and death. Ultimately, West's faith in justice transcends the predicament of the individual criminal and the seriousness of his crime. She is less concerned with the pathology of the condemned than with the collective health of whole communities, countries, civilization—entities that, in her view, are also on trial in these proceedings. It's not the cruelty of hanging that alarms her so much as what that cruelty can trigger in human nature: "For when society has to hurt a man it must hurt him as little as possible and must preserve what it can of his pride, lest there should spread in that society those feelings which make men do the things for which they get hanged."

This astonishing book makes us long to know what Rebecca West would have made of the trials of O. J. Simpson, Susan Smith, and the Menendez brothers—all the grisly mass entertainments, these gory cockfights staged on a colossal scale, that we have come to accept as legitimate legal procedures on which men and women's lives depend. *A Train of Powder* makes us look harder to see what she might have seen: her flashes of insight into the minds of criminals and victims, her long gaze into the future to discern the distant shock waves, the social repercussions of these sensational trials and the ways in which justice is served or betrayed. How terrible that it should be out of print, this book that makes us pay a different sort of attention to the legal battles that periodically turn our living rooms, our offices, our neighborhood barber shops and bars into annexes of the courtrooms on which all the rest depends.

THE BUNKER
Jeffrey Eugenides

We hadn't been installed more than three days before we heard about the bunker. It was right under us, apparently, directly beneath the elegant lakeside villa that had once housed a Jewish banking family—the Hans Arnholds—and that now housed us, a small group of scholars and artists staying at the American Academy in Berlin. Well, this was Germany, wasn't it? Across the lake stood the Wannsee Conference House, where the Final Solution had been formulated over coffee cake. In such a neighborhood, why be surprised to find a Nazi bunker in your backyard?

Nevertheless, we were. The villa had been recently renovated. A Francisco Clemente—on loan—hung in the living room. Also a Rauschenberg. During media events when politicians showed up, movie screens unscrolled from the ceilings. Glittery, Klimt-like tilework decorated the tympanum of the dining room. The paneled library might have been Bruce Wayne's.

This hotel or conference center gloss was only the latest transformation of the old house, however. During the 1930s Hans Arnhold had taken his family out of Germany, and the villa, like many mansions in this affluent part of Berlin, had been taken over by the National Socialists. Hitler's economics minister, a man named Rust, had lived in the house until the end of the war. After that the villa had been occupied by American officers, serving as a recreation center for American troops.

It was Herr Rust who had put in the bunker. In her memoir of those years, *The Past Is Myself*, a book remarkable for its depiction of the incremental, frighteningly organic process by which National Socialism slowly wrapped its tentacles around social institutions and the minds of her fellow German citizens, Christabel Beilenberg writes: "It was common knowledge that the party bigwigs were building air raid shelters under their lakefront mansions." Hitler himself had inspected the bunker under the academy.

It was inevitable that we would all become obsessed with the bunker. Over that fall and early winter, we talked about it constantly at dinner. We asked the academy's executive director, Gary Smith, to describe it. The chef, Reinhold, had to go down there occasionally. "What it's like?" we asked. "I'll show it to you sometime," said Gary. But with one thing and another he never did. And so we stopped talking about the bunker for a while. And then a week later somebody would bring it up again, and we would start asking the usual questions: How big was it? How deep? What did it look like inside?

Sometimes while working I would look out the glass door of my office at the sloping lawn that led down to the plane trees and the glaucous lake. There was a large drained swimming pool on one side of the property and a smaller one, a kind of wading pool, in the middle of the lawn. The grass itself was browning or weedy in spots. Gatsby would have had a bigger staff of gardeners, but there were still a few around during the week, mowing and pruning, digging. Sometimes a frog hopped along the walkway outside my door. Impressive clouds, somehow Prussian, boiled and marched over the lake. The lake itself was gray most days but could suddenly fool you and turn blue. Ferries plied the water. The American Yacht Club was right next door, as was, rumor had it, a brothel patronized by business executives. My attention would be taken up by all these things and then, often enough, I would lower my gaze from the dramatic sky and the speckled plane trees and would look at the grass and think about the bunker below.

Our obsession with the bunker came partly from the word itself. You can hardly say the word *bunker* without adding a certain name before it: "Hitler's bunker." *Bunker* and *Hitler* are inseparable. (I suspect it was the fascistic connotation that led Norman Lear to name his great, bigoted character "Archie Bunker.") But if you step back and think about it rationally for a minute, it's clear that there is nothing especially historic or significant about a bunker. As Christabel

Beilenberg points out, a bunker is really nothing but an air-raid shelter. How many WWII-era bunkers must there be in Berlin, in Germany, or in all of Europe for that matter? Winston Churchill had a bunker of his own beneath the streets of London. He prosecuted the Second World War largely from underground. Still, the image we have of Winston Churchill isn't subterranean. Churchill descended to the underworld during the winter of life. Down there he overcame death and returned above ground, like spring wheat. Hitler didn't. Down in the bunker was where he perished. Something about this appeals to the imagination. It feels right. Down in the dirt, down with the earthworms and the creepy blind unsunned moles, down where corruption takes place, that's where Hitler belonged.

Then one night a terrible thing happened. August Kleinzahler, the poet, got to see the bunker all by himself. One evening I arrived for dinner and felt hands grasping my lapels. It was Michael Meltsner, a constitutional scholar. "Gary took August down to the bunker," he told me in a grave tone. Was this true? I found Kleinzahler in the library, sitting in his usual armchair. He looked shiny cheeked, pleased with himself.

"You saw the bunker?"

"Yes, I did."

"What's it like?"

"It's not much."

"Is it true Hitler was down there?"

Kleinzahler gave me a level stare. "I didn't see him," he said. Over the fireplace in the library hung a portrait of Hans Arnhold himself. Arnhold's daughter, Anna-Maria, and her husband, Stephen Kellen, are the primary benefactors of the American Academy in Berlin. Anna-Maria Kellen had grown up in this very house. When the idea arose to start an American Academy in Berlin, the Kellens had been the first to give financial support. She had been kept apprised of the progress, was told that a building had been found and that it would be renovated. Only later did she discover that, by an amazing coincidence, this building was her childhood home.

Anna-Maria Arnhold became an American. In the early fifties, after her marriage, she came back to Berlin with her husband. The plane coming into Tempelhof flew low over the Wannsee. Anna-Maria looked out the window to try and find her old house. The woman seated next to her then spoke.

"Do you know that house, too?"

"Yes," Anna-Maria replied.

The woman smiled. "My husband and I spent many wonderful nights there. Herr Rust used to throw wonderful parties."

It was from her seatmate that Anna-Maria Kellen learned about the bunker. After landing in Berlin, she and her husband drove out to the Wannsee. The old family gardener was still there. He had been Rust's gardener, too, throughout the war. Coldly, he showed the Kellens around the house. When they asked to see the bunker, he took them down.

After they had come out, as they were driving away, Mrs. Kellen said to her husband, "You know, that gardener could have shut the door behind us. No one would have ever found us."

"I know, my dear," replied Stephen Kellen. "That was why I made sure to walk behind him."

Weeks passed. The plane trees lost their leaves, revealing their stunted, twisted arms. A winter fog began to cover the Wannsee. One night there was a lecture. When the guests had gone, we went into the library to talk and smoke. Reinhold brought out a tray of liqueurs. A plum-flavored schnapps began making the rounds.

Two historians, one linguist, one novelist, one poet, a composer who lived in Paris, a Harvard law professor, and a visual artist, we were talking, that night, about the bad smell that had been gathering in the basement where our studios were. It had started in Milad Doueihi's office.

"I can't even work there anymore," he complained.

I insisted to everyone that it was the worst smell I had ever smelled. "They think it might be coming from under the kitchen. There's a tube where all the fat drains out. Maybe it's clogged."

"It's the *shmalts*! I knew it."

"It's not the *shmalts*" I said. "It's the bunker."

We had a laugh over that. In the next moment, providentially, the executive director entered the room.

We were on him at once.

"When are you going to show us the bunker, Gary?"

"You promised you'd show it to us."

"How come Augie got to see it and we didn't?"

We were unstoppable, fueled by Pomeranian schnapps. We had eaten an obscure Baltic fish for dinner. We had been living and working on top of a Nazi bunker for nearly three months now and we wanted to see it. Tonight was the night.

Gary knew there was no putting us off any longer. The signal was given. Reinhold lit candelabra and handed them around. We crossed the living room and the dining room and entered the kitchen. At the back a door led to a flight of stairs. Laughing, fluttery, already making cracks, we each held a candelabrum and followed our leader down the dark stairs into the earth.

"I'm trying to raise the money to build a health club down here," Gary joked.

"Ve haf vays of making you get in shape!"

"How come you know this place so well, Reinhold?"

"We keep the Riesling down here."

"Ah, it's not a bunker. It's a wine cellar."

Holding the candelabra, with flames streaming backward and thinning as we moved, we descended the stairs. We were in our dinner clothes. The women wobbled on high heels. Right in front of me was Meltsner. Folksy and tough, he usually wore sweatshirts. Now he was in a blue blazer and white shirt. Even a tie. Finally, at the bottom, we came to the bunker door. We grouped there, silent, staring at it. The joking stopped as we contemplated the fact of this heavy armored door. The joking had been, in a sense, like whistling past the graveyard, but now we had stopped at the gates. The door to the bunker was slightly convex, like the hatch of a tank. Greenish gray, cobwebby, rusted at the edges. The glass spyhole was protected by a metal shield. Bullets wouldn't have penetrated it. At length Reinhold pulled the door open and we went inside.

Kleinzahler was right. It wasn't much. No artifacts remained, no furniture. The ceiling was low, the walls chalky. There were two or three long, narrow rooms. At the end another door led up to the back lawn. We might have been in a basement anywhere.

Only one thing showed the underground space for what it had been. Just inside the front door was a small engineering room. Here were the controls for ventilation and plumbing. Elegantly designed manifolds and valves, the height of modernity back in 1942, lined one wall. Each, in slanting *Fraktur* script, proclaimed the element it brought into the bunker: *Luft. Wasser.*

What did we expect to find? What do we seek by going to the sites of atrocity? There was no difference, at bottom, between our trip to the bunker and a visit to the concentration camp of Sachsenhausen outside Berlin. We wanted to draw near to historical evil, to see and touch it if we could, and somehow comprehend it. Such ghoulish sightseeing has become a kind of perverse pilgrimage, marked by necessary stops and full of ritualized thoughts. Therefore, I couldn't help staring at those beautifully designed controls and thinking about "the rationality of evil" or "the mechanization of the death camps." All true, no doubt, but not my thoughts. Only borrowed, recited like a litany.

It was cold down in the bunker. Meltsner had backed into a wall. His blue blazer was all white behind. I slapped his back. Meltsner grew up in New York and became one of the big civil rights lawyers. He defended Muhammad Ali when they tried to take his heavyweight title away. Now this Meltsner, originally from the Upper West Side, was down in the Nazi bunker with me, and I was pounding him on the back.

"You've got white stuff all over," I said.

The white dust flew up, sparkling in the light of the candles we had brought down there with us.

GRAHAM GREENE'S VIETNAM
Katie Roiphe

I.

I spent more time than was strictly necessary in the plush red corridors of the Hotel Metropole in Hanoi. For some reason, I had convinced myself that I needed to see the inside of suite 228, which was otherwise referred to in the voluminous hotel literature as "the Graham Greene Suite." Greene, whom I had been mildly fixated on for some time, had stayed there during the fifties. I was staying next door in suite 226, and after several days of wondering how I was going to get into his room, I noticed the maid's cart outside. When she finally ducked out to refill her stash of aloe shampoo and little almond soaps, I slipped into the half-opened door. Inside was a bare mahogany desk, a brass lamp, a king-size bed with a modern, striped duvet, and several spindly French sofas, also striped. I couldn't help feeling vastly let down. The setting was devoid of both Greene's seediness—he later regretted popularizing the word *seedy*—and his elegance, which should not, of course, have come as a surprise. The Metropole was gutted after the war and rebuilt. And even if it hadn't been, I knew from experience that this sort of literary pilgrimage is always anticlimactic: the writer is dead and what remains of him is in his books.

Luckily in Greene's case the books are everywhere. It's almost impossible to walk down the street in Hanoi without stumbling across a sky blue Penguin edition of *The Quiet American*. If one looks closely enough, the black-and-white photograph of a gun emerging from long grasses on the cover is slightly blurred, and if one flips through the pages the words themselves are also blurred, which is because they are pirated copies, Xeroxed from the originals. When I first spotted the cheerful, familiar blue covers, I was taken aback. My private relation to the novel felt cheapened. It bothered me to see Greene's morally complicated vision hawked to tourists, but then everything was hawked to tourists, and wasn't I, when it came down to it, a tourist myself? Weren't there, in fact, dozens of tourists sitting in cafes thinking that their private relation to *The Quiet American* was cheapened? In a way, its commercial ubiquity is something the book could have predicted of itself. The novel foretells a Vietnam in the thrall of what it calls "dollar love," and Westerners in thrall right back.

By the time we reached Hanoi, my husband and I had been traveling through Asia for almost a month. I had begun to see that everywhere we went there were a million minor transactions taking place beneath the surface. At first I was oblivious to these transactions, but slowly I began to recognize them: if a driver takes you to his friend's hotel, he is getting a cut; if a waiter sells you an expensive dish, he is getting a cut; if a guide takes you to a silk shop, he is getting a cut; and there are bound to be other people getting cuts of his cut. If you watch these transactions closely enough, you begin to get the feeling of an ant farm, a honeycomb, thousands of tiny gestures replicating themselves.

On one of our first days in Bangkok we made our way to the Grand Palace. We could see the gold roof of the main pagoda glinting behind a wall. A man pointed us down a street to the entrance. It seemed a long way, so we asked again and two other men pointed us in the same direction. When we got to the end of the street a cyclo driver told us that the Grand Palace was closed, and he would take us to another temple and then back for a dollar. An old man came over to translate his offer. In fact the Grand Palace was not closed. The entrance was in the other direction. This scheme employed five men for an afternoon.

After a while, we began to get used to the idea that nothing was solidly what it seemed. For small amounts of money, the facts were willing to alter themselves. At a jumbled antique store across from the Metropole, we picked up a coy-looking stone Buddha with its hands on its hips. "It is from the seventeenth century," the woman with serious glasses behind the counter informed us. When we returned later that afternoon it was from the nineteenth century.

We bought it, whatever it was, and went out for a late lunch. I looked over at my husband dipping a dumpling in sauce, and I noticed that he had been physically transformed. He is one of the few people I know who looks most himself in a suit and tie. In his closet at home, he keeps wooden shoe trees in his shoes. But as soon as we arrived, he stopped shaving. He started wearing sandals that Velcroed across the toes. At some point, without my realizing it, his appearance had passed beyond scruffy into the netherworld of international drifters who float through Asia staying in guest houses without sheets. I am not sure whether this was a subliminal attempt at disguise, but if it was, it didn't work. There was no way to evade looking prosperous.

One staggeringly hot day, we took a motorcycle through the rice paddies to a nearby beach and stopped at a stretch of creamy sand with mountains rising from the ocean. But as soon as we took off our shoes, dozens of children clustered around us trying to get us to sit under their umbrellas.

When we finally laid out our towels and settled down with our books, two sturdy-looking girls came to offer pedicures and necklaces. "My name Hong Kong," one of them said. They crouched next to us. They showed no signs of moving. The one that was not Hong Kong sulked theatrically. "Bad day. No one buy Buddhas." She fanned out the jade necklaces she was selling.

"I don't have any money," I told her.

"He has money," said Hong Kong, gesturing toward my husband.

"He doesn't want to buy anything."

"He change mind."

"I never change my mind," he said.

"You change mind."

"Madam, you want? Tell him you want, he change mind."

"But I don't want one."

The green Buddhas glittered in the sand.

"If we stay he change mind."

"I never change my mind," he said again.

They squatted near our feet. One of them rested her head on my arm. We tried to look out at the ocean.

"You need souvenir? You remember day?"

They sat with us for an hour, resuming their sales pitch every now and then. "You buy one?" "You buy two?" They were harassing us, but sweetly. Their presence changed the nature of the activity. We were not sitting on the beach the way we think of sitting on the beach at home.

"You change mind?" They went over to my husband. Hong Kong put her hands on her hips and studied him.

"No."

The shadow of a cloud moved across the sand. Suddenly I needed a souvenir to remember the day.

"Let's just get one," I said. We bought a jade Buddha on a strip of leather.

"He change mind!" they said triumphantly. "He change mind!" We gave them a dollar. Interestingly, it was my husband who put the Buddha around his neck.

We paid in dollar bills because they prefer them here. In other countries one pays for familiar-looking items with brightly colored bills that look and feel like Monopoly money. But here it is opposite: every element of life is different, the air, the sun, the dense, sweet coffee, the dragon fruit we eat for breakfast with its curling fuchsia rind like lapping tongues, the lizards that dapple the walls of elegant restaurants like patterned wallpaper. The only thing that is familiar, the only thing that moors us to our regular lives, is the green face of our president.

II.

In Phnom Penh, the proprietors of our hotel have placed a discreet gold plaque on the reception desk that reads, NO CHILD SEX TOURISM. If this sign is regarded at all, it is regarded quite literally, because outside on a chaise longue near the pool lies a sullen-looking Khmer girl in a leopard print bikini who looks no older than fourteen. The

German next to her has graying, wiry hair, tortoiseshell glasses, and a perfectly round, pregnant-looking stomach emerging from his Speedo bathing suit. He is talking avidly into his cell phone. After a little while they go into the pool. She lies on her back and closes her eyes. He holds her up as if she were a child learning to float.

They flock here, men too lonely, too fat, too ugly, too lazy, to pick up a woman in their local bar in Marseille, Duluth, or Baden-Baden. They seem to find it reassuring that the line between prostitution and normal life is blurred; that a man can go to a bar and pick up a beautiful woman who will be his girlfriend if he buys her things, and who will continue to be his girlfriend, if he continues to buy her things.

One night in Bangkok at a pretty outdoor restaurant on the canal, we are seated next to a little dumpling of a man with pale blue crinkling eyes. He is wearing a crisply ironed white shirt and a black suit and his face is overwhelmed by an enormous black cowboy hat.

"You like shrimp?" he says in heavily accented English.

"Very much," murmurs the Thai woman across from him.

"You are very pretty."

The evening smells of smog and burning leaves. The lights of the restaurant flicker in the black water.

"More champagne?"

"Thank you."

The eye is drawn to the improbably wide brim of the cowboy hat with its braided tassel and turquoise tips. One can feel how hard the man is trying, how deeply he aspires toward a certain kind of masculinity—it is all there in the wide planes and felted surfaces of the hat.

The man flags down the waitress for another bottle of champagne. It's clear that he is going all out. No romantic flourish will be spared. He is determined to be a man enjoying a romantic evening instead of a man paying for a woman, determined to experience seduction, even in a situation where seduction is ludicrous. This, it occurs to me, is where one can find Graham Greene. Here in the relationships between Western men and the Eastern women whose company they are purchasing or half purchasing. Whenever Greene describes the allure of the East, women are always intricately involved: he wrote, "The spell was first cast by the tall elegant girls in white silk trousers, by the pewter evening light on flat paddy fields." And in *The Quiet American*, his British and American characters cannot help developing dangerous romantic fantasies, and his Vietnamese heroine remains cool, untouched.

Greene himself was attracted to both the idea and reality of prostitutes and taxi girls. When he was in Saigon he frequented the House of Four Hundred Women on the Ruc de Catinat, which he fictionalizes in *The Quiet American* as the House of Five Hundred Women. In fact his view of ordinary romantic relationships was so bleak that it is easy to see how the simplicity of a purchased evening would appeal. For him, love affairs caused endless amounts of savagery and bitterness, and watching love fade, he observed over and over, was like death itself. Marriage, it goes without saying, was even worse; he wrote coolly, "There is nothing so charmless as the company of a woman who is no longer desired." And in the end, what is interesting about Greene is the strain of desperate emotional blackness. Beneath the surface of his bestselling adventure stories was a sensibility so bruised that prostitutes seemed purer than the demanding women from home. In my favorite photograph of him, Greene, in a cable-knit Irish sweater, is stretched out lankily on a beach blanket with his great love, Catherine Walston. But even with her he is irritable and gloomy. He could never rid himself of his obsession with the transactions beneath relationships, the transactions that we keep hidden in the West, the transactions that surface so easily here.

A few weeks later, we find ourselves in a cafe in Hanoi that serves lattes and cappuccinos to Westerners who have grown tired of thick, sweet Vietnamese coffee with condensed milk.

I hear a man's voice saying, "When we get home you shower with me—I will wash your back."

The voice is coming from a chunky American in his fifties with a long mustache and a plaid button-down shirt, short sleeves rolled up to reveal an elaborately fanged dragon tattoo. He is sitting across from a young, not quite pretty Vietnamese woman.

"Lots of the girls there want to be my girlfriend. There is one girl, I spend many nights with her. She wants to be my girlfriend."

I can't hear how the woman responds because she speaks too softly.

"Shouldn't your sister be helping to pay for your father?"

She murmurs something unintelligible.

He says, "I will send you two, maybe three million dong."

The waiter swoops down to clear their plates. The man places a ten-dollar bill on the table. "You're staring," my husband points out. I have the terrible habit of turning to stare at the people I am eavesdropping on. I try to turn my attention back to my Croque Monsieur.

We watch countless scenes like this everywhere we go. At first, I feel a twinge of superiority, but over time this superiority dissipates. And in the end the trip is quite humbling. It reminds me of one of the ancient temples at Angkor Wat, which is made up of a series of concentric walls, each one ringed around another. The doorways carved into the stone are made progressively lower as you move toward the shrine at the center. The architecture physically forces you to bow.

III.

From the moment I stepped onto the boat on Cambodia's vast Tonle Sap lake I had a premonition that something bad was going to happen. For one thing, it lacked seriousness. It looked like the kind of brightly painted wooden boat that children play with in fountains. Emerging from the dashboard was an unpromising collection of wires in various states of unravelment held together by duct tape, and the usual accoutrements of safety, such as radios or life preservers, were notably missing. The windows were so small that if the boat tipped over, as it was known to do from time to time, our guidebook pointed out that we would all be trapped inside and drowned. And the captain had sold so many tickets that half of the passengers had to sit cross-legged on the flat roof. Sixty people were crammed with luggage into a boat made for twenty-five. Greene wrote that what attracted to him to this part of the world was "the exhilaration which a measure of danger brings to a visitor with a return ticket," but I didn't feel anything like that exhilaration. When the engines started and the nose of the boat began to bounce on the choppy water, and everyone else started clapping and cheering, it seemed to me that we were casually ferrying to our deaths.

After an hour or so, we were in the middle of the giant, milky brown lake. The trees were a distant fringe around the shore. And suddenly an alarm sounded, a mournful electrical cry from the depths of the water. It meant, though none of us knew at the time, that we had run aground. The reason none of us knew it at the time was that the crew spoke no English. The passengers, with the exception of one Chinese-speaking man, spoke no Khmer.

The boat sat motionless. There was nothing we could do but wait. The heat was astonishing; temperatures had been hovering around 120 degrees and the low roof of the cabin seemed to press in on us. Some of the passengers began sticking their heads out of the tiny windows to get air. Others became annoyed that they were getting less air because of the people who were plugging the windows with their heads. One man, a French chef vacationing with his parents, had a cooler abundantly packed with beer, ice cubes, and pâté sandwiches on French bread. The rest of us eyed him suspiciously. On the way to the dock, my husband and I had picked up a dust-coated bottle of water from one of the floating villages, but I noticed we only had a few sips left. I thought about our bodies swelling on the glassy brown surface of the lake, the parching of our throats, the slow blackening of our skin; My husband leafed through the *Herald Tribune*.

Eventually I climbed up on top of the boat where the younger passengers were already roasting and pinkening in the sun. An American college student was trying to get a signal on the international cell phone his parents had given him in case of emergencies; a British woman with a kerchief around her head had taken out a water filter that she claimed would clean the typhoid and bacteria from the murky lake water. Narrow sampans glided by, little children squatting in the bows. They looked up at us with wide eyes: foreigners stuffed into a unmoving boat.

At this point the sun was still swollen and high in the sky, but in a few hours it would be dark. Even if we somehow made it to shore, the surrounding jungle was not necessarily safer than the middle of the lake. There were not necessarily roads with cars. The jungle floor was laced with land mines. The day before we left we had stopped to listen to a band made up entirely of musicians with various limbs blown off.

The American student mentioned the possibility of the embassy sending a helicopter to lift us to safety. I was willing to entertain the idea. But the British couple chuckled. The Australians exchanged glances. Here was an American attitude of the type Greene satirized so elegantly in *The Quiet American*. And, of course, he was right. The assumptions about movement that we generally take for granted, namely, that there will be someone we can pay to take us to where we want to go, suddenly seemed naive and oddly irrelevant.

If only we had flown. We had thought of flying. Most tourists, with the exception of grubby backpackers and committed bohemians, fly from Siem Reap to Phnom Penh. From the sky you can see how astonishing the landscape is: Rivers the color of chocolate milk running through grassy fields. Sugar palms sticking up from the flat earth. The rich green and gold brush of rice paddies divided neatly into squares. But then, in Cambodia even flying involves all of the country's eccentricities: according to the local papers, a plane was recently delayed for hours by a stray dog wandering onto a landing strip.

I climbed back into the cabin because I could feel my face getting burned. I took my old seat next to my husband, who was still immersed in the *Herald Tribune*. In fact his nonchalance was beginning to attract attention. The round, merry Malaysian man on my other side started calling him "Moon Man" and "Man from the Moon," since he was the only person on board who did not seem to be alarmed by our situation, this when he wasn't congratulating me on having such a tall husband.

Six hours later, a rickety wooden boat with a motor tied to it with string sputtered up next to our ferry. Half of us got off and stood on the boat in the sun. There wasn't room to sit. Water pooled at our ankles, seeping in through the gaps in the wood. The makeshift boat tugged the other boat, slowly, to deeper waters. We could see the angled silhouettes of pagodas and palm leaves against the flame-colored sky. Eleven and a half hours after we set out, we arrived in Phnom Penh.

As we stood on the dock in the gathering dusk I felt shaken. One of the shirtless crew members standing on top of the boat with a cigarette dangling from his lips tossed my luggage to my feet. I tried to smile at him but he didn't smile back. And it was suddenly clear that what had distressed and slightly shocked me about the boat ride was the hostility, the contempt of the crew. When a group of passengers went up to try to talk to the captain, he waved them away like an emperor dismissing the girls coming to fan him with banana leaves. In fact the crew was finding it amusing, if anything, to watch white faces turning various shades of fuchsia in the beating sun. They sat on the roof and smoked. They plumped up our luggage like pillows and sprawled across it, joking with each other in Khmer. When the resourceful British woman with the water filter tried to ask them if someone was coming to help us, they imitated her question in a shrill, mocking tone, "Excuse me, is a boat coming to help us?" Normally, when there is not a crisis, one doesn't feel this kind of hostility; the language barrier is strong enough, the moving boat itself enough distraction, but there, stuck in the middle of the lake, in the stillness, the brilliant green of the jungle melting into the sky, it was impossible not to see. I felt like I had been experiencing this hostility, this mocking, all along: in the faces of the children hawking postcards, in the sinewy necks of the cyclo drivers who pedaled our heavy foreign bodies up hills. I suppose it is always there in a tourist culture—when the people are poor and the tourists are rich, the power smolders and turns very easily into something ugly. It is the modern version of the rage against colonials in *A Passage to India* or *The Jewel in the Crown*. It is the contempt of the seller for those who are sold to.

IV.

During our eleven and a half hours on the boat, I conceived a desire to stay at the Royal Hotel in Phnom Penh. The Royal is more expensive than any of the hotels that we encountered on the trip, and we encountered expensive hotels. In a city renowned for its lawlessness, a city where guidebooks warn that armed theft happens regularly—rumors abound that it may be the local police doing the robberies—a city where the streets are still unwalkable at night, the rates are nothing short of astonishing. But this, of course, is part of the point. I picture a lobby with soaring ceilings, sweeping staircases, milk-white columns and marble floors; rooms with mahogany four-poster beds, burnished Buddha heads with tight gold curls, plates of croissants, fluffy bathrobes, and slippers with little insignia on them. I am feeling unsafe.

Even under normal circumstances, I find grand old colonial hotels infinitely comforting: the rattan chairs, the potted palms, the ceiling fans, the general atmosphere of gin and tonics about to arrive with a slice of lime. These hotels tend to overdo themselves, like movie sets, but the overdoing itself is what makes them comforting. The bars have names like "Elephant Bar." The gift shops have glass cases, where rings and necklaces nestle in velvet cushions. The doors are manned by turbaned doormen who bow deeply as you enter. Outside a man prods you with his stump and smiles; the air smells of incense and rotting fruit; the sound of motorcycles pierces the night like gunfire. But the bombardment of the street is somehow framed and miniaturized by a hotel like this; it is put in perspective; it is the culture that you have flown all this way to observe, manageable as a postcard.

"Let's stay at the Royal Hotel," I say when we slip into the taxi. I say this knowing that my husband prefers another sort of hotel. His taste runs toward the ramshackle, the family-run. He prefers inns like the tiny three-hundred-year-old house in Hoi An where we rented a room with intricately carved mahogany walls and ceilings, and a red velvet bed draped in frothy mosquito netting. He finds the theatrical colonialism of places like the Royal off-putting.

"The Royal Hotel?" He raises his eyebrows. "Expensive taste for a housewife."

I look out the window. I am filled with rage. I am coated in a layer of dirt from the boat. My luggage is coated in a layer of dirt from the boat. Could I have misheard? Is he actually saying that I don't have a right to choose our hotel because I am a housewife? It is true that I have spent the last year musing on my next book, reading and plotting and taking notes, and he has largely been supporting me. I hadn't thought of it so starkly, but when it comes down to it he is paying for the trip. The money for the hotel room is his, I realize; he should decide where we stay. I am suddenly overwhelmed by my own helplessness. How have I allowed myself to slip into this maddening, 1950s-style dependence? Why hadn't I noticed it before? A line from *The Quiet American* comes to mind: "The hurt is in the act of possession: we are too small in mind and body to possess another person without pride, or to be possessed without humiliation."

The car weaves through throngs of motorcycles, some of which are piled high with entire families, and stops at a red light. Outside the city menaces. The dusty, saffron-colored buildings have crumbling walls and peeling wooden shutters and wrought-iron terraces spilling over with bougainvillea. Everything looks charming and decrepit and chipped. It looks like Paris, if Paris had sunk to the bottom of the sea for decades.

"What's wrong?" my husband asks.

I look out the window.

"We can stay there if you want. I was just kidding."

In fact, he was only referring to my filling in the occupation "housewife" on my visa application so as to avoid the complications that would arise from filling in "writer" or "journalist." He was not calling me a housewife, though for a moment our relation to each other feels jittery.

The truth is that this exchange would never have happened anywhere else. It involves a way of thinking that is alien to both of us. What is mine. What is his. The misunderstanding surfaces here because of the perpetual marketplace; because female company is so easily, so ubiquitously, for sale.

V.

Our guide in Cambodia is tiny and immaculate, his plaid button-down shirt tucked into black khakis, a belt around his waist. He is so nervous and self-effacing that we pick him out of the crowd of touts who have been waiting on the dock for eleven and a half hours for our boat to arrive. They are all waving signs and shouting, "Taxi! Hotel! Taxi! Hotel!" But our guide seems embarrassed by the idea of having to sell his services. He is wincing with embarrassment. He has the floppy hair of an English schoolboy, and his voice is so soft that we have to lean in close to him to make out what he is saying.

Early the next morning, he takes us to the abandoned high school, once known as Security Prison 21, where the Khmer Rouge tortured and killed thousands of their own people. It is a low, undistinguished-looking cement structure built around a courtyard and surrounded with barbed wire. There are people milling around with cameras around their necks. But it is not a museum the way we have museums; it is not polished the way we think of museums being polished. There are bloodstains on the stone floors, for instance. There are rusting bed frames where prisoners were tortured. There are wooden bars that they were chained to lying down. There is not enough light. Our guide leads us quickly from one room to the next. He goes out of his way to touch everything with his hands. As we make our way through the courtyard, it feels more like a crime scene that had been blocked off with yellow tape than a museum. The tragedy feels fresh, the air disturbed.

Afterward our guide drives us to the Killing Fields. Within blocks the stone edifices of the city dissolve into palm-thatched huts on stilts. The pavement gives way to a rough dirt road embedded with stones. Our driver's silver Timex looks bulky on his fragile wrist as he steers around the larger rocks and holes. It is impossible to tell how old he is—he could be twenty or forty-five. People here tend to look very, very young until all of a sudden they look very, very old. As the car bounces along, we manage to look out the window at the jackfruit trees. I have never seen jackfruits before. They are green and bumpy and scrunched up: they look like women's handbags hanging from trees.

The ride takes longer than we expected. We hadn't really wanted to go to the Killing Fields in the first place. We anticipated the eerie lushness, the indifferent, picnic-ground green common to sites of mass murder. But our guide, in his gentle, unassuming way, was adamant.

When we finally arrive, as we had suspected, there is not much to see. There are ditches and delicate, drooping trees. There are several clusters of tourists murmuring in cemetery tones. Our guide calls me "Lady," as he directs me to the best view, "Lady, you stand here."

He tells us that the Khmer Rouge killed babies by swinging them against a tree. He mimes the gesture and says, "They like for mothers to see."

At the end of our tour, our guide brings us over to a blossoming frangipani tree and says softly, "Now I will tell you about my family." The fragrance of the white blossoms fills the air. We lean in closer to hear him. With the wind it is almost impossible to make out what he is saying. It occurs to me that as we were jostled on the dock, with all of the touts trying to shepherd us toward their taxis, our guide had said, "I will tell you about my family's experiences." I hadn't been paying attention at the time. But now I feel an almost shameful curiosity opening in myself.

Our guide tells us that planes circled his village on the border of Vietnam, spraying white napalm onto the thatched roofs. His three-year-old brother and four-year-old sister died of burns as the family fled with all of their belongings through the jungle.

He speaks quietly and without expression in his far-from-perfect English. He mimes the situations he can't find words for, holding his arms around his stomach to communicate that his other sister was pregnant when she stepped on a land mine, years later, at around the same time that his uncle and cousins were abducted by the Khmer Rouge. "It is still difficult here," he concludes. "I have to pay money to send my children to school." He leads us past a monument of skulls piled high in a glass case. Three Cambodian schoolgirls are chatting up a group of Japanese men, their giggles rising to the trees. And as we walk back to the car, I have the sullied feeling we have just paid for something you are not supposed to pay for.

A few days later, we fly home. As soon as we unpack, the trip recedes into a series of benign and picturesque images: the pink dawn against the pineapple towers of Angkor Wat, the tall elegant girls in white silk trousers, the pewter evening light on flat paddy fields. But there on our mantel is the chipped stone Buddha from the seventeenth or nineteenth or twenty-first century; the shifting, bought object, plundered, beautiful, faked; it stands there, smiling, in our house.

NO, BUT I SAW THE MOVIE
Russell Banks

For many years, or maybe not so many—for some years, anyhow—I'd be out on the book-tour hustings and after a reading would be signing books at a table in the lobby, and a lovely thing would happen. A stranger, a total stranger, would appear in line and volunteer that he or she loved one of my books (one other than the book that I was at that moment signing, of course, and was now embellishing with endearments and fawning declarations of lifelong gratitude). There is, of course, nothing more satisfying to an author of serious literary fiction or poetry—which is to say, an author who does not write for money—than to be told by a stranger that one's work has entered that stranger's life.

And whenever a person told me that he or she had enjoyed *Affliction*, say, or *The Sweet Hereafter*, I assumed the reference was to my book, and I might say in a surprised way, for it was, after all, to me still somewhat surprising, "Oh? You read the book?" As if the reference were possibly to another affliction, like cholera or extreme poverty, or to a different Sweet Hereafter, a designer drug, maybe, or a chic new soul-food restaurant on Manhattan's Upper West Side. Inviting, I suppose, what usually followed, which was a description of the circumstances or conditions under which the book was read—a book club, my brother-in-law gave it to me for Christmas, a college course, I read it in prison, in the hospital, on a train/plane/slow boat to China, et cetera.

It's what we talk about when we talk about a book that one of us has written and the other has read. We're inevitably somewhat self-conscious, at a loss for the appropriate words, in a bit of a blush, both of us. Writing and reading literary fiction and poetry are activities almost too intimate to talk about. Literature is intimate behavior between strangers, possibly more intimate even than sex, and it occurs between *extreme* strangers, who sometimes do not even speak the same language and thus require the services of a translator. Sometimes one of the strangers (the writer, usually) has been dead for centuries; sometimes he or she is utterly unknown, anonymous, or someone, like Homer or the author of the Upanishads or the Song of Solomon, whose individual identity has been mythologized and absorbed by an entire people.

My point is simply that this activity of writing involves at its center the desire on the part of the writer to become intimate with strangers, to speak from one's secret, most vulnerable, truth-telling self directly to a stranger's same self. And it's so central to the impulse that it actually does not work when one's readers are *not* strangers, when one's readers are one's friends, lovers, or family members (it's well-known, after all, that no writer takes pleasure from the praise of his mom or kid sister, and we're all conditioned from our apprenticeship on not to take seriously the critiques offered by our husbands and wives and best friends). Either way, people who know us personally have motives and knowledge that disqualify them as readers. No, it's only the kindness of strangers that counts, that shyly offered gift, "I have read your novel." (With the clear implication, of course, that it was not an unhappy or unrewarding experience.)

I know this, because I am a reader, too. I am other writers' intimate stranger, and I have sat next to an author at dinner and have felt the same odd, embarrassing need to declare, as if revealing a slightly illicit or inappropriate interest in baseball cards or negligee mail-order catalogs, that I have read his or her novel, and I know that, in saying so, I am confessing that I have traveled out-of-body deeply into that stranger's fictional world and have resided there, dreamed there, hallucinated there, and have been moved, comforted, and frightened, have laughed aloud there and maybe even wept. The author, I can always tell, is slightly embarrassed by my confession, but pleased nonetheless—the more so inasmuch as he or she and I have never met before and never will again, and he or she has never read anything of mine and, if the author wishes to preserve our beautiful relationship as it is, never will, either. Reader and writer from two different solar systems, our orbits intersect for a second, and we reflect back the flash of each other's light, take brief comfort from the actual physical existence of the other, and then speed on, safely back in our own imagined universe, as if the other were not circling far away in another universe, around a different, possibly brighter sun than ours.

In the last few years, however, there has been a subtle but important change for me in this exchange between writer and presumed reader. Nowadays, when at the book-signing table, I'm often approached by a person carrying a copy of *Affliction*, for example, the paperback with the picture of Nick Nolte and James Coburn on the cover, or maybe the Canadian edition of *The Sweet Hereafter* with Ian Holm and Sarah Polley staring mournfully out, and the person will say, "I loved *Affliction*," or "*The Sweet Hereafter* meant a lot to me," and pleased and slightly embarrassed, as usual, I will say, "Oh? You read the book?" And the person will look at me somewhat quizzically, and say, "Uh . . . no, but I saw the movie."

I honestly don't know how that makes me feel, how I *ought* to feel, or what I ought to say in response. What *do* we talk about when we talk about a book I wrote whose movie version you saw? Or a book I wrote that you know of solely because you heard about the movie and saw the clips on the Academy Awards television show? What is the relationship generally between literary fiction (that relatively esoteric art form) and film (the most popular and powerful art form of our time), and in particular between my literary fictions and their film adaptations?

These are not simple questions, and literary writers have historically been reluctant to discuss them, except in dismissive ways. Hemingway famously advised novelists to drive (*presumably* from the east) to the California-Nevada state line and toss the novel over the line, let the movie people toss the money back, then turn around and drive away as fast as possible. Which is what most novelists have done, and is what most producers, directors, screenwriters, and actors have wanted them to do. Let us buy your plot, they say, your characters, setting, themes, and language, and do whatever we please with them, that's what the money's *for*, Mr. Shakespeare, so we can leave dear old Lear happily ensconced at the Linger Longer Assisted-Living Facility in Naples, Florida, with his three daughters, Melanie, Gwyneth, and Julia, living together in adjoining condos nearby, heavily into Gulf Coast real estate, romance on the horizon, fadeout and hit the credits soundtrack. "Stayin' Alive" by the Bee Gees, and let's get Newman for the old guy, and for his pal, whatzisname, the guy with glaucoma, get Jack—we'll keep the title, sort of, only we'll call it *Shakespeare in Retirement.*

Writers who didn't, or couldn't, afford to take Hemingway's advice almost always paid for it dearly with their pride, their integrity, often their reputations, and sometimes even their whole careers. The story is that Hollywood is like Las Vegas—if you have a weakness, they'll find it. Everyone knows Fitzgerald's sad tale of depression, booze, and crack-up, and there are dozens more. Faulkner seems to have managed only by staying solidly drunk from arrival to departure. Nelson Algren sold the film rights of *The Man with the Golden Arm* to Otto Preminger, contingent on Algren's being hired to write the screenplay; later, safely back in Chicago, he said, "I went out there for a thousand a week, and I worked Monday, and I got fired Wednesday. The guy that hired me was out of town on Tuesday." S. J. Perelman said of Hollywood, "It was a hideous and untenable place when I dwelt there, populated with few exceptions by Yahoos, and now that it has become the chief citadel of television, it's unspeakable." A native of Providence, Rhode Island, and a great writer about boxing and horse racing, Perelman is not someone you'd think of as especially fastidious, but Hollywood he saw as "a dreary industrial town controlled by hoodlums of enormous wealth, the ethical sense of a pack of jackals, and taste so degraded that it befouled everything it touched." (Sort of the way I see Providence, now that I think of it.) More or less in the same vein, John Cheever said, "My principal feeling about Hollywood is suicide. If I could get out of bed and into the shower, I was all right. Since I never paid the bills, I'd reach for the phone and order the most elaborate breakfast I could think of, and then I'd try to make it to the shower before I hanged myself." Strong

statements, but not at all atypical, when serious literary writers found
themselves obliged to work in, for, and with the makers of movies. Ben
Hecht put it in depressingly simple terms, "I'm a Hollywood writer; so
I put on a sports jacket and take off my brain."

And yet, one is forced to ask, was that then and this now? And how
do we account for the difference? Because, when one looks around
today, one notices an awful lot of very respectable fiction writers
having what appears to be a very good time in bed with Hollywood,
both as authors of novels recently adapted to film, like Michael
Ondaatje's *The English Patient*, Toni Morrison's *Beloved*, Peter
Carey's *Oscar and Lucinda*, David Guterson's *Snow Falling on
Cedars*, and Mona Simpson's *Anywhere but Here*, and as fiction
writers turned screenwriters, like Richard Price, John Irving, Amy
Tan, Jim Harrison, and Susan Minot. Paul Auster has even *directed* his
first film and is planning to try a second. There are others waiting in
the wings. And we're not talking about the Crichtons and the Clancys
here, whose fiction seems written mainly to fit the template of
blockbuster movies—a respectable line of work, but not one I myself
identify with. No, we're talking about writers whose fiction aspires to
the somewhat more Parnassian heights where literature resides, work
composed without consideration of financial reward and meant to be
compared, for better or worse, to the great literary works of the past.
And there is a growing phalanx of such writers, whose often difficult,
morally ambiguous novels, complexly layered books with unruly
characters, have been eagerly sought out and adapted for film. I
honestly can't remember a period like it. We could easily make a
very long list of novelists and story writers, serious, literary writers,
almost none of whom actually lives and works in Hollywood, as it
happens (thanks to fax machine, modem, and e-mail), but all of whom
are making a fairly good living from the film industry these days, a
much better living, certainly, than they could make on the sales of their
books alone or than many of them used to make teaching in university
creative-writing programs.

I now must add my own name to that list, and confess that in the last
few years, not only have I made a pretty good living from the movie

business, I've had a heck of a good time doing it, too. And furthermore, I'm not ashamed or even slightly embarrassed by the movies
that have been adapted from my novels. Well, that's not altogether
true: there are a few moments in each that make me cringe and crouch
low in my seat when I see them. But overall I am delighted to have been
associated with the making of those two films, *Affliction* and *The
Sweet Hereafter*, and am grateful to the people who made them and to
the businesspeople who financed them. I think they are interesting,
excellent films on their own terms, and I feel they honor the novels on
which they are based. And I don't believe I'm alone in having had such
a delightful experience—most of the writers I listed earlier, if not all of
them, feel the same about the films adapted from their works. Oh,
Rick Moody might grumble about aspects of *The Ice Storm* and
William Kennedy might quibble with some of the decisions made in
the making of *Ironweed*, but unlike the Faulkners, Cheevers, Perel-
mans, and Hechts of previous generations, none of the writers mentioned here feels demeaned, exploited, or deceived. The contrast
between my experience and that of so many of my colleagues on
the one hand, and the experience of our predecessors on the other, is so
great as to raise an interesting question. Simply, has the movie industry
in the last ten or fifteen years, and especially in the last five years,
become uncharacteristically hospitable to serious works of fiction, or
have the sensibilities and needs of the writers of fiction been coarsened
and dumbed down to such a degree that they no longer feel offended
by Hollywood?

Obviously—since, rightly or wrongly, I feel neither coarsened nor
especially dumbed down—I believe it's the former. It's Hollywood
that's changed. And it's possible that my own experience there, since it
hasn't been especially uncharacteristic, can illustrate *how* it has
changed, if not suggest *why*. Although *Affliction* was not released
until December 1998, and *The Sweet Hereafter* was released a year
earlier, in December 1997, both movies were shot within weeks of
each other between January and March of 1997. Both were filmed in
Canada, *Affliction* in Quebec, less than two hours' drive from my
home in upstate New York, and *The Sweet Hereafter* in Toronto and

British Columbia. The most salient aspect of this (other than the fact that, because they were nearby, I got to hang around the sets a whole lot) is merely that neither movie was filmed in Los Angeles. A far more important fact, however, is that the director of *Affliction*, Paul Schrader, and the director of *The Sweet Hereafter*, Atom Egoyan, although a generation apart, are both auteur-style, independent film-makers, serious cinematic artists with highly developed artistic imaginations. Crucially, they are men with no studio affiliations, who finance their projects by hook and crook, pasting together support from half a dozen sources, foreign and domestic, risking their mortgages, their kids' college educations, and next summer's vacation every time out, in a game that for them is high stakes and personal, but leaves them with maximum control over what ends up on the screen. Final cut, in other words, all the way down the line. And this is only possible because of budget size. Paul Schrader likes to point out that somewhere around fourteen million dollars you have to put white hats on the good guys and black hats on the bad guys. It's practically an immutable law of filmmaking. Fourteen million dollars, adjusted to inflation, is the point where you're told by the person with the checkbook: no more shades of gray, no more contradictions, no more ambiguities. *Affliction* cost a little over six million dollars to make, *The Sweet Hereafter* cost about $4.7 million, and you can be sure that Nick Nolte, Sissy Spacek, James Coburn, Willem Dafoe, and Ian Holm did not receive their usual fees. These actors, movie stars who command salaries equal, in a couple of cases, to the entire budget of the movie, worked for far less because they admired the director and the other cast members and wanted to work with them, they were excited by the screenplay and the source material for the film, and they wanted to portray characters who were colored in shades of gray, wanted to inhabit lives made complex and believable by contradiction and ambiguity, dealing with serious conflicts that matter in the real world. They believed in film as an art form and in their craft and the abilities of their colleagues, and were trying for that rare thing, a collaborative, lasting work of art.

Two important factors, then, contributed mightily to getting these rather difficult and, some might say, depressing films made: the directors, both of them artists with strong personal visions of the world, were independent filmmakers free of studio affiliation, with track records that attract great actors; and both films were budgeted low enough to keep down the debt service, so that an investor could recoup his money and even make a profit without having to sell tickets to every fourteen-year-old boy and girl in America. Without, in other words, having to turn the movie into a theme park or a video game. Also, there may have been a third factor, which underlies both of these first two: technology. The technology of filmmaking has changed considerably in recent years. From the camera to the editing room, from the soundtrack to the projection booth, film making has gone digital, as they like to say, so that it's possible, for instance, as in *The Sweet Hereafter*, to send a school bus careening over a cliff and skidding across a frozen lake to where it stops, then slowly sinks below the ice, a horrifying sight—all composed in a few days in a dark room in Toronto, pixels on a computer screen, a *virtual* school bus, cliff, frozen lake, et cetera, for one-tenth the price and in one-quarter the time it would have taken to stage and film in 35 millimeter an *actual* bus, cliff, lake, et cetera. The enormous and incredibly expensive technological resources and hardware available to a studio will soon be available to almost any kid with a credit card or an indulgent uncle, and that kid can set up shop with a laptop anywhere—from SoHo to Montreal to Toronto to Seattle—and compete with the Lucases, Disneys, and Hensons of the world.

American independent film making seems to be entering a truly brave new world, and it will create a transition comparable, perhaps, to the transition between silent films and talkies, one in which, thanks to technological change, the old controlling economic structures undergo seismic shifts and rearrangements, with the result that the prevailing aesthetic and thematic conventions will have to give way. The boom in recent years of independent moviemaking is just the beginning. The trend toward multinational corporate bloat and gigantism will no doubt continue, if for no other reason than, thanks to that same technological change put to other uses, it *can*—unifying theme parks, professional sports, retailing, and gambling under one all-season stadium roof, so that the distinction between shopping and entertainment eventually disappears altogether, and Las Vegas and Orlando become our national cultural capitals, the twenty-first-century Model Cities of America. But at the same time, thanks to the very same technology, the equivalent of a cinematic samizdat is beginning to evolve right alongside it. This is where the real filmmaking is being done; the rest is little more than consumer advertising, tie-ins, and product placement. And this is where we'll see the bright young directors, screenwriters, cinematographers, and actors going to work. The Atom Egoyans and Paul Schraders of the future will be making their films rapidly and cheaply, editing them as fast as they're shot, and releasing them as independently as they're made, by the Internet or on video and DVD. Films like *The Blair Witch Project* and *Being John Malkovitch* and *The Celebration* and the recently released *Last Night*—inventive, unconventionally structured, freshly and bravely imagined movies—are not anomalies in today's film world, although five years ago they would have been. Five years ago they probably would not have been made at all. Nor, for that matter, would *Affliction* and *The Sweet Hereafter*.

This is why I think you're seeing so many serious novelists hanging around the filmmakers these days. They sense there's something marvelous happening here, and if it doesn't take too much time away from their fiction writing and pays reasonably well, they'd like to be a part of it. Just consider the writing itself—until fairly recently, the conventions of screenwriting were, from a late-twentieth-century novelist's perspective, moribund, stuck in linear time, glued to the old Aristotelian unities of place, time, and character, a three-act tale as anachronistic and predictable as . . . well, as a late-nineteenth-century novel. What self-respecting postmodernist fiction writer would want to work in a form so limited and so inappropriate to our times? Yet for the writers of screenplays, until recently, it was as if, five generations after Faulkner, Joyce, and Woolf, modernism never existed, or if it did, that it had no relevance to narrative except between the covers of a book. No wonder Ben Hecht felt he had to take his brain off when he went to work in Hollywood. No wonder Hemingway couldn't be bothered even to cross the state line. And no wonder there was such a fuss a few years ago when Quentin Tarantino in *Pulp Fiction* pushed the envelope a little and played with narrative time and point of view. At the time, it was a radical move for a screenwriter, perhaps, but all he was doing was employing a few of the tools that practically every second-year fiction-writing student keeps at the ready, switchback and replay, and a *Rashomon* split point of view.

Consider, again, our two examples, *The Sweet Hereafter* and *Affliction*, not just *how* those screenplays were written, but the (to me) amazing fact that the novels got adapted for film at all. Never mind the subject matter—although it is amusing to imagine pitching the stories to an old-time studio executive. "Mr. Warner, I've got this very dark story that starts with a school-bus accident in a small north-country town, and a large number of the children of the town are killed, and the movie is about the reaction of the village to this mind-numbing event." Or this: "An alcoholic, violent, forty-five-year-old small-town cop tries and fails to overcome the psychological and moral disfigurement inflicted on him as a child by his alcoholic, violent father." The door, Mr. Banks, is over there.

Let's look at just the narrative form and structure of the two novels. *The Sweet Hereafter* is told from four separate, linked points of view, four different characters, each of whom picks up the story where the previous narrator left off and continues for seventy-five or so pages before handing it off, in the process remembering and recounting his and her past, offering reflections, ruminations, observations, and grief for the lost children. *Affliction* is told from the point of view of an apparently minor character who is gradually, indirectly, revealed to be an unreliable narrator and thus by the tale's end has become the central figure in the story, displacing the person we *thought* the story was about. Neither form lends itself to a conventional three-act screenplay with the usual plot points and fixed unities of time, place, and point of view, and if for no other reason than that (never mind subject matter), I was amazed that anyone even wanted to *try* to make a movie from them. Happily, both Atom Egoyan and Paul Schrader did, and they both felt free to invite me into the process of adaptation from the start and allowed me to look over their shoulders, as it were, all the way through to the editing room and beyond. It was fascinating and very instructive to see the liberties they took, not with the books, but with the old conventions of filmmaking, from screenplay to casting to camera placement to editing and sound.

For instance, to preserve the multiple points of view of *The Sweet Hereafter*—in the novel one can think of them as being structured vertically, like four columns of type, or four members of a mile relay team, which in the "real-time" constraints of a movie (as opposed to the more interactive "mental-time" freedoms of fiction) would have resulted in four separate, consecutive, thirty-minute movies—Egoyan essentially tipped the story onto its side, ran the several points of view horizontally, as it were, almost simultaneously, the relay runners running four abreast instead of sequentially, so that the story moves back and forth in time and from place to place with unapologetic ease. Egoyan trusts his viewer to reconstruct time and place and reunify point of view on his or her own, just as one does when reading a modern novel. No big deal. Similarly, Schrader with *Affliction* felt no compunctions against letting the narrator of the novel, a minor character, it seems, one outside the action, function in the film as the witness and recapitulator of his older brother's deeds and misdeeds. This is the character who would surely have been eliminated at once from a studio production of this film, but Schrader makes him slowly, subtly, become the center of the story, using voice-over to establish his presence at every crucial juncture and giving us explicit, dramatized inconsistencies, conflicting versions of events, to establish his unreliability, so that Willem Dafoe's voice-over at the end, "Only I remain . . ." can be heard and felt with a terrible chill of recognition by all of us in the audience, we who—unlike poor Wade Whitehouse, the ostensible and long-gone hero of our story—*also* remain. And in that way, the story of *Affliction* becomes our story, Wade's affliction becomes our culture's affliction.

Working closely with Egoyan and Schrader, I received a crash course in filmmaking, and what I learned *can't* be done in film was just as interesting and instructive to me, the fiction writer, as what I learned *can* be done in film was interesting and instructive to me the neophyte screenwriter. A particularly useful, and typical, insight, for instance, came to me early on in the writing of *The Sweet Hereafter*'s screenplay. Egoyan had told me that one of the aspects of the novel that most excited him was the final scene, a demolition derby. We even drove to the Essex County Fair in upstate New York and videotaped one. It was the most cinematic scene in the book, Atom said. But when it came time to write it into the screenplay, he just couldn't. It was too big, too loud, crowded, too crammed with action. What to do? He asked me, "What's the underlying function of the scene in the *novel*?" I explained that it served as a social rite, a familiar but strange, rigidly structured ritual that could embrace, embellish, and reconfigure the roles of the various members of the community. With the devices and artifices of fiction available to me, I could keep the noise down, thin out the crowd, slow down the speed—distancing the demolition derby, so that it could function in the novel as an emblem for everything else in the story. He got this. Also, all along I'd told him that, to me, the novel only *seemed* realistic; that actually it was supposed to be experienced as a moral fable about the loss of the children in our culture, an elaboration on a medieval fairy tale. That's when he proposed cutting into the film the whole of the Browning poem "The Pied Piper of Hamelin," inserting a literal reading of the book. At first I said no way, too literary. There's barely a mention of it in the book, one or two passing allusions, maybe. But the more I thought about it, the more I realized—too literary for a *novel*, maybe, but not for a film. Just as the demolition-derby scene was too cinematic for a film, maybe, but not for a novel. Film, I was discovering, is in your face; fiction is in your head.

Here's a further example: something I learned a full year after *The Sweet Hereafter* was released. In Toronto one night, Atom and I gave a presentation to benefit a small theater group there and decided that I would read scenes from the novel, and he would show a clips of the film version of the same scenes, and then we'd discuss why we'd each done our respective work the way we did. One of these scenes was the incest scene, which a number of people who had, and some who hadn't, read the book complained about in the film. "It was like a dream," and "I thought maybe I'd imagined it," the fourteen-year-old Nichole tells us over and over in the novel—distancing us from the actual act, the incest, by placing her account of her *response* to it between it and us, so that we simultaneously imagine the act and the girl in two different time frames, both during and after. Egoyan tried to find a cinematic way to show that from Nichole's point of view it was like a dream, maybe something she imagined, et cetera, and as a result he presented it as if it *were* a dream, i.e., dreamy, with candles, music, a father who almost seems to be her boyfriend, which has the effect, not of distancing the incest and allowing us to pity the victim and fear for her in an appropriate way, but of romanticizing it, making the victim seem way too complicit and fear and pity nearly impossible.

These lessons don't suggest to me that fiction is in any way superior to film. Merely different, in fascinating and challenging ways. Furthermore, the freedom to make movies this way, to be inventive, imaginative, and complex in the formal and structural aspects of the screenplay, and to deal with life-and-death issues that affect us all in our day-to-day lives, this is what attracts novelists like Paul Auster, Peter Carey, John Irving, and so many others like them to the movie business. It's not, as in the past, merely the business of the movie business that attracts; it's the movies that can be made there. It's certainly what has attracted me. And as a direct result of my experience with *The Sweet Hereafter* and *Affliction*, in the last few years I've become a screenwriter myself. I'm a dues-paying member of the Screenwriters Guild of America, having adapting two of my novels: *Rule of the Bone*, for Chris Noonan to direct, with Chris, his partner Barry Mendel, and me to produce; and *Continental Drift*, with Willem Dafoe and me to produce. I am also now at work on an adaptation of a novel by a different novelist, *On the Road*, by Jack Kerouac, for Francis Coppola, and am planning soon to write an original screenplay, too. And the people I'm working with, the directors, actors, producers, even the agents, are smart, and they are exceedingly skilled at what they do. They know all kinds of things that I don't, and in no way do they make me feel that, to work with them, I've got to put on a sports jacket and take off my brain. Quite the opposite.

Eudora Welty once said, "The novel is something that never was before and will not be again." That is the reason why we write them. When it begins to appear that a film can also be that new, that uniquely itself, then, believe me, men and women who otherwise would be writing novels will want to make films, too. We are fast approaching that point. Oh, sure, it is a lot of fun to hobnob with movie stars and go to Cannes and Sundance and ride to the Oscars in a limo the likes of which you haven't seen since your senior prom, but the thrill fades faster than cheap cologne. The thrill of becoming intricately and intimately involved in the process of making a true work of narrative art, however, and the chance to make that work of art collaboratively in the most powerful medium known to man, that's as thrilling as it gets; at least for this old storyteller it is. And, too, as Peter DeVries once said, "I love being a writer. What I can't stand is the paperwork."

But I don't want to leave the mistaken impression that I or any of the other novelists I've mentioned, my blessed colleagues, is likely to give up writing fiction to devote him- or herself to film. Despite the paperwork. That's inconceivable to me. These dalliances with film—however thrilling, remunerative, and instructive they are—can't replace the deep, life-shaping, life-*changing* response one gets from creating a fictional world, living in that world for years at a time, then sending it out to strangers. *Perfect* strangers. A novel, like a marriage, can change your life for the rest of your life; I'm not so sure that can be said of a movie, any more than it can of a love affair.

What, then, *do* I say to that very kind stranger who tells me, "No, but I saw the movie?" I can answer, "Ah, but that was in another country, friend, and in a different time. If you read the book, you will now and then be reminded of that country, perhaps, and that time, but only dimly and incidentally." For when we open a novel, we bring to it everything that we bring to a film—our memories and fears and our longings and dreams (our secrets, even the ones we keep from ourselves)—all of which the film either displaces or simply disregards as it unspools in the dark before us. All of which—our memories, fears, longings, and dreams—the novel engages and utilizes wholly as it takes us out of our lives into another that's as much of our own making as it is of the novelist's. That intimacy, that secret sharing among strangers, is what no novelist and no reader can give up. No matter how remarkable it is, a film is what it is, regardless of our presence or absence before it. The darkened theater can be empty, and it won't affect the essential nature of the film being shown there. But a novel simply does not exist until it's read, and each time it's read, even if it's read a second time by the same person, or a third, even if it's read a thousand years after it was written, it's just as Eudora Welty said, it is "something that never was before and will not be again."

THE MAGNIFICENT FRIGATE BIRD
Abigail Thomas

R ich was a birder, dyed in the wool, we have lists from his fourth-grade sightings in Central Park. He wrote with a dark pencil and he pressed down hard. Bluejay, house finch, crow . . . Once, in his teens, he sighted a magnificent frigate bird off the coast of Connecticut, blown there by a hurricane. This was the proudest moment of his bird-watching life. On top of his dresser now are a bunch of birds, a small, haphazard collection. There are the shorebirds, long-legged wading creatures; a bufflehead duck he made of clay in the seventh grade; two drab decoys we bought at an auction; a red plastic chicken (mine) that neatly lays three white eggs if you push down gently on her back; a papier-mâché crow, mascot of Old Crow, with his jaunty top hat that I fell in love with because something in its expression reminded me of my father. There is also a little box of grain Rich saved from a cross-country trip he took when he was seventeen; he and a friend worked on farms along the way. It goes with the birds. What used to be on top of his dresser? A small tray for change, his wallet, scraps of paper with things to do, a picture of us taken at his brother's house a couple of weeks after we were married. A flashlight, just in case. A backup alarm clock, just in case. Rich was prepared for everything. He was a man who carried a couple of Band-Aids in his wallet and always had an extra handkerchief if somebody needed one. I've put a corn plant next to the bureau, green and leafy. They never die.

I go up to see my husband every Wednesday. My friend Ruth picks me up at eight, so I get up at six in order to have the dogs walked and the paper read and the coffee drunk. It's a couple of hours north, depending on traffic, and we have become close friends over the last few months. Our destination is Kingston, and once there Ruth and I stop in Monkey Joe's, a coffee shop with fantastic cappuccino and great pumpkin muffins. We sit together for twenty minutes, then she goes to work at Benedictine Hospital and I head for the pay phone behind a Hot Wings joint that seems to be always on the verge of reopening and call a cab to the rehabilitation center where my husband has been for nine months.

Sometimes when I arrive Rich is still asleep, his face relaxed, looking so like himself that I can't believe he won't wake up and be all better. Other times he is up, stalled in the middle of whatever he began to do, his back to the door, his arms raised like a conductor, motionless, as if he were playing some cosmic game of statue. Or maybe he sits on the bed, a pair of socks in one hand, his trousers laid out beside him. After our usual greeting, "Absie! How did you find me!" or "What time did you get up? I didn't hear you," he lapses into silence. The nurses say he can stand in front of the bathroom mirror (made of shiny metal) for an hour or more, toothbrush in his hand. In brain-injury jargon, perhaps this is what is meant by "difficulty completing a task."

The first time I heard this term I imagined a child who can't manage tying shoelaces, a grown-up who forgets how to scramble eggs, some kind of visible difficulty, frustration, something that could be re-learned. I didn't know about the getting stuck. For my husband, there is no such thing as a minute ago, there is no *but we've been sitting here for an hour and a half.* That information has nowhere to lodge in Rich's consciousness. He has a collapsing past. If he doesn't remember, he doesn't believe. And if everything is now, what's the rush? I used to try and coax him, nudge him on (the TBI term is "redirect"), but that only made him angry and confused. So I have adapted. I join him. We sit and steep ourselves in 10:37, a single moment, while outside this room an hour disappears, bypassing us. I am always surprised when I look at the clock to find how long we've been there.

Once he's moving, I see how slowly he puts himself together. We select the clothes. "These aren't mine," he insists, but somehow we get past that. He puts his socks on the way he always did, rolling them back to get his toes in, unrolling them carefully over the rest of his foot, inch by inch, then pulling them over his heel. Next trousers, then shirt carefully buttoned, and everything tucked in neatly. Rich hasn't shaved in some time, instead he pulls his beard out. This has a name but I forget what it is.

Last week he didn't smile or greet me. He wouldn't hold my hand. "What's wrong?" I asked, this was so unlike him. "We're divorced," he said, as if I were an imbecile. "We're married, Rich," I told him. "We've been married fourteen years. You're my husband," I said, touching his arm. "I'm your wife." He looked at me coldly. "Transparent window-like words." He doesn't believe in his brain injury, so he has come up with an explanation for my absence: I have left him. "I'm alone," he says, waving his arm down the hall. "Hundreds of single beds," he says, "hundreds of single beds with old men lying in them with their boots on."

Time has gotten skewed, as tangled as fish line, what means what anymore? How could it be two years since the accident? I calculate it in months, weeks, but the numbers don't feel real or important. One hundred and four weeks. Twenty-four months. Whole handfuls of time have slipped through my fingers. Seasons rush by before I have grasped "winter," "spring." Somehow I have gotten to sixty; in no time Rich will be seventy. We would have had parties to mark the place, but the last birthday slid by unnoticed, the last anniversary. Twenty-four months since the accident. If it were a child, it would be talking, walking, climbing into everything. "Time flaps on its mast," wrote Virginia Woolf in *Mrs. Dalloway*. For us time hangs off its mast. Sometimes I'm not even sure about the mast. Something stopped ticking April 24, 2000. Our years together ended, our future together changed. In one moment of startling clarity he told me, "My future has been dismantled." Last week he wouldn't look at me for an hour. "If I may navigate this already swollen stream of self-absorption," he said at last, "people borrow things without asking."

"What things?" I asked gratefully, and with that the subject had changed. We spent the rest of the afternoon looking at the *Sibley Guide to Birds*, which I'd bought him a year ago. We spent a long time with ducks, with woodpeckers and thrushes. He didn't recall having

ever seen a magnificent frigate bird and I didn't insist. Long-term
memory is sometimes intact, but he's forgotten that long-gone windy
day in Connecticut.

A friend of mine, a bereavement counselor, tells me that most
widows remember more vividly the last weeks of their husband's
lives than the span of their lives together. I am not a widow, but my
husband as he was is gone. I concentrate on who Rich is at any given
moment and I lose sight of who he was, who we were. It takes my
friend Denise to recall how when we had company at our house in
Greenport, Rich went out early in the morning to buy several newspapers, bags of warm scones and croissants and muffins. I had
forgotten, and remembering was painful. Rich used to make a mean
omelet. On nights when I was cooked out and there was nothing much
to eat, Rich fixed an omelet for himself, did I want one, he always
asked, and no thanks, I always said. But the look of it sliding out of the
pan, perfect with that mottled brown, smelling of butter, sometimes a
little lox thrown in at the last minute, weakened my resolve, and Rich
would slide the better part of half onto a plate and urge me to eat. I
remember how he used to wake me in Greenport with a cup of
cappuccino from Aldo's. One weekend when our friends Sarah and
Cornelius and Kathy were visiting we looked up the magnificent
frigate bird in the Audubon book and discovered that the male has
a red pouch that he inflates to make himself attractive to the female,
but it takes him thirty minutes to get it done. "Phoo phoo—be there in
a minute, honey—phoo phoo!" We laughed ourselves sick at the
kitchen table. How long ago was that? The only way to contain
catastrophe is to cordon it off with dates, but the numbers mean
nothing. If I think instead of how much dust would have settled on
Rich's bureau, then I can feel it. There is nothing like dust.

When Rich is ready, we obtain the pass that lets us out of this locked
ward and downstairs to the cafeteria. This week his mood is better,
and we look forward to lunch. Rich takes the tray and passes all the
baskets of condiments along the right wall. He examines carefully
everything in every basket, then drops two onto the tray. Slippery
packets of mayonnaise, ketchup, jelly, something unspeakably awful

called "table syrup," tartar sauce, margarine, salad dressing, soon the tray is crowded with these silvery foil-wrapped items. Napkins, two knives, two forks, two spoons. Lots and lots of saltines. I meanwhile am slapping together an egg salad sandwich for him, bowls of salad, a few bananas. We meet at the cash register. "I don't have any money," says Rich anxiously, but I tell him it's on me. (My cheese sandwich after weighing comes to thirty-two cents.) We find a table and unload the food. Last week, the week we were divorced, he looked around and said, "All these people dunking their doughnuts in a cup of sorrow, I hope it's not contaminated by the River Styx." Today we are holding hands again, happy to be together. We eat, go back for more coffee, unwrap the saltines. When the food is gone Rich starts in on the condiments, carefully opening each one, inspecting it, and scooping or squeezing out the contents and eating them on saltines. He is like a curious determined child.

I want to be upstairs at one-thirty, the designated smoking time. In the lunchroom for the Behavioral Unit, cigarettes are rationed out after lunch, and heavy steel ashtrays gotten from the cupboard. The techs hand out the cigs and light the smokes for those who smoke; most everyone does. God knows I do. One of the patients, Mr. Mendez, has a beautiful voice, and having been asked, is now singing "The Star-Spangled Banner" in Spanish. He clasps his hands on the table, his feet tapping in time, and before each phrase he draws a solemn breath from his diaphragm without compromising the pace of the anthem. He sings for fifteen minutes without coming to the end, somewhere his needle is stuck, and soon I don't know where or how the song does end. At last he finishes, or rather, stops singing. We applaud and Mr. Mendez is modest but not humble. When the clapping subsides he looks around smiling, "This is America." He bows.

I went to Mexico for a week last winter, a place on the Yucatán Peninsula where time stops, or at least the importance of telling time. You get up at dawn, eat when you're hungry, go to bed when it's dark. The rest of the time you lie in the sun, float in the water. There were pelicans smashing into the water in their ungainly fashion. One afternoon five impossibly pink flamingos flew by and everyone suddenly got to their feet, shielding their eyes against the sun, like a stadium full of people rising to watch a grand slam. Later I saw two other birds, and I knew what they were right away although I'd never seen one before. By the time I got out my camera they had embedded themselves higher and higher in the blue sky until they were specks. I snapped a picture but you'd never know. They could have been anything up there.

THE ONLY SOLUTION TO THE SOUL IS THE SENSES: A MEDITATION ON BILL MURRAY AND MYSELF
David Shields

A few years ago Bill Murray said in a radio interview: "I was one of the first people to really devote my entire life to the Weather Channel, which is what I do. I love the Weather Channel. The charm and the power of the fronts, you know. You get to see something really important happening. And it's dealt with in a really . . . there's even more talk about it, but nothing can be done." I'm in a swoon over Murray because he takes "my issues"—gloom, rage, self-consciousness, word-weariness—and offers ways out, solutions of sorts, all of which amount to a delicate embrace of the real, a fragile lyricism of the unfolding moment. He thus flatters me that under all my protective layers of irony I, too, might have depth of feeling as well. I admire his slouching insouciance but don't possess it, admire it precisely because I don't possess it. I realize, of course, that a certain redemptive posture is the unique property of movies and movie stars, but Murray's grace is manifest at least as often outside movies as in them. The first line of his book, *Cinderella Story: My Life in Golf*, is "The light seems to come from everywhere."

In the last decade there have been a few exceptions—primarily *Groundhog Day* and *Rushmore*—but Murray has been so good in so many bad movies that it's as if he makes bad movies on purpose as a way to demonstrate the truth of Denis Leary's dictum (to which I subscribe): "Life sucks; get a fuckin' helmet." Murray's movies, in general, suck; he's the fuckin' helmet. In a self-interview in which he asked himself to explain why so few of his films have succeeded, he replied, mock-solemnly, "I've had lots of good premises." *The Razor's*

Edge being, again, an interesting exception, Murray seems to believe that, given the horror show of the universe, the supreme act of bad faith would be to appear in a pretentious work of art aspiring to be beautiful, whereas my impulse has always been to try to find in art my only refuge from the storm.

Murray's metaphor for the Sisyphean struggle is: "In life, you never have to completely quit. There's some futile paddling toward some shore of relief, and that's what gets people through. Only the really lucky get a tailwind that takes them to the shore. So many get the headwind that they fight and, then, tip over and drown." Life is futile; failure is a sign of grace; Murray is fuck-up as existential fool. His loserdom is the exact opposite, though, of, say, Woody Allen's, who seems intolerably sniffly by comparison. I'm much, much more like Allen than I am like Murray, which is why I admire Murray (Jewish adoration of un-Jewish stoicism). Asked to name people he finds funny, Murray mentions Bob Hope, David Letterman, Conan O'Brien, Eddie Izzard—Waspy wise guys, *goyischer* slackers, no whiners allowed.

In *Meatballs*, Murray is a counselor at a summer camp for losers. When they're getting demolished in a basketball game against a much tonier camp, Murray instructs his charges to run around pantsing their opponents. Forget the score; fuck the rules; do fun things; give yourself things to remember. Camp director Morty takes himself and the camp way too seriously (so many blocking figures in Murray movies are officious Jews; what's that about—Hollywood's knee-jerk self-hatred?) and so Murray leads all the kids in always calling him "Mickey," turning him into a mouse. The great crime in any Bill Murray movie is self-seriousness, because as Murray's fellow Irishman Oscar Wilde said, "Life is too important to take seriously." Wilde also said, "The only solution to the soul is the senses," which is a key to Murray's appeal: he's in touch with his animal self and teaches the kids to be in touch with theirs. We're all meatballs; we're all just bodies. If I were a girl or gay, I'd have a searing crush on him in this movie, because just the way he carries his body seems to say, *Here is fun. I'm where fun happens.* When he (crucially: unsuccessfully) courts another counselor, he does so without an ounce of earnestness. Losers are winners; they get that life is an unmitigated disaster. At one point he leads the campers in a chant, "It just doesn't matter, it just doesn't matter, it just doesn't matter." My problem is that even though I know on an intellectual level that "it just doesn't matter," on a daily level I treat everything like it does. Murray is notorious for and proud of the degree to which he makes up his own lines in movies; I suppose I could look up whether "It just doesn't matter" is in the original screenplay of *Meatballs*, but I'd rather not. I want to believe it's his invention.

Murray's shtick—antistar Star, antihero Hero, ordinary-guy Icon—is built in part upon the fact of his unglamorous appearance. In sketches on *Saturday Night Live*, Gilda Radner would often call him "Pizza Face," and it's obvious he's never done anything to improve his deeply mottled skin. Seemingly half my adolescence was spent in a dermatologist's office. *Saturday Night Live* producer Lorne Michaels said about Murray, "He never had much vanity. There was a way he always told the truth." The qualities are, of course, intricately intertwined; it's his absence of vanity that allows him to get to emotional truths in a scene, as opposed to, say, Ethan Hawke, who you can tell is always only concentrating on one question: how do I look? I was cute enough as a little kid to appear in an advertisement for a toy store; my father took the photographs, and here I am in the family album, riding a plastic pony and brandishing a pistol with crypto-cowboy charm. Although now I'm certainly not handsome, I don't think I've ever quite outgrown that early narcissism. Murray's not fat, but he has a serious paunch; as opposed to some middle-aged buffster like Harrison Ford, Murray's fifty and looks all of it. Bless him for that: it's a gift back to us; he makes us all feel less shitty. He posed for a *New York Times Magazine* profile wearing a drooping undershirt and with uncombed, thinning gray hair. It's a comparison Murray would surely loathe for its la-di-da-ness, but the photograph reminds me of Rembrandt's late self-portraits: a famous man who understands his own mortal ordinariness and is willing to show you the irredeemable sadness of his eyes, in which that knowledge registers.

Murray's sadness is not other movie stars' pseudo-seriousness; he seems genuinely forlorn—always a plus in my book. Speaking to Terry Gross on *Fresh Air*, Murray said, "Movies don't usually show the failure of relationships; they want to give the audience a final, happy resolution. In *Rushmore*, I play a guy who's aware that his life is not working, but he's still holding on, hoping something will happen, and that's what's most interesting." Gross, stunned that Murray would identify so strongly with someone as bitter and remorseful as Herman Blume, tried to pull Murray up off the floor by saying, "I mean, you've found work that is meaningful for you, though, haven't you?" Murray explained that Blume is drawn to the energetic teenager Max Fischer, who is the founder and president of virtually every club at Rushmore Academy, but "sometimes it makes you sadder to see someone that's really happy, really engaged in life when you have detached." He said this as if he knew exactly what he was talking about. "Murray's glazed expression sees no cause for hope in the world," the film critic Anthony Lane once said of him. Nothing can be done. In *Quick Change*, co-directed by Murray, he plays a clown named Grimm. "What kind of clown are you?" he's asked. "The cryin'-on-the-inside-kind, I guess," he says, which—maybe it's me—I take both as goof on the cliché and true confession.

The Razor's Edge, co-written by Murray, is the only completely serious film he's ever done, the film which he had desperately been wanting to do for years and which the studio agreed to finance only after Murray first agreed to do *Ghostbusters II*. It's Murray's ur-story. The first part of the Maugham novel is set in Chicago, but Murray moved the first part of the film to Lake Forest, next door to Wilmette, the North Shore suburb in which he grew up. The bulk of the book and film are set in Paris, where Murray spent a year, studying French and Gurdjieff and fleeing from post-*Ghostbusters* fame. Surrounded by cripples and sybarites, amoralists and materialists, Murray's character in *The Razor's Edge*, Larry Durrell, travels to China, Burma, and India searching for meaning, and the best he can come up with is: "You don't get it. It doesn't matter." It just doesn't matter. Such is the highest wisdom a Murray character can hope to achieve: a sort of holy detachment, which only deepens his dread.

Angst translates easily to anger. Wes Anderson, explaining why he'd been somewhat anxious about directing Murray in *Rushmore*, said, "I'd heard about him throwing someone in a lake on one thing, and I'd heard that if he didn't like the situation he's going to change it." Discussing megalomaniacal celebrities, Murray said, "Whenever I hear someone say, 'My fans,' I go right for the shotgun." In *Kingpin*, Murray plays an impossibly arrogant bowler who, in one scene, says hello to the two women sitting at the next table. The less attractive woman responds by saying, "Hi," and Murray says, "Not you [nodding to the less attractive woman]. You [nodding to the more attractive woman]." Murray explained to Terry Gross how he had ad-libbed the line: "It just came into my mind at that moment. And it was so horrible—such a horrible thing to say that there was a moment of complete disbelief and then everyone [on the set] laughed really hard because, you know, the guy should be taken out and shot. It was what I think would be the most offensive thing you could do. I was trying to paint a picture of a guy who was really, really a bad guy, so that any second that Woody [Harrelson]'s character stayed with this guy was an investment in bad time." Murray can access his own cruelty but isn't defined by it. He simply doesn't radiate malevolence, as, say, James Woods used to do, but neither is he cuddlesome-cute, à la Tom Hanks; this mixture keeps me productively off balance, makes me unsure whether to embrace him or be slightly afraid of him. I strive for the same mystery in my own persona but fail miserably, since it's so evident how much neediness trumps coolness. When Murray gave his protesting-too-much explanation to Terry Gross, she responded, "I guess I've always wondered how you, so intuitively, seem to understand a certain type of really crude, ego-driven personality." With genuine hostility in his voice, Murray said, "Well, that's a loaded question, Teri." Then he quickly downshifted back to a more mild tone—again, that nervous-making mixture: "But how do I understand that? I don't know. I think show business can enrich that. You can see people manifesting in a bizarre way that, you know, other people don't try to get away, wouldn't try to get away, with. But people get lost in a vanity space and just start going. You know, people that just take themselves too seriously—it's ripe for re-creation."

He seizes the regenerative power of behaving badly, being disrespectful toward condescending assholes, telling truth, as they say, to power. In his self-interview, in which he pretended to be discoursing with Santa Claus, he said, "I was at the New York Film Critics Circle Awards one year. They called me up when somebody canceled two days before the thing, and asked me to present some awards. So I went, and one of the funniest film moments I've ever had was when they introduced the New York film critics. They all stood up; *motley* isn't the word for that group. Everybody had some sort of vision problem, some sort of damage. I had to bury myself in my napkin. As they kept going, it just got funnier and funnier looking. By the time they were all up, it was like, 'You have been selected as the people who have been poisoned; you were the unfortunate people who were not in the control group that didn't receive the medication.'" This is a little amazing, even shocking to me; I fancy myself something of a literary troublemaker, but I can't imagine being quite this publicly dismissive toward the powers that be in the book world (privately, I'm acid etched in acid, of course—what bravery). I suppose his career is less dependent than mine is upon good reviews, i.e., he's actually popular. "If you're not angry, you're not paying attention," goes my favorite bumper sticker. Murray's edginess is a product of the fact that he actually pays attention. He has what Hemingway said was the "most essential gift for a good writer: a built-in, shock-proof shit detector."

Hemingway's hometown of Oak Park is about twenty miles southwest of Murray's hometown of Wilmette; both men have or had a gimlet-eyed view of the disguises the world wears. It's more broadly midwestern, though, than only Hemingwayesque, I think. I should know. My wife, who was born and raised in Lake Forest, has it. Dave Eggers, who also grew up in Lake Forest, has it. Johnny Carson, who was raised in Nebraska, and David Letterman, who was raised in Indiana, have it as well—this quality of detachment which is a way of not getting sucked in by all the shit sent your way, of holding on to some tiny piece of yourself which is immune to publicity, of wearing indifference as a mask.

He is, in other words, ironic. He's alert to and mortified by the distance between how things appear to be and how they are. On *Charlie Rose*, the unctuous host kept trying to get Murray to brag; in every instance, Murray deflected the praise, lightly mocking himself (his irony is bottomless but never particularly self-lacerating). In *Polyester*, Murray sings "The Best Thing," a love song; it's telling, I think, that John Waters cast Murray to sing the parody love song in the parody love movie. In *Michael Jordan to the Max*, a grotesquely worshipful IMAX film-paean, Murray, as a fan in the stands, says, "It's like out of all the fifty thousand top athletes since, you know, prehistoric times—brontosaurus and pterodactyls included—he [Jordan]'s right there." These are modest examples, but they betray Murray's impulse: to unhype the hype, to replace force-fed feeling with something less triumphal, more plausible and human and humble. In *Stripes*, Murray delivers a rousing speech to his fellow soldiers to encourage them to learn overnight what they haven't learned during all of boot camp—how to march. "We're Americans," he says, "we're all dogfaces, but we have within us something American that knows how to do this." Murray saves the speech from sentimentality by mocking the sentimentality. *I'm not really in this situation*, Murray's character seems to be thinking; *I'm not really in this movie*, Murray seems to be thinking. That reminds us, or at least me, of our own detachment and puts us in the scene, thereby making the moment credible and, ironically, moving. Here, as in so many other Murray movies, Murray somehow manages to install a level or two of Plexiglas between himself and the rest of the movie. "What's funny about Murray is not his performance," the film critic Tom Keogh has written, "but the way he hangs back from his performance." At its most dire, Murray's persona is simply anti-feeling; at its most fierce it's anti-faux-feeling. This is what gives his persona such an edge: it's unclear whether his self-mockery is saving grace or Nowhere Man melancholia. It's both, obviously, to which I can attest or hope to attest. Maybe detachment is a way to get to real feeling; maybe it's a dead end from which no feeling arises. That's the Murray bargain.

Murray's characteristic manner of delivering dialogue is to add invisible, ironic quotes around nearly every word he says, as if he weren't quite convinced he should go along with the program that is the script, as if he were just trying out the dialogue on himself first rather than really saying it to someone else in a movie that millions of people are going to see, as if he were still seeing how it sounds. The effect is to undermine every assertion at the moment it's asserted. As a stutterer and writer, I'm a sucker for Murray's push-pull relationship to language; it's undoubtedly one of the main sources of the deep psychic identification I've always felt toward him. Commenting upon Murray's performance as Polonius in the most recent film adaptation of *Hamlet*, the film critic Elvis Mitchell said that Murray's Polonius is "a weary, middle-aged man whose every utterance sounds like a homily he should believe in and perhaps did many years ago." Murray simultaneously embodies and empties out cliché, showing how much we don't believe it, how badly we want to. In *Tootsie*, as Dustin Hoffman's roommate who's a playwright/waiter, Murray says about his work in progress, "I think it's going to change theater as we know it." Murray says the line in a way that no one else could: we're aware that he's full of shit, but we're also aware that he's aware he's full of shit. For which we adore him, because he reminds us how full of shit we are every hour of every day. He's also a welcome relief from Dustin Hoffman's earnestness.

His pet technique for underlining his self-consciousness is knocking, loudly, on the fourth wall. Serving as guest broadcaster for a Chicago Cubs baseball game, which Murray once said is the best thing he's ever done, he answered the phone in the adjoining booth, stuck out his tongue at the camera, called down to the players on the field. On the first episode of the David Letterman show, Murray ran into the audience and led them in an insanely spirited rendition of Olivia Newton-John's "Let's Get Physical." In *Stripes*, when his girlfriend leaves him, he turns to the camera and says, "And then the depression set in." At pro-am tournaments, Murray wears goofy outfits, jokes with the crowd, hits wacky shots—in an effort to tear a hole in the sanctimonious veil surrounding the game of golf. In *Michael Jordan to the Max*, Murray shoves his tub of popcorn at the camera and asks, "Hey, can I ask you: how big does that look on IMAX? Does that look like a gigantic bucket of popcorn or not that big?" At a Carnegie Hall benefit concert with a Sinatra theme, Murray, backed by a full orchestra, sang "My Way"; Murray told an interviewer, "I basically rewrote the lyrics and changed them around to suit my own mood. I started getting laughs with it, and then I was off the click track. I mean, there's a full orchestra playing to its own charts, so they just keep playing, you know. And the fact I'm off the lyric and talking and doing things—it doesn't matter to them. They don't keep vamping; it's not like a piano bar. They just keep going to the end. So I said let's see if this big band is going to stay with me here, and they didn't. They just kept barreling right ahead. But I managed to catch them at the pass. I headed them off at the pass and turned it around and got out of it again." It's crucial to Murray's comedy that the orchestra is there, playing away, serious as society—the formal straitjacket he wriggles out of. By far my favorite joke my daughter has brought home in the last year goes:

> Knock-knock.
> Who's there?
> Interrupting Cow.
> Interrupt—
> Moo.

Murray and I—other people, too, obviously—share an impulse to simultaneously annihilate and resuscitate received forms. I have an extraordinarily vivid memory of a very brief video clip I saw twenty years ago of a juggler who was riding a unicycle and pretending to have great difficulty controlling the knives he was juggling. He was in absolute control, of course, but I loved how much trouble he pretended to be having; I loved how afraid he pretended to be; I loved how much it was both a parody of the form and a supreme demonstration of the form. I loved it so much (an artist pretending death was going to win, but art had it under control all along, thank you very much) that it brought me to tears.

Murray's acute self-consciousness is paralyzing, but also curiously freeing: it frees him up to be a rebel (just barely). In *Razor's Edge*, he's the only character who is both (just) sane and (beautifully) whimsical, which is the balance he strikes in nearly every movie, his signature mixture of hip and square. He knows better than anyone else that you don't always have to do what they tell you to do, but he also tends to realize that the way out of the slough of despond is delight in other people, making him clubbable. In *Stripes*, asked by the drill sergeant what he's doing, Murray's character says, "Marching in a straight line, sir." It's not a straight line, but what he's doing is still, finally, marching. Although Murray is utterly insubordinate toward the sergeant, he winds up earning the sergeant's admiration by leading a rescue mission at the end. Murray is a goof-off and antiestablishment, but he winds up having the right stuff. He gets it together but on his own terms, if "own terms" can be defined unambitiously. Asked by an interviewer what he thought of the television show *Cheers*, Murray said, "That was like prime-time TV; I never really got into it or anything." Such is the extent of Murray's rebellion—late-night vs. prime-time TV. One of the many good jokes of *Tootsie* is that Murray, playing an avant-garde playwright, is nobody's idea of an avant-garde playwright: everything in his body—his competence, his responsibility—screams acceptance of things as they are. He defies without sabotaging authority. When an interviewer asked Murray whether *Rushmore* director Wes Anderson's gentle approach toward actors was effective, Murray replied, a bit huffily, "Well, that's good manners, you know? That's tact." Murray went to Loyola Academy, a prep school, in Wilmette, and all his hell-raising is, in a way, the unthreateningly bad behavior of a slumming preppy. The ultimate effect of all his hijinks on the links is to deepen golf's hushed, moneyed silence (Murray's antics would seem redundant at a football game). There's the official way and then there's your own way; Murray does it his own way, he never gets co-opted, but—and this is his magic trick, this is the movies, this is what is so deeply reassuring about his persona—he still succeeds (rids the city of ghosts, gets the girl, leads the rescue mission). He therefore is a perfect bridge figure between, to paint in broad strokes, fifties conformity, sixties rage, seventies zaniness, eighties and nineties capitalismo; hence his appeal—he convinces us that we're still a little rebellious inside even as we're finally doing what everyone else is doing. As the child of left-wing activists, I'm frequently embarrassed by how bourgeois my yearnings are; Murray's relatively unangry versions of *épater le bourgeois* coat my conformity in glee.

This very deep contradiction in Murray is directly related to the way corrosive irony, in him, sits atop deep sentimentality. (So, too, for myself: walking out of the theater after *Terms of Endearment*, I subjected it to a withering critique while tears were still streaking down my face.) When he was guest commentator at the Cubs game, he mocked every player on the opposing team in a parody of fan fanaticism ("That guy shouldn't even be in the major leagues, and he knows it. He's lying to himself; he really should go back into some sort of community service in his hometown"), but he refused every opportunity the cameraman handed him to score easy points off the enormously fat African-American umpire Eric Gregg, whose uniform had been lost and who just couldn't get comfortable in his borrowed clothes. Before the Cubs played their first night game at Wrigley Field, Murray visited the booth again, this time for just a few minutes, mercilessly ribbing the legendary announcer Harry Caray before suddenly declaring, "This is the most beautiful park in the world." I feel so earthbound compared to Murray, so uncelebratory. In *Ghostbusters*, he pretends to be a self-absorbed asshole, but we're meant to understand that underneath the mordant pose he's a pussycat. Murray's MO is in a way classic American cowboy—Gary Cooper, John Wayne, heart of gold encased in steel. I'm the opposite—sensitivo surface masking homicidal maniac. Had the actors in *Mad Dog and Glory* been cast according to type—De Niro playing the mobster and Murray the neurasthenic police photographer—the movie would have made no sense. The movie wouldn't be funny,

the violence wouldn't seem silly, if we didn't understand that approxi-
mately credible though Murray is as the Mafia don, he's really not a
killer; he's just joking, we don't believe him for a minute. Murray has
an amazing ability to deliver mean lines that somehow don't sound
mean; this is because he is, I'm almost sure of this, a gentle man (who
also possesses of course perfectly repressed rage—giving the gentleness
its edge). With just a few exceptions (*Kingpin*, say, or *Mad Dog and
Glory*), Murray is almost always the character in the movie who
embodies and articulates the vision of the movie, precisely because he's
so hard to dislike. Asked about his parodies of bad singers, Murray
explained, "You have to see what the original center of the song was
and how they destroyed it. It's the ruining of a good song that you
want to re-create. You have to like the stuff and you have to, I guess,
know that when you have the microphone you have the opportunity
to touch somebody. And when you don't do it with the lyric of it, and
your own excuse for technique comes in and steps on top of it, that's, I
guess, what I object to when I'm mimicking something." That old
story: rage is disappointed romanticism.

Disappointed romanticism, however, isn't romanticism. Murray
isn't Tom Hanks; he never, or almost never, does romantic comedy.
He likes himself too much, for as Murray says, "The romantic figure
has to behave romantically even after acting like a total swine. It's 'I'm
so gorgeous you're going to have to go through all kinds of hell for
me,' and that isn't interesting to me. Romance is very particular.
There's something about romance, that if you don't have to have
someone, you're more desirable." Murray has the dignity of not
having to have someone, or at least not going on and on about it.

He is, in short, male, a guy's guy, still extremely boyish though he
was born in 1950, broad-shouldered, tall (six foot one), upbeat about
his masculinity in a way that seems quite foreign and enviable to me.
My voice is high and soft, as a way to control my stutter, but also as if
in apology for my Y chromosome. His father, who died when Murray
was nineteen, was a lumber salesman. One of five brothers (and nine
siblings), Murray now has five sons (and no daughters) from two
marriages. So much of his persona, his shtick, his appeal is that he

revels in and excels at the brutal but obviously affectionate teasing that is characteristic of large families, whereas more than one person has asked me, apropos of nothing in particular, whether I'm an only child (I'm not).

Occasionally psychotic but never neurotic, Murray plays well against nervous types, as I'm trying to make him do in this essay. He's not me. He's not Woody Allen. He's not Dustin Hoffman. In *Tootsie*, in which Dustin Hoffman plays an obnoxious actor, Michael Dorsey, who pretends to be a woman in order to get a part in a soap and, by "becoming" a woman, learns to be a better man, Murray is the true north of "normal" masculinity, our ordinary-guy guide, the big galoot around whom the gender-bending bends. "I think we're getting into a weird area," he informs Hoffman when Hoffman gets preoccupied with his female alter ego's wardrobe. "Do you know what my problem is?" Hoffman asks him at one point. "Cramps?" Murray replies. When Hoffman asks Murray how he-as-she looks, Murray says, "Nice, but don't play hard to get. Instead of trying to be Michael Dorsey the great actor or Michael Dorsey the great waiter," he advises Hoffman before ushering him in to his surprise birthday party, "why don't you just try to be Michael Dorsey?" This line isn't in even fairly late drafts of the screenplay; it's pure Murray; I'd bet he came up with it. He is the king of hanging out. He already knows how to be himself and how to be kind, how to be male but not be a jerk, whereas Hoffman needs to learn how to do this. Hoffman, the high-strung Jew, must learn how to do what Murray already does instinctively—to like life, to like the opposite sex, to embrace his own anima. *Live, live, live,* as Strether, that priss, finally realizes in Henry James's *The Ambassadors*, and as Murray has always known, as Murray always conveys.

Murray's boyishness is, at its most beguiling, childlikeness: openness to surprise. In *Cinderella Story; My Life in Golf*, Murray writes, "The sum and substance of what I was hoping to express is this. In golf, just as in life—I hoped I could get that line in the book somewhere [Murray's relentless ironic gaze, his ear for cliché]—the best wagers are laid on oneself." In *The Man Who Knew Too Little*, Murray plays Wallace Ritchie, a dim American man who, visiting his businessman brother in London, thinks he's attending an avant-garde "Theater of Life" performance and unbeknownst to him is caught up in an international spy-versus-spy scheme. Murray, as Ritchie, wins the day—defeats the bad guys, gets the girl—because he just goes with the flow, is cool and relaxed, never stops believing that he's watching and participating in an unusually realistic performance. Ritchie's relaxedness is Murray's relaxedness, Ritchie's distance is Murray's: life is theater with arbitrary rules. His bemused bafflement toward everything that happens is a handbook for Murray's acting technique and his approach to life—recognizing the absurdity of all action, but (and therefore) grooving in the moment.

When Murray was the guest commentator at the Cubs game, he somehow made anything the camera focused on—a hot-dog wrapper, an untucked shirt—seem newly resonant, of possible interest, because unlike every person to ever broadcast a baseball game, Murray talked about what was actually going on in his head, was actually seeing what was going on in front of his eyes rather than viewing it through a formulaic filter, was taking in the entire ballpark rather than just the sporting event per se. His eyes haven't gone dead yet. Life, seen through such eyes, becomes existentially vivid. Broadcasting this game, Murray seemed as interested in the physical universe as a beagle, sniffing the ballpark for new sensory input. He's demonstrating the Wildean wisdom that the only solution to the soul is the senses. He's a combination of two characters from the movie *American Beauty*: the kid with the video camera who can see ribbons of beauty in a plastic bag being blown around in the wind, and the Kevin Spacey character, who processes everything through his sulfur-spewing irony machine. I'm Spacey and want to be the kid with the video camera.

It's his attempt to be authentic, and his underlining of his attempt to be authentic, that I admire most in Murray; all of my current aesthetic excitements derive from my boredom with the conventions of fiction and my hope that nonfiction (autobiography, confession, memoir, embarrassment, *something*) can perhaps produce something that is for me "truer," more "real." Lorne Michaels once said, "It's a cliché, but Bill is always Bill. So much of my generation's approach to comedy was a reaction against the neediness of performers. When Bill was onstage, he didn't much care whether they [the audience] liked him. Because of that, he had enormous integrity. There was a way he always told the truth." The tape I have of Murray broadcasting the Cubs game has live audio rather than commercial breaks between innings; Murray sounds exactly the same off air as he does on. He is incapable of doing Stentorian Announcer, let alone Star Turn. I adore this about him. At one point in his life he was strongly influenced by the philosophy of Gurdjieff, whose Madame Blavatsky-esque work I can't bring myself to read but one of whose titles is *Life Is Only Real, Then, When "I Am."* A bad translation, to be sure, but the self-conscious quote marks around "I Am," the slight or not so slight inscrutability, the deep yearning to apprehend and embody reality—that's Murray's program.

The royal road to the authentic for Murray is through the primitive. Look at the Stanley Kowalski way he kicks open the door to the barracks in *Stripes*. In his self-interview, he told a joke about how Ralph Lauren's dog is named Rugby, but his real name is Stickball. People who pretend that they are civilized Murray finds completely ridiculous. In *Caddyshack*, a movie about class warfare phrased as a golf comedy, he plays a groundskeeper who is obsessed with killing gophers. Chevy Chase is the embodiment of the golfing fop—moneyed, charming, handsome. Murray is riddled by doubt, self-pitying, working class ("I got a blue-collar chip on my shoulder," Murray said. "That part of it was not hard"). Chase, for all his bonhomie, isn't in touch with the primitive force of the universe; Murray is (he's the only one capable of recognizing that a dark brown clump floating in the country-club swimming pool isn't a turd but a Baby Ruth bar, which he eats). The movie teaches the young golfer protagonist that Chase is wrong, Murray is right. The only way for Young Golfer to grow up is by learning how to say fuck you to the "snobatorium"—the country club's version of golf and life. Would that rebellion were so easy. Still, when the interviewer Charlie Rose advised Bill Murray to take a sabbatical, because lawyers do, Murray said, "If law firms do it, Charlie, it probably can't be right." (That "probably" is quintessential Murray—antiestablishmentarian but not utterly.) Rose also advised him about the importance of "proportionality" in one's life—balance between work and play. "I want to learn that one, too," Murray said, pretending to search for a pencil. "Let me write it down." In *Wild Things*, Murray is the lone actor among several other middle-aged actors in the movie who is granted the privilege of grasping the movie's vision: human beings are beasts, life is a scam, manipulate the other beasts in the jungle to your own advantage. It would be impossible to cast Murray as someone who didn't understand this.

Maybe it's not much of a revelation to anyone else, but to me it always seems to be: we're finally just physical creatures living in the physical world. Murray knows this in the bottom of his bones. If Murray didn't ad-lib the following lines in *Tootsie*, he should have: "I don't want a full house at the Winter Garden Theater. I want ninety people who just came out of the worst rainstorm in the city's history. These are people who are alive on the planet, until they dry off. I wish I had a theater that was only open when it rained." Explaining to an interviewer that *Rushmore* director Wes Anderson isn't just knowledgeable about film and clever about alluding to film history but also able to convey strong emotion in his work, Murray said, "Let's get right down to it. It's like the French. You know, they can't play rock-'n'-roll to save their lives. They can't play the blues to save their lives. But if you play a song by somebody, you know, Son House, they go, 'That's Son House, the famous musician and blues player. That is from the session he did in Meridian, Mississippi. I believe that is the January 24th . . .' You know, they'll know the date, the time, and the take. They couldn't give you an ounce of the feeling of it, you know. But this guy, Wes, and it's the difference, you know—mind and body, he just knows how to get these things together in one place." Murray does the same thing; all his verbal play happens atop a foundation of understated physical grace. In *Space Jam*, Murray isn't Michael Jordan, but it's crucial that he isn't Wayne Knight, either. He's halfway between jock god and blubbery nerd—someone we can identify with. After kibitzing with Michael Jordan at the golfing tee, wearing madras shorts and cornball shirt and shoes, he finally whacks the hell out of the ball. So, too, at pro-am tournaments it wouldn't work if, after goofing around for twenty minutes, he couldn't finally play the game. By being both ridiculous and competent, he becomes beautifully contradictory—the unicycle-riding knife juggler who pretends to be anxiety-stricken but isn't; without the contradiction he's just pathetic (Wayne Knight) or boringly excellent (Jordan). It's that stage in between that Murray occupies so movingly.

I imagine that Murray would be a bit of a bully in the way a hip older brother or popular camp counselor might be—making you feel bad if you just don't want to have fun right now as Murray defines fun, not allowing you to just mope if that's what you want to do. I imagine he would be such a drill sergeant on this score—toward his sons, say—because a frenetically kept-up joie de vivre is how he's managed to paper over his fairly real despair, and if he can, he's going to bring everyone along with him out of hell. I admire this and resent it a little; why can't we mope if we want to mope? Maybe the only solution to the soul isn't the senses; maybe it's deeper soul-searching (probably not); maybe there is no soul. "To be, to be, sure beats the shit out of not to be," he writes at the end of *Cinderella Story*. At the very end of *Where the Buffalo Roam*, in which Murray plays Hunter Thompson, Murray quotes Lord Buckley's epitaph: "He stomped on the terra." This is the nucleus of Murray: we're made of clay; we'd better cause a little ruckus while we can. He's the anti-Malvolio in our midst; he's Tigger versus the suits. Life is absurd—make it your own absurdity. Instead of wearing artiste basic black—my dumb uniform—Murray typically wears his own weird mix of plaids and prints of different patterns and colors—a tartan vest, for instance, with a paisley tie and a sky-blue shirt. Or black pants, a brown striped shirt, and a tan vest. Nutty clothes—so out they're in, cool because he's wearing them. In *What About Bob?* Murray, as Bob Wylie, the patient of anhedonic psychiatrist Leo Marvin (Richard Dreyfuss), visits the Marvins' summer home and succeeds in making even dishwashing, for Chrissake, fun for Marvin's family (all except Dr. Marvin, course). Murray and Dreyfuss reportedly came to despise each other during the making of the movie—Murray's unscripted silliness drove Dreyfuss crazy, in exactly the same way Bob drives Leo mad in the movie—and I know we're supposed to love Murray and hate Dreyfuss, and I do, I do, but I'm much closer to serious, striving Dr. Marvin than I am to antic Bob, which is, I suppose, what this essay is about: my distance from Murray, my yearning to be him, the gap between us, the way he makes life seem bearable (fun, amusing) if I could only get with his giddiness. (I can't.) In Murray's golf book, Cheryl Anderson, a golf pro, says, "I was practicing at the far end of the grand cypress range one morning. There wasn't another soul there. Just a set of clubs in one of the stands a few yards away from me. Then a figure appeared in the distance. He was on a bicycle, at the same time carrying a boom box. It was Bill. He gave me a quick nod, then walked to the clubs, set down his box, and flipped on a tape. It was an out-there rock group called Big Head Todd and the Monsters. He hit balls to the music for a while, then picked up the box, nodded goodbye, and pedaled off."

Physical grace as a container, then, for spiritual grace, if that's not putting too fine a point on it. "A lot of *Rushmore* is about the struggle to retain civility and kindness in the face of extraordinary pain," Murray said shortly after the film was released. "And I've felt a lot of that in my life." This is what Murray knows so well and what I have been trying to learn from him: life is a shitstorm; laugh (somehow and barely). In his self-interview, he tells Santa a story about the making of the movie *Scrooged*: "We're shooting in this Victorian set for weeks, and [Buddy] Hackett is pissed all the time, angry that he's not the center of attention, and finally we get to the scene where we've gotta shoot him at the window, saying, 'Go get my boots,' or whatever. The set is stocked with Victorian extras and little children in *Oliver* kind of outfits, and the director says, 'All right, Bud, just give it whatever you want.' And Hackett goes off on a rant. Unbelievably obscene. He's talking—this is Hackett, not me—about the Virgin Mary, a limerick sort of thing, and all these children and families . . . the look of absolute horror. He's going on and on and on, and finally he stops. It's just total horror, and the camera's still rolling. You can hear it, sort of a grinding noise. And the director says, 'Anything else, Bud?'"

Murray loves the director's dignity against the shitstorm, his refusal to be cowed or fazed.

In his article "The Passion of Bill Murray," Greg Solman says about Murray's performance in *Mad Dog and Glory*, "What's remarkable about the performance is how well Murray can now convey the intrinsic humor of his characters and situations . . . but differentiate them from others in his past by eliminating irony, sarcasm, and self-reflexivity." This seems to me wrong, or at least in opposition to the premise of this essay: namely, that in the twenty-five years Murray has been acting he's gotten better not by ever going away for a second from irony but by finding deeper and deeper levels of emotion within it. That's why I value his work so much: he embodies the way—not around but through. At the end of *Groundhog Day*, after being forced to repeat February 2 over and over again until he discovers real feeling, he finally says to a sleeping Andie McDowell, "I think you're the kindest, sweetest, prettiest person I've ever met in my life. I've never seen anyone that's nicer to people than you are. The first time I saw you, something happened to me that I never told you about. I knew that I wanted to hold you as hard as I could. I don't deserve someone like you, but if I ever could, I swear I would love you for the rest of our life." This is awfully sweet, and the only reason I believe it is because of the way Murray teases her when he's teaching her how to flip cards into a hat. At the end of *Scrooged*, Murray, the scabrous president of a television network who recovers the Christmas spirit, walks onto the set of the cheesy live Christmas special he's produced, announcing: "It's Christmas Eve. It's the one night of the year where we all act a little nicer, we smile a little easier, we cheer a little more. For a couple of hours out of the whole year we are the people that we always hoped we would be. It's a miracle, it's really a sort of a miracle, because it happens every Christmas Eve. You'll want it every day of your life, and it can happen to you. I believe in it now. I believe it's going to happen to me now. I'm ready for it." A few moments later, when he has trouble dragging his long-lost beloved, Claire, in front of the camera, Murray, clearly improvising, says, "This is like boning a marlin." It's Murray's fidelity to his own mordant consciousness and the locating of joy within that mordancy that is, to me, the miracle. This is getting a little overadulatory, so I'll stop.

An unfortunate fact about stuttering is that it prevents you from ever entirely losing self-consciousness when expressing such traditional and truly important emotions as love, hate, joy, and deep pain. Always first aware not of the naked feeling itself but of the best way to phrase the feeling so as to avoid verbal repetition, you come to think of emotions as belonging to other people, being the world's happy property and not yours—not really yours except by way of disingenuous circumlocution. Hence my iron grip on ironic distance; hence my adoration of Murray; hence my lifelong love of novels (*The Great Gatsby*, *A Separate Peace*, Ford Madox Ford's *The Good Soldier*, Gunter Grass's *Cat and Mouse*) in which a neurasthenic narrator contemplates his more vital second self; hence this essay. My first novel is about a sportswriter's vicarious relationship with a college basketball player; my most recent book, a diary of an NBA season, is largely given over to my obsession with Gary Payton. What is it about such a relationship that speaks so strongly to me? Art calling out to Life, Unlife wanting Life? Are these just parts of myself in eternal debate or am I really this anemic? Murray, for all his anomie, likes being in the world. Bully for him. I love standing in shadow, gazing intently at ethereal glare.

LITTLE AUDREY
Ann Hood

I n 1982, my thirty-year-old brother Skip died when he fell in the
bathtub and drowned on a warm June evening. The details are
fuzzy, because he was home alone that night. Perhaps he had leaned
over too far to adjust the water temperature and bumped his head,
falling facedown into the tub of water, unconscious for just enough
time to drown. A small bruise on his forehead gave credence to this
theory, but we will never know for sure what happened.

All I know for certain is that for fifteen years after he died, I cobbled
together a life without Skip, a life as an only child of sorts. Again, the
details of those years are not important. What matters is that during
that time I slowly began to reclaim my heritage. I liked the shock on
people's faces when they learned that I, with my dark blond hair and
green eyes, was Italian, a fact I no longer kept to myself. But rather
than embrace my traditions, I reinvented them. My Italian cooking
came out of cookbooks, and was never southern. When I visited Italy,
I went to its cities—Venice, Florence, Rome. Inside churches, I
remembered how to light a votive candle in someone's memory,
and lit them for my brother. I began to collect religious artifacts—
statues and crucifixes and candles, the things of my childhood.

But when my father died in 1997, and our once-indestructible
family of four was now cut in half, I felt a desperate need for comfort.
Those religious things from my childhood took on a new importance.
Still, in my search for miracles, I mostly looked for the external kind,
the kind you take a journey to find. By the summer of 1998, with an
advance on a contract for a book about miracle sites, I began to plan
trips in search of a genuine miracle. I doubted that anything could cure
me of my despair and restore my faith again, unless my father could

intervene. I longed so much for his conversation, his laugh, him, that the sight of intact families made me weep. Desperately, I made plans.

I am a modern pilgrim.

That means many different things. For one, I am disconnected from any organized religion. How much simpler it would be to know my pilgrimage must be to Mecca or the Western Wall. How much simpler to know, as the Hopi Indians do, that every July the kachinas (spirits) go home to the San Francisco Peaks after serving the people all year; the Hopi honor them and bid them farewell in a dance called Niman, the Home Dance. But we modern pilgrims have a mixed culture that leaves nothing clear.

I am an Italian-American woman. I could go to Italy and visit the homes of saints: Catherine, Francis, Clare. I could wait until September and visit Naples to see if San Gennaro's blood liquefies, as it has done most years since he was martyred in A.D. 305. I was raised a Catholic. I could go to Fatima or Medjugorje or any of the other places where the Virgin has appeared. I could go to the principal shrine of the Catholic Church, Saint Peter's Basilica in Rome.

I am a mother. Can I expect a two-year-old, a five-year-old, and a nine-year-old to climb mountains, crawl into caves, visit third-world countries, all so I can find whatever this elusive thing is that I am seeking? There are school vacations to coordinate, limited time to travel, the children's pressures of learning how to read and divide—these loom larger than my spiritual yearnings.

I am a wife. For two years my travels have centered on my search for miracles. I have gone alone or with one of the children or with my whole family to shrines and feasts. There was my original trip to Chimayo, in New Mexico, a visit to Mexico City for the Feast of the Virgin of Guadalupe, a return to Chimayo, our family's trip to San Giovanni Rotundo, Italy, where a now dead monk named Padre Pio is said to perform miracles. My husband, despite his patience for my search, would like a vacation that can satisfy my quest and our family's need for relaxation and fun. We are not a family that enjoys vacations spent lying on the beach at a resort in Aruba, but the children have walked the stations of the cross a lot lately. One day I came home to find my five-year-old son, Sam, lying on the kitchen floor, his arms spread wide.

"What are you doing?" I asked him.

"I'm Jesus on the cross," he said.

Like most families I know, we are paying a mortgage and school tuitions and American Express bills. I have spent more than our usual funds allotted for vacations as I've traveled. Despite a little money from my publisher and some expenses paid by magazines, we have a budget to consider. I cross off Japan, Sri Lanka, Peru from my list of miracle sites.

Close to home, only an hour's drive away, a miracle is supposed to be happening. While I continue my search for a longer miracle journey, I decide to drive to Worcester, Massachusetts.

Worcester, Massachusetts, is an unlikely place for miracles. For the most part, places associated with miracles and visions, shrines and even the birthplaces of saints are beautiful. Think of the Pyrenees, in France, where Lourdes is nestled, or the dramatic Himalayas, in which, according to Hindu tradition, lies the country of the gods. Think of Tuscany and Umbria, two regions of Italy rich with miracles and saints. A volcanic rock formation shaped like a sleeping bear, Bear Butte is rich with conifers and ash trees that the Lakota Sioux and Cheyenne believe is sacred. It is said that Crazy Horse prayed there before Little Bighorn. Today, people still go to Bear Butte and leave small bundles of cloth filled with tobacco as offerings to the Spirit. These colorful "prayer ties" blow gently in the South Dakota breeze.

Ancient sacred traditions often revolve around mountains and rivers and springs and caves, majestic demonstrations of nature at her best. So it is surprising to find the industrial city of Worcester as a modern miracle-healing site. Worcester, in central Massachusetts, is known for other pursuits. Its location on the Blackstone River led to its rapid industrialization in the early nineteenth century. Producing mainly machinery and metal goods, Worcester later added chemicals and pharmaceuticals to its industrial output.

Worcester has a violent history too. In 1675 and 1683 it was the scene of Native American attacks. One hundred years later, Daniel

Shays led an armed rebellion of economically depressed farmers demanding relief. The Shays Rebellion, as it came to be called, was put down by state troops and Shays escaped. In 1788 he was pardoned.

Today, Worcester is the home of Holy Cross College and Clark University. But it is better known as the site of a large complex of shopping outlets. Glimmers of a more beautiful city can be seen in the maze of one-way streets and traffic circles that perplex visitors. Grand Victorian houses line one main boulevard. A grassy park forms the center of downtown. The Worcester Art Museum is a proud and still lovely building.

Mostly, though, one sees strip malls with convenience stores and fast food restaurants, small and often shabby houses, and churches. Everywhere one looks in Worcester a steeple jabs the sky.

In one neighborhood, off the appropriately named Pleasant Street, in an ordinary ranch house of the type that became popular in the early 1960s, lies a fifteen-year-old comatose girl named Audrey Santo. The sign outside the house asks people not to ring the bell or knock on the door. PLEASE RESPECT OUR PRIVACY, it says. Anyone who wants to can show up at the house between ten and two any Tuesday, Wednesday, or Thursday and go inside. Inside, it is said, miraculous things are happening.

At 11:03 A.M. on August 9, 1985, Audrey's mother, Linda, found the toddler floating facedown in the family's aboveground swimming pool in their small backyard. The family was told that Little Audrey would not live. Linda Santo refused to believe that. When in fact Audrey did survive, they were told she would never wake up from the coma that was brought on by a combination of her near-drowning and an overdose of hospital-administered phenobarbital. Linda refused to accept that either. Instead of putting Little Audrey in a long-term nursing facility, she brought her daughter home.

Audrey requires round-the-clock care. She breathes through a tube in her trachea and eats through a tube in her stomach. Her pediatrician, Dr. John Harding, says that Audrey is not in a coma, but rather suffers from what is called akinetic mutism. People in a coma show no signs of awareness of what is going on around them. The Santos and Dr. Harding believe that Audrey is aware of her surroundings. They know when she is agitated or happy and say that she expresses herself with her eyes.

In 1988, Linda Santo took her six-year-old daughter, who had been in a coma already for three years, to Medjugorje, in Bosnia, the site of apparitions of the Virgin Mary where people have reportedly been miraculously cured. In an interview with Lesley Stahl, Linda Santo said that she believed that Audrey would be cured at Medjugorje. Instead, Audrey went into cardiac arrest and had to be flown home.

It was after the Santos returned to Worcester that inexplicable things began to happen in their home. Nurses hired to help with Audrey's care reported smelling roses in the room when there were no flowers there at all. Many Catholics believe that the scent of roses is believed to be a sign from God. Padre Pio was said to emanate an intense fragrance of roses. His followers called it the Odor of Sanctity. The technical name for this phenomenon is osmogenesia.

Besides osmogenesia, the religious statues in Audrey's room supposedly began to weep what appeared to be an oily substance. The *Catholic Free Press* reports that initial analysis of this substance has determined that the oil is neither animal nor vegetable. It is of a mysterious origin.

Priests who have said mass in the Santos' garage chapel have stepped forward to say that spots of blood have appeared on the Communion host. At present, the Catholic church is investigating the strange occurrences around Little Audrey. The process is a slow and careful one. The church does not embrace situations like the one in Worcester. Even revered and famous shrines such as those at Fatima and Lourdes are designated by the church as sites of "private revelation." Catholics may accept or reject them. However, even in the early stages of the investigation, the church has already eliminated trickery as a cause for the weeping statues and bleeding Communion wafers.

Then, of course, there are the miracle healings.

Hartford Courant religion writer Gerald Rener reported that through Audrey's intercession, Joey Parolisa of Methuen, Massachusetts, recovered from injuries sustained in an automobile accident in 1994. Joey had been told he would probably never walk again (doctors unconnected to his case claim that injuries of the type he suffered result in about a 50 percent recovery rate). His mother, Sheryle Parolisa, went to Worcester and prayed through Audrey for her son to walk again. When she returned home, Joey was on his feet. His mother said that he just had a feeling he could walk.

Several years ago, Audrey developed a terrible, unexplainable rash. A dermatologist biopsied it and learned that it was caused by a certain type of chemotherapy. Audrey had never received any chemotherapy. Rumors have circulated since then that shortly after the rash appeared, the Santos received a letter from a cancer patient who had visited Audrey and prayed for a cure. She was undergoing the type of chemotherapy that produced the rash Audrey had. And her cancer had disappeared after she prayed to Audrey to intercede.

There is a term in Catholicism for someone like Audrey: a victim's soul. A victim's soul takes on the suffering of others. She takes on the pain and suffering of those who file past her three days a week on what is called on the instruction sheet distributed by an organization called the Apostolate of a Silent Soul, Inc., "Pilgrimage Day at Little Audrey's Chapel." The Xeroxed sheet has a boxed picture of the comatose Audrey, eyes open, lips parted, seemingly gazing at a distant spot, with the words *Little Audrey Marie Santo, Our Precious Gift* beside it. "Praise be Jesus and Mary," it begins, "the moment has arrived—the Holy Spirit inspired us to open the doors to Audrey's Chapel."

Fourteen instructions follow, including directions for where to park, when you can arrive, and warnings that police will tow cars. Number six reads: "You may drop off anyone who cannot physically walk to Audrey's." You are told that you can bring a priest/priests and that oil from the weeping statues will not be distributed, though you can write and request some. Numbers ten and eleven read: "You will not see Audrey, but she is present in the home where the chapel is." "Audrey will know you are here."

At the end of the sheet, as if the Apostolate were a bunch of teenagers signing off in a letter, it reads: "Hope to see you soon!"

The other side of the sheet is an order form for the video of Little Audrey's life and the monthly newsletter. The two-hour video includes "moving and touching footage" of Audrey's birthday party, miracles, the four Eucharistic occurrences, and oil and blood exuding from the images in Audrey's room.

Oddly, many Worcester residents are not even aware of what is going on in the house on South Flagg Street. The news is being spread by a coterie of Catholics who believe that Jesus and Mary are calling for prayer and repentance by creating the weeping statues and bleeding Communion wafers. After Mother Angelica, a television evangelist, reported on Little Audrey for the Eternal World Television Network, four thousand people showed up at Christ the King Church in Worcester. In 1998, Holy Cross's twenty-three-thousand-seat football stadium was filled for a mass on the anniversary of Audrey's accident.

In 1999, the Catholic Church made an unofficial request that people pray for Audrey, not to her, an interesting request considering that her mother, Linda, has said that each time she was pregnant she prayed God would give her a saint. After what has happened to Audrey, the *Hartford Courant* asked, would Linda still pray for God to give her a saint? "I can give them life but I can't give them eternal life. God answers your prayers," she replied. "And it may not be the answer you want but it is much better to give him the issue. It works for me." Still, in that interview and others in newspapers and television, Linda Santo has said that she too is praying for a miracle: that her daughter Audrey wake up.

Fearing that Little Audrey is becoming a spectacle, the church has asked that the Holy Cross debacle, in which she was rolled on a stretcher into the stadium, not be repeated. Weeping statues and bleeding wafers are not part of Catholic pedagogy, and the church does not support such events.

Still, especially on the August 9 anniversary of the accident, people flock to Worcester. Last year, in an effort to respect the church and Little Audrey's followers, the Santos arranged for a prayer vigil at Christ the King Church. From 1 to 5 P.M., the crowd filed into the church two by two and viewed Little Audrey behind a glass partition.

Remembering the twenty-three thousand at Holy Cross a year earlier, I arrived at the church in Worcester at 10 A.M. with my cousin Gloria-Jean, my children, Sam and Grace, and a bag full of snacks and crayons.

A bus from Pennsylvania had already deposited a large group, who stood saying the Hail Mary in front of the modern yellow-brick church. The parking lot was not yet full, though it would be jammed by the time we left that afternoon. Cars with New York, New Jersey, and Pennsylvania license plates were parked there when we pulled in. Leaflets had been tacked up to posts. There was the same black-and-white photograph of Audrey at the top, and in big letters: NO MASS OR BENEDICTION. ATTENTION: READ CAREFULLY, followed by seven items. Number one read: "Little Audrey will be in the church—you will see her."

We joined the line of people. Many had brought coolers and sat comfortably on lawn chairs on the grass. Poking from shopping bags were large crucifixes and statues. People fingered rosary beads as they waited. A Mexican family posed for pictures, snapping happily away. In front of us, an Indian man cradled an infant wrapped in a bright Barney blanket. His wife looked solemn and sad despite the cheerful pale green flowered dress she wore. Her eyes were ringed with dark circles, as if she had not slept well in a long time. Their five-year-old daughter chattered happily and skipped in circles around them.

The large group's elderly bus driver came to tell them he had parked in a shady spot down the street. Now he was off to McDonald's for some breakfast. Many of them tried to convince him to stay. "No," he said loudly, addressing all of us, it seemed. "It's a political decision."

The priest in the group pleaded with him. "But you're so close." The bus driver smiled. "I'm closer than you know," he said. He explained to the growing crowd that he never missed church once until 1968. "I didn't fall away from the church," he said, "I walked away."

Behind us, an elderly couple commented on Grace's glasses.

"Isn't she cute?" the woman said. Her denim hat had a large artificial daisy pinned to it and the daisy bobbed as if it were nodding agreement.

"Where did you come from?" I asked her. Everyone in the crowd was eager to talk.

"New Mexico," she said.

Her husband, a gaunt man with skin tinted yellow, grinned. "Yup," he said. "She wanted to come."

I assumed he was ill and she had come hoping for a miracle.

"Did you come to get a miracle?" I asked her softly.

"I came for strength to accept what comes my way," she said.

I nodded, admiring her knowledge that perhaps that was all she could get here, or anywhere.

"Yup," her husband said. "She's got cancer."

Startled, I looked at the robust woman standing beside me. "You?" I blurted.

"I've had three operations and almost died twice," she said. "Ahh," she added almost dismissively, "I've had hard times my whole life."

The Indian family had rearranged itself. Now the mother held the baby while the father quizzed the little girl from Brain Quest cards for ages seven to eight. 1000 QUESTIONS AND ANSWERS TO CHALLENGE THE MIND, the box boasted.

"How do you spell baby?" the father asked.

"B-A-B-Y," the girl said slowly.

That was the first time I saw her baby brother convulse. He had several more convulsions as the morning passed.

I turned from the mother and her sick baby to see a family setting up lawn chairs in the shade beneath a tree. It was easy to see who was who in the family: parents in their late sixties and their two daughters. Both appeared to be around my age, somewhere in their forties. One was tanned and blond and apparently healthy except for a cast on her foot. The other, I could see, was dying. She was thin and sallow. Her body seemed to sink into itself, and she moved as if she were in pain. Her eyes were glazed, her mouth set hard. Her husband buzzed around her, arranging the chair and making sure she was comfortable. His gentleness broke my heart. Behind them a Benedictine monk dressed in a long black robe appeared to hear confessions in folding chairs. He was from Latrobe, Pennsylvania, the oldest all-men's monastery in the country.

I went to talk to him, sitting in the wobbly chair across from him.

I meant to ask him what he thought of all this—Little Audrey, the weeping statues, everything. But instead I blurted my own story of my father's illness and how I'd gone to Chimayo to find him a miracle. I started to cry, but continued to talk to him. He had a long gray beard and dark eyes. In his robes he looked like a visitor from another era, and somehow that appealed to me. If he was surprised to hear my story instead of a confession, he didn't show it.

When I finished, I felt drained.

"Why did God do this?" he said. "He didn't do it. He allowed it and we choose to either grow from it or let it ruin us. God allowed your father to die. Now you must choose what you will do. Through God's grace you have a talent, the ability to write. With this you can comfort others in grief." Then he leaned toward me the slightest bit. "This is real, you know," he said. "Something is really happening here."

I looked back at the crowd. Two more buses had pulled up, along with news teams from Channel 6 and Channel 4. A woman stepped out of the crowd and posed for one of the news cameras with her statue of the Virgin Mary. Another bus arrived. It was bright green with a picture of a leprechaun on its side and the words CATCH THE MAGIC. Something was happening here. But what was it?

I moved back to my place in line, where the Indian father was removing a tube from the baby's mouth in the mother's arms.

"Wouldn't it be weird if Little Audrey woke up today?" Sam asked me. I wondered how many people here were hoping for that very thing. The mother with the sick baby was talking to a man from Wisconsin. Although he wore a priest's collar, he was standing with his wife, both of them draped with large wooden rosary beads. The Indian woman explained how her husband hadn't wanted to come. But she prayed that he would change his mind and he did.

"What can you give me?" she asked the man. Her eyes darted from his face to his wife's.

"When you have a baby who will never be normal—" he began.

"I'm not ready to say he will never be normal," she interrupted passionately.

"Fine," the man said. "But children like this are little saints. He is a little saint."

Disgusted, the father walks away.

Seeing such pain and desperation makes me want to walk away too. I propose a trip to the bathroom with the kids. The bathrooms are in the basement of the church, a cool plain place where it is easy to imagine bingo games and Girl Scout meetings and Christmas bazaars. But today it is filled with smiling women wearing pink ribbons beneath that black-and-white photograph of Little Audrey. They answer questions and point the way to the bathrooms. As we wait for a stall to open up, a woman from a bus group with a name tag that SAYS HELLO MY NAME IS VERA says to another woman, "Someday she will just get out of that bed."

"That's right," the other woman says. "You're right."

It is noon. In one hour we will be allowed inside the church. As we make our way back to our place in line, more buses arrive.

The Indian woman is still talking to the man and his wife.

"Life is valuable at any level," the man tells her.

The woman has grown frustrated. She tells a story that she has clearly told many times and that she believes no one understands. Her eyes grow feverish as she talks.

"I am telling you," she says forcefully, "that there are mysterious things with him. The similarities with my son and Audrey are unbelievable. Even with the things the nurses did. I read about what they did to Audrey. The same thing with my son. The things she can move, he can move. The very same things!"

She holds out a sheet of paper that she received in the mail when she wrote to the Apostolate of a Silent Soul for some of the oil from the weeping statues that the family collects in plastic cups.

"I don't have all the dates and things like they do. But I am telling you the similarities are incredible."

I listen carefully as she talks. Does she think her baby is also a victim's soul? I am not certain. The only thing that is clear is how desperate she is. She wanders back to her place in front of me in the line. I smile, hoping to emit the compassion I feel.

"Did you drive far to be here?" I ask her.

"We came from New Jersey," she said. "My husband didn't want to come. We are Hindu. We don't believe . . ." her voice trails off. She obviously believes.

She grabs my arm conspiratorially. "Everything about my baby is mysterious. The seed came from nowhere. Do you understand? We had taken care of it so we had only the one child." She points toward her daughter, who is playing a game of tag with Sam and Grace. "An astrologer told me I would have two children and I laughed. 'It's impossible,' I explained to her. Then one week later I am pregnant." She shakes her head as if she still cannot understand the course her life has taken. "At first, when you have a baby like this, you can't believe it."

"Well," says the woman from New Mexico with the nodding daisy on her hat, "what's wrong with him anyway?"

"It's mysterious," the woman says, now turning her full attention to her new listener. She hopes, I suppose, that someone will hear what it is she is trying so desperately to say. "He is fifteen months old, but he is like a three-month-old."

"I noticed how he just lays there," the woman says, clucking her tongue sympathetically.

"Yes! But the doctors cannot figure out why. Whenever they do tests, the results disappear. There is mystery here, I tell you!"

It is 12:50 when an ambulance pulls up. A murmur spreads through the crowd: Little Audrey is here. The church group at the front of the line resumes its long-since-abandoned Hail Marys.

I chat briefly with a reporter from the *Catholic Free Press*. I tell him about my book and how it started with my own trip to Chimayo. When he leaves, I turn to find the husband and wife with the two adult daughters looking at me. Their faces are so open that I touch the wife's arm.

She motions toward her daughter, the one who looks so sick. "She's got it," she says. "Like your father."

The family is pressed together in the line. I recognize my own family in their good-natured teasing, and in their solidarity. The five of them have come here together to save this woman. I remember my family crowded together in hospitals and doctors' offices. Our faces had once been this open too. We had believed that the power of family could save my father. I realize I have not let go of the woman's arm. The sick daughter has religious medals, maybe six of them, hanging around her neck. She seems already apart from the others, as if she has begun to leave them, even though she stands close by.

"She's worried now," the woman says. "She heard you say about the chemo and she's scared."

"Oh," I say quickly, "but he was not in good health. He had emphysema."

"And he was old, right?" the mother asks, her eyes hopeful.

"Yes," I lie. My father was hardly old; these parents were probably older than him.

Now the sick woman's father speaks. "For two months we've had a black cloud over our head," he says. His wife concurs. "Two car accidents. One with the baby right in the backseat. That one broke her foot," he says. "And now this."

They both look at their daughter's drawn face.

"How do you feel about all this?" I ask her. "About coming here?"

She rolls her eyes and walks away, to stand back in the shade. Her husband and sister follow.

"But maybe this will change our luck," the woman says. "First we went to Boston to have both their auras changed. So they'd quit smoking. It's too late for that one, but still. This Indian man can get you to stop. So we went and she told him about her pain and that went away too. Plus they haven't smoked since Friday."

Hearing this, people in the crowd ask for the name of the man in Boston who changes auras.

The line begins to move forward. We finally enter the church.

The first thing I notice about Little Audrey is that she is not little. She is a teenager, with the face of a teenager. The second thing I notice is that whether it is called a coma or akinetic mutism, she is not aware. Her eyes flutter the way those of a person in a coma might. They flit around without ever landing anywhere. Then they close, only to flutter open again. The tubes that creep out of the blanket discreetly pulled over her reinforce the fact that she is very ill. I have read descriptions of her, how saintly she looks, how like a Dresden doll. But I am struck only by how vulnerable she is, like the very ill people I saw all those months I sat by my father's bed in the hospital.

The sight of Audrey Santo, her mother at her side, behind a glass partition so people can view her, haunts me. Did her mother get the saint she so desperately prayed for? Or does she simply have a child who will never recover from a tragic accident? The girl's uncle contends that whether her eyes are open or closed, she knows you are there. Does Audrey Santo know that thousands of people are walking past her, dropping to their knees, praying to her, not for her? I think not. I think she responds to the love and care her family showers on her, just as I believe my family's love kept my father alive when medicine said he should be dead.

Of course, this does not answer the question of why and what those statues weep. Or how blood appears on Communion wafers. There are some things, perhaps, for which there are no answers.

In the car on our way back home, I asked Sam and Grace what they thought when they looked through that glass at Little Audrey.

"I think she's very sick," Grace said somberly.

"Her hair is so beautiful," Sam said.

Her hair, a rich chestnut color, has never been cut, and spreads out on the stark white sheets, cascading by her feet.

Then Grace asked simply, "But, Mama, why did Little Audrey fall in the pool?"

"It was an accident," I said.

"But Mama," Grace asked again, "why?"

Finally I answered, "No one knows why."

I drive to Worcester a second time that summer, to the Santos' house. My son Sam is at Farm Camp, so today I have Grace and my nine-year-old stepdaughter, Ariane, with me. As we get out of the car, it is hard not to notice the large inflatable rafts, of the type used in swimming pools, stacked on the side of the Santos' house. The irony of their presence seems to go mostly unnoticed by the people who come to visit Audrey's Chapel. The chapel is a makeshift one in what was once the Santos' garage. Two white-haired men greet us. They tell us not to park on the street, directing us back to the main road. They point out where there are rest rooms for us to use. Finally we are ready to enter.

Despite the reminders posted everywhere to pray in silence and not to touch anything, the homemade altar at the front of the room, and the statues and crucifixes that occupy every surface, I cannot stop feeling that I am in a garage. I have a morbid curiosity that embarrasses me in the reverent silence. These statues are supposed to weep and I have come to see them.

There are little plastic cups taped under the Virgin Mary's chin and at Jesus' feet, and the cups have liquid in them. Some are more than half full; others have a few drops in the bottom. On the altar is a Communion wafer in a gold display. The wafer has a spot of what appears to be dried blood on it.

This is the truth: I want to believe that these statues weep.

Believing it means something important to me. Perhaps it gives me faith that there are things that we cannot understand, miraculous things. Perhaps it lets me believe in a greater power, something like God. I will take comfort in the knowledge that things happen—fathers die even after they have had a miracle, statues weep mysterious oil— that we cannot understand.

But I am in Audrey's Chapel in Worcester, Massachusetts, and I am cynical. The Virgin Mary is everywhere, in plastic and plaster, as the Virgin of Guadalupe with her golden rays around her and as the young innocent girl in a blue shawl. She is all around me and I know that these statues of her cannot weep.

Loss has made me bitter. Sometimes I find myself thinking terrible thoughts: that our acts are meaningless, that there is nothing after death but emptiness, and worse, even darker thoughts. I try to remind myself that if this is true, then how did my long-dead grandmother, Mama Rose, come to me one September night and warn me of my father's death? How do I explain the power of love, the miracles around me that I still believed until recently? Hadn't I still been willing to accept Augustine's "miracle of miracles," even right after my father's death? Now another quote from Augustine rings more true: "I became to myself a barren land."

I sit on the wooden bench in the chapel and try to clear my mind. The room is an assault on my senses, an overload of images. There is Audrey as a healthy, normal little girl, before the accident. And there she is in picture after picture in her coma, with priests and statues and a close-up blown up so large that I can see a tear in the corner of her eye. There are collages of sayings and photographs. One has as its center: AUDREY: THE NAME MEANS GOLDEN. There is one collage that refers to the bombing of Hiroshima on August 9, the date on which, more than forty years later, Audrey fell into the family pool. This place is not unlike all of the shrines to saints I have visited, except this shrine is to a living teenager who lies in a coma somewhere on the other side of the closed door.

As I sit trying to sort out what I see and what I feel, people keep coming in. A steady stream arrives, grandmothers with their grandchildren, elderly women alone, a few young men. Sometimes there are twenty of us inside, then it drops to about a dozen. But people never stop arriving, walking the few blocks from the main street, through the well-tended neighborhood, to this house at the end of the dead-end road.

Everything in here glistens. The neck on the tall statue of Jesus. The foot of the Virgin of Guadalupe. The tip of a crucifix, at the foot of which a cup is almost overflowing with oil. A framed picture of the Shroud of Turin is so stained with moisture it is hard to see it clearly. Even the walls are tear-streaked. That is what it looks like: rivers of tears running down the walls, staining them.

I think of the living room in an old house we rented. A large, irregularly shaped damp spot appeared on the wall there and no one could determine its origin. Plumbers and carpenters and contractors remained stumped. Until finally, years after we moved out, someone found a leak above and a hole in a pipe and the mystery was solved.

I think too of the way the lights that hang over the altar shine on the statues. Could they not be the source of Mary's glistening face? I understand the sign that says: DO NOT TOUCH, MARY AND JESUS WILL TOUCH YOU. There is nothing I want more than to sneak a touch, to run my fingers along one of the statue's cheeks and see if it is, as it appears to be, wet.

From the house beyond the garage come the sounds of children laughing. I can hear small feet running, and then more laughter and squeals of delight. When it grows quiet, one of the white-haired men appears and gives the children inside the chapel rosary beads. Then a priest leads us in a prayer. I am struck by how easily the words of Catholic prayers come back to me, even though I have not said them in three decades. The familiar soothing words tumble from my mouth.

The priest begins to recite the Our Father, and the voices around me join in. Suddenly I am back in my father's hospital room on the Easter weekend when he almost died. A priest was called in to give the Sacrament of the Sick, what the church used to call the Last Rites. Our family was around my father, all of us crying. The priest sprinkled him with holy water. Then he began to say the Our Father. Unbidden, we joined him, our voices coming together as these voices are today. That April morning, I was filled with a fear so large I could not imagine living with it. In his book *A Grief Observed*, C. S. Lewis says that grief feels like fear. Perhaps that day I took my first giant step into the grief that was about to take over my life.

Now, sitting among these strangers, the still face of Audrey Santo looking down upon me in black and white, beside tear-stained walls, I am saying those words again for the first time since that day at my father's side. I realize there is no fear now. It has been replaced by something else. I think of Emily Dickinson's phrase "quartz contentment." Although she referred to her own isolation, she meant it as something more, the settlement the soul makes in the face of the unfathomable.

My soul is beginning to settle. Now I have to understand how and where.

"Well," I asked Ariane and Grace as we walked up Audrey's street to our car, "what did you think?"

"I wanted to touch one of those statues," Ariane said.

"So did I," I agreed.

"I mean, they were wet. But what was that stuff?"

I frowned, remembering how willing I had been to blame a trick of light.

"Are you sure they were wet?" I asked her.

"Oh, yes," she said.

Grace touched her own cheeks. "Mama," she said, "they were crying."

We had reached the car and while I fumbled for my keys Ariane said, "That was amazing."

"You're right," I said. "It is amazing."

Amazing, but not enough to restore my faith. Odd that I could accept the possibility that something unexplainable is happening in Worcester but not have it open the door for me to find my way out of despair. We make the drive back to Rhode Island, and I continue my research.

THE MANDARIN AND THE HIPSTER
Gerry Howard

Do you remember when the word *dildo* first, um, penetrated your consciousness? I do, vividly. It was during Parents Weekend in fall 1968 at Cornell University, in my freshman dorm room. My roommate Scott Brown was regaling some of us with a reading of the climactic scene of Gore Vidal's notorious new novel *Myra Breckinridge*. Myra, the self-proclaimed avatar of vengeful feminity, has her sacrificial victim, the would-be Hollywood stud Rusty Goldowsky, secured to an examination table, his pants pulled down and his "tiny sphincter" exposed to her greedy gaze. She straps on a dildo (helpfully specified as "over two inches long at the head and nearly a foot long"), puts her "battering ram to the gate," and proclaims triumphantly, "Now you will find out what it is the girl feels when you play the man with her." Her exertions end with this ecstatic apostrophe:

> I was like a woman possessed, riding, riding my sweating stallion into forbidden country, shouting with joy as I experienced my own sort of orgasm, oblivious to his staccato shrieks as I delved and spanned his innocent flesh. Oh, it was a holy moment! I was at one with the Bacchae, with all the priestesses of the dark, bloody cults—

At which point my roommate's father and mother entered the room, the book was hastily shoved under a pillow and we all strived to pretend that we'd been shooting the breeze like healthy college boys rather than being in the thrall of a dildo-wielding bacchante. But that passage had been quite a revelation all right in terms of both physiology and rhetoric, and I was soon, perhaps not coincidentally, to change my major from biology to literature.

Not that the farther shores of erotic desire hadn't already touched my imagination. A paperback copy of Terry Southern and Mason Hoffenberg's raunchy comic satire *Candy* had burned its way through my circle of teenage horndogs the year before, and full-throated cries of "I need your warmth!," "Give me your hump!," and "Good grief, it's Daddy!" were heard to echo enigmatically in the Brooklyn streets. So I was well prepared to encounter another exercise in the sort of smart, subversive smut that made the sixties so much fun to be a reader in. Both Vidal, in his high-mandarin way, and Southern, in his irreverent hipster fashion, knew how to take aim at the groin, the funny bone, and the literary sensibility all at once—a difficult feat to pull off and never better accomplished than in these two books.

But then, it is interesting to recall how central breakthroughs into the erotically proscribed were to some major American literary careers in that period. Consider: Norman Mailer's *An American Dream* (heterosexual buggery); William S. Burroughs's *Naked Lunch* (buggery of every conceivable description, erotic strangulation); John Updike's *Couples* (suburban adultery, sacramental cunnilingus); Philip Roth's *Portnoy's Complaint* (masturbation and plenty of it). Authors and publishers had stormed through the gates opened by the 1958 publication of *Lolita*, and the bluenoses had been routed, seemingly for good. And women authors were soon to seize the opportunities afforded by these new freedoms, most notably in Erica Jong's *Fear of Flying* and Lisa Alther's *Kinflicks*. It is also interesting, and a little depressing, to contemplate how little new literary capital has been created from the unlimited freedoms now afforded. In the past two decades the only notable dirty book I can recall is Nicholson Baker's lubricious novel of phone sex, *Vox*. Oh sure, Nerve.com purveys what it calls "literate smut," but it feels a bit tame and beside the point in comparison to the Himalayas of hardcore now endlessly available. Which makes it all the more surprising that *Candy* and *Myra Breckinridge* still retain their power to amuse and arouse after all these years.

Candy, as most people know, is roughly modeled on Voltaire's *Candide* and relates the erotic misadventures of Candy Christian, a naïve All-American sexpot perpetually ready to minister to the sexual needs of others, no matter how bizarre or disingenuously stated. Her odyssey of serially debauched innocence leads her from the classrooms of Racine, Wisconsin, to the fleshpots of Greenwich Village to a utopian cult community to the mountains of Tibet as she gives herself to her college professor, a Mexican gardener, a slavering hunchback, and a disconcertingly familiar guru, among others. All this is related with delicious high spirits, a sort of faux-porn diction ("honey pot," "fabulous lamb pit," "seething thermal pudding," et cetera), and a winking elaborateness that marries parody with put-on. I particularly cherish Candy's filthy-minded and foul-mouthed Aunt Livia, who is given to such effusions as "I'm in the mood for cock and plenty of it. About ten pounds, please, thick and fast," "Get me out of these sopping wet pants and into a dry martini," and "When I was in Italy I got so much of that hot dago cock that I stopped menstruating and started minestroneing." Resistance was futile.

While it reads today like an *echt*-sixties novel, *Candy* was in fact written in 1958 as a "db" (dirty book) for the erotic Traveller's Companion series of Maurice Girodias's Olympia Press under the pseudonym Maxwell Kenton. Both Mason Hoffenberg and Terry Southern were cash-strapped American literary expats at the time, and the job was undertaken for some easy money. Hoffenberg, a poet/junkie who claimed (fascinating fact) to have hooked Anita Pallenberg, Marianne Faithfull, *and* Nico on heroin and had already written two earlier books for Girodias, played renegade Jew to Southern's Texas hipster aesthete and the two got along famously. According to Lee Hill's biography *A Grand Guy*, it was Hoffenberg who contributed such elements as Dr. Krankheit, a Wilhelm Reich send-up, and Aunt Livia's filthy repartee. But it was Southern who did most of the literary heavy lifting, and nobody familiar with his delicious script for *Dr. Strangelove* or his satirical masterpiece *The Magic Christian* can doubt for a second that *Candy* is essentially his book. Its refusal to take sex seriously was of a piece with his subsequent treatment of nuclear war and the grotesque—then and now—American way of life. *Candy* was a proleptic novel of the first order and one of the main reasons that Southern was immortalized by having his photo collaged on the cover of *Sgt. Pepper* by the Beatles. It was finally published by Putnam in 1964 and was an immediate sensation, one that made Terry Southern famous but not rich; a copyright technicality put the book in the public domain, breeding numerous pirated editions and an interminable, byzantine dispute over royalties. What is remarkable about *Candy* from this distance is how accurately its over-the-top satire and its demolition of sexual pieties anticipated and even helped to create the irreverent counterculture sensibility: *Candy* was love-bead ready when the inevitable and mediocre film adaptation rolled around in 1968.

Gore Vidal was a friend and admirer of Terry Southern, calling him "the most profoundly witty writer of our generation," and he could not have failed to have had the example of *Candy* in mind as he embarked on his own adventure in black-humored sexual satire, *Myra Breckinridge*. Like *Candy*, the book had its inception in a high-porn enterprise: Kenneth Tynan had asked Vidal to contribute a sketch to his planned erotic review *Oh Calcutta!* But as soon as he set to work, the mysterious sentence "I am Myra Breckinridge whom no man will ever possess" sprang to mind and Vidal knew he was heading somewhere else entirely. The book became an outrageous theater of polymorphous perversity, a heady cocktail of Aristophanes, Marcuse, and Nietzsche married to an encyclopedic knowledge of the American cinema of the thirties and forties. One of the great creations of postwar fiction, Myra has come to Hollywood claiming to be the widow of Myron Breckinridge, a deceased film critic and Parker Tyler aficionado. She lays claim to his inheritance, one-half ownership of the Academy of Drama and Modeling, ran by Myron's uncle Buck Loner, an old-time cowboy actor. While Buck and Myra dice over the estate and she teaches classes there, she concentrates sub rosa on a larger, madder project: the final sexual demoralization and conquest of the increasingly irrelevant heterosexual male (". . . the phallus cracks; the uterus opens, and I am at last ready to begin my mission, which is to recreate the sexes and thus save the human race from certain extinction," she explains with no hint of false modesty). "She"—the quotes are necessary, for Myra is, of course, a transsexual, if just—is quite cracked, of course, but divinely so, in the pagan sense.

Vidal has never been more Nabokovian than in *Myra Breckinridge*. His heroine's unshakable sense of her own mission is of a piece with that of the narrator of *Pale Fire*—"Alone of all women I know what it is like to be a goddess, enthroned and all-powerful." Then there is an ecstatic quality to the prose quite unique in Vidal's oeuvre, not unlike Nabokov's at high lyric flood—she released something in his usually cooler sensibility. Myra became a wonderful vehicle for Vidal to channel his late-sixties anger and despair over a Vietnam-mired America in the midst of a violent crack-up, as well as a fine mouthpiece for some witty asides on the French nouveau roman, then all the critical rage. The book is very aware of itself as a literary performance—postmodern before the term had gained any currency. Finally, and most originally, Vidal lavishes the sort of attention on the movies that Nabokov reserved for butterflies. Myra's sole and encyclopedic frame of reference is the classic Hollywood movie—Pandro S. Berman and James Craig have had no more ardent student—and *Myra Breckinridge* is a real monument in the growth of film consciousness in this country. Too bad it, like *Candy*, was made into a mediocre movie.

That switch of majors didn't turn out too badly, and when I became a book editor it afforded me the opportunity to repay the favor to the creators of these wonderful books, which came along right at the moment when I needed them. I now serve as Gore Vidal's editor, not that he needs me. And in the middle eighties I was able to bring *Candy* as well as *The Magic Christian* back into print in paperback editions, which was a kick, to say the least. Heh-heh-heh. And this occasioned one of my best publishing anecdotes.

Soon after the deal for the two books was agreed on I arranged to lunch with Terry Southern. We met, for the first time, in the basement of O'Neal's, at Fifty-seventh Street and Sixth Avenue, and while we were waiting to be seated in this rather crepuscular restaurant, we somehow got onto the subject of race and my teenage envy of black guys for their superior basketball skills, their superior dancing moves, and, I had to believe, their superior sexual abilities. Which last launched Terry—by that stage in his life a fairly disheveled being—into the following monologue, delivered in a broad Texas drawl:

"That reminds of a story about old Jim Brown. You know who *Jim Brown* was, don't you? [I assured Terry that I did.] Well, back in the early sixties I was dating this model poon, and when we got back to her apartment her roommate, also a model poon, was on the phone telling someone all about her date the night before with the football player *Jim Brown.* And I wasn't listening very hard until I heard this model poon say, quite clearly, 'And it was so big I couldn't get my *mouth* around it!'"

Deeply dirty and appreciative chuckle. "Jim Brown."

That set the tone for one of the most bibulous lunches of my publishing career, little of which I remember. But two hours and five bourbons apiece later we stumbled up the stairs into the bright summer sunlight. And as we strolled in a thick and pleasant alcoholic fog along Fifty-seventh and then up Madison in the direction of the Penguin offices I looked across the street and noticed a handsome and very athletic-looking black man walking in conversation with a smaller white man. The black man was built like some sort of superbly fashioned logging tool, wide at the shoulders and narrow at the waist, a leather jacket hanging off his muscular frame. He was wearing tight blue jeans as well, so tight that they left little doubt that this man's love muscle was as developed as all the rest. And there was something familiar about this guy. Very familiar . . .

And so I turned to Terry and declared to him delightedly, "Look over there, Terry. See that black guy? My God, do you know who that is? That is . . . *JIM BROWN!*"

THE RESURRECTIONIST
Richard McCann

Here is what happened:
I was cut apart.
The liver of a dead person was placed inside me so I might live again. This took twelve hours and thirty-three units of blood.

But who was I afterward?

I could still recall the body I'd had when I was ten, the body in which I carried what I called "myself," walking along the C&O Railroad tracks or crossing the divided highway that separated our house from the woods; a heavy, modest body, dressed in husky-size jeans from Monkey Ward and a brown corduroy car coat that my mother chose, identical to those my uncles wore back in the mining towns they lived in. I could recall the body I'd had, nervous and tentative, when I first made love at seventeen. But these bodies were gone, as was the body into which I'd been born, these bodies I'd called "mine" without hesitation, intact and separate and entire.

Three months after my liver transplant I flew to Nashville to visit my mother in the nursing home. She sat in a blue housecoat at a folding card table, slowly spooning a Dixie cup of ice cream to her mouth. "Marie, your son's here," the nurse kept telling her. But my mother wouldn't look up except to look through me. She'd begun her own metamorphosis since the last time I'd seen her, withdrawing into the form of a bony old woman who only sometimes recognized my brother or me.

"Is this your son Richard?" the nurse asked, a grade-school teacher prompting a forgetful pupil. My mother shook her head: no, no.

At night I sat at her bedside. "I'm here," I whispered as she slept. "I made it through. I'm here."

I didn't know if she could hear me. For a while I tried to work on the letter of gratitude I was planning to send to the strangers the transplant coordinator referred to as my "donor family," though I knew nothing about them or their loved one whose liver I'd received. I couldn't figure what to write to them that would seem neither too rehearsed nor too intimate, though I planned to repeat some remarks I'd heard in a support group meeting, thanking them for "the gift of life" and assuring them that the highest form of giving occurred, as theirs had, when neither the donor nor the recipient was known to one another.

For a moment my mother shifted beneath her blanket, murmuring in her sleep. I put down the pencil and closed my eyes. *In just a second*, I thought, *she'll say my name.*

"Mother," I said, though she said nothing further. I wanted us back as we had been, restored to what I felt were our real and original bodies, my mother smoking a cigarette on the stoop of our old house in Silver Spring and me beside her with a bottle of Pepsi in my hand, though I knew if my mother were able to ask what had happened to the liver I was born with—the one she'd given me, I sometimes imagined, for it had once been a part of her as well as of me—I could have told her only what the surgeon had told me: "It was sent to pathology and burned."

I flew home the next morning. On the plane I noticed the man beside me staring as one by one I swallowed the half-dozen immunosuppressants that kept my body from rejecting the organ it would forever perceive as foreign, and for a moment I felt my own sudden strangeness, even to myself, as if I were a distinct biological phenomenon, constructed in a manner different from that of my fellow passengers hurtling though space in a pressurized cabin, drinking coffee and reading their magazines.

"I'm a liver transplant recipient," I told my seatmate.

He wanted to know if my new liver was male or female or white or black.

I said I didn't know; he said that if it were him he'd sure want to find out.

But I didn't, or at least I didn't think so, and I was relieved when the plane began its descent. Somewhere over the Alleghenies my seatmate had asked if I'd heard about a man with AIDS who'd gotten a liver from a baboon.

No, I hadn't.

But in my transplant support group I had heard of recipients who'd waived their rights to anonymity to arrange what they sometimes called "reunions," inviting their donor families over for yahrzeit rituals and barbecues, and I'd heard of donor families who'd secured the names of recipients, showing up unannounced on their doorsteps, bearing bouquets of mixed flowers and brightly colored mylar balloons.

"Maybe it's kind of like discovering you're adopted or finding your birth mother," one woman said, confiding to our support group her anxious plans for meeting the mother of the teenage boy whose lungs she'd received.

No one dared the obvious: the mother was the mother of a child who was dead, even if his lungs were still drawing breath on earth.

Sometimes I too fantasized that I had an alternate family that was eager to receive me as flesh and blood, especially as my mother retreated farther and farther into a world from which I was excluded, as when she imagined that I was her dead brother and called me by his name. But my fantasies of a happy meeting with a donor family were vague and unspecific, even less concrete than the fantasies I'd concocted as a child, waiting for George Maharis from Route 66 to pull up to the house in his Corvette, ready to speed me away to what I felt sure was my real future.

My fantasies of a painful meeting, however, were explicit and detailed with dread. What would I say if my donor family were to ask to place their hands on my belly so they could feel the liver softly pulsing within?

How could I refuse them? I owed these people everything. I was alive because of a decision they'd made while standing in the bright fluorescence of a hospital corridor. Wasn't the liver more theirs than mine?

I imagined myself hesitating when they reached to touch me, and I imagined them demanding of me, with what I would have agreed was a rightful anger, "Who do you think you are?"

We are made of the dust of old stars, our grade-school teacher told us; we are made of leaves and sediment and the mulch of life. But I was made also of something rescued from the graveyard, I realized after the transplant, and if I was now among the resurrected, I was also the resurrectionist—the name given in the nineteenth century to the grave robbers who sold corpses for dissection to physicians and anatomists, trafficking in bodies and parts.

I don't recall when I began to think of what is medically called "the non-heart-beating cadaver donor" as neither a noble but faceless benefactor nor as a nonhuman organ source, but rather as someone particular and separate who'd lived his own life before he died. I don't recall when I began to think of a donor organ as a bearer of its own set of cellular memories and not just as some sort of bloodied and perishable apparatus that one could airlift a great distance in an Igloo cooler marked HUMAN HEART or HUMAN EYES. In the eleven months I spent waiting for a transplant, I could barely acknowledge what was happening to my own body as my liver rapidly failed: abdomen grossly distended from accumulated fluids; muscle wasting as my body cannibalized itself for nutrients and proteins; pale stools streaked with bile; profound and constant exhaustion; brief spells of aphasia; cramps and sudden hemorrhages, blood puddling in my mouth from ruptured esophageal varices; skin the color of copper and eyes the color of urine.

I do recall a spring afternoon a month before my transplant, when I was lying on the grass in Rock Creek Park, back from the transplant clinic where I'd overheard a nurse telling someone in the next room—I couldn't see who—that a high number of teenage donors die not from car wrecks but from suicide.

I didn't want to know this, not as I myself was growing so desperate for a donor. As soon as I left the clinic, I asked a taxi driver to take me to Rock Creek Park—"Are you all right?" he kept asking, afraid of my appearance—where I'd often gone when I was well to sunbathe with my friends, though now I was alone. I paid the fare; then I was lying on the unmowed grass, attempting to lose myself in the song I could hear playing on a far-off radio, pretending that my whole life consisted of just one word: *sunny, sunny* . . .

But it didn't work. My donor had begun to claim me, or so it seemed; I felt as if he'd somehow been constructing himself inside me without my knowledge as I was dying, though he was still alive and waiting for nothing unforeseen. Perhaps he's here right now in this park, I thought, or perhaps he's in another part of the city, crossing a street against traffic or standing at a pay phone or waiting for the bus that will bear him home from work. For a moment it seemed as if there were but the two of us left in the world, me and my blood brother, though one of us would soon be dying.

Don't die, I wanted to whisper, though I didn't know if I was speaking to him or myself.

I suppose I found out four weeks later: the hospital paged me past midnight to say they'd located a suitable donor.

My friend Sarah drove me to the E.R. The whole way I kept checking and rechecking the contents of the small suitcase I'd packed six months before—silk dressing gown, twenty-dollar bill, packet of Dentyne, razor and toothbrush and comb; I couldn't stop touching these things, as if they were all that was left holding me to earth.

I knew what would happen when we got to the hospital—X ray, EKG, and enema; introduction of IV lines, one in the left hand and another beneath the collarbone, for sedatives and cyclosporine and antibiotics. For months, I'd been trying to prepare myself for the transplant surgery, studying the booklets the doctor had given me, one with drawings of abdomens marked with dotted lines to represent incision sites, and another with a diagram showing how a pump-driven external system of plastic tubing would route my blood outside my body during the time when I would have no liver.

I was prepared to wake in the ICU, as in fact I did, unable to speak or move, brain buzzing like high voltage from prednisone.

But I was not prepared for what came the week after that: the impact of the realization that I had participated in the pain and violence and grief of a human death. *You have to face what you've done*, I kept telling myself as, each day, I watched myself in the mirror, growing healthier, until even my jaundiced eyes were white again: I had taken a liver from a brain-dead corpse that had been maintained on a ventilator during the removal of its organs, so that it looked like a regular surgical patient, prepped and draped, with an anesthesiologist standing by its head to monitor blood pressure and maintain home-ostasis, its chest visibly rising and falling with regulated breath.

"It's not like you killed him," my friends kept telling me.

"I know, I know," I said to quiet them, though I didn't know, not really. But I did know, as perhaps my friends did not, that it isn't just children who believe they can kill with the power of a thought or a word. After all, I had sat in the clinic waiting room with other transplant candidates, joking that we should take a rifle up to the roof to shoot some people whose organs we might like. "I wish we'd been at the Texas Book Depository with Oswald," one man had said.

At night in bed I often thought of the person who'd died; when I was quiet, I could feel myself quietly grieving him, just as I was grieving my own body, so deeply wounded and cut apart, though still alive.

"I'm sorry," I wanted to tell him.

Sometimes I woke in the middle of the night, troubled to realize that I had taken a piece of him inside me, as if I had eaten him to stay alive. When this happened I often forced myself to think of it longer, though I didn't want to, as if I were a member of a tribe I'd read about a long time before in an old ethnographic text that described how the bereaved dripped the bodily fluids of the dead into their rice, which they then made themselves eat as an act of reverence and love.

In this state, I could not console myself. I got up and sat on the sofa. *So here I am*, I thought, *right on the edge of the unspeakable . . .*

Other nights I thought of the donor with a great tenderness, sometimes perceiving him as male and sometimes as female. These nights, I placed my hand over what seemed to be still her liver, not mine, and slowly massaged the right side of my body—a broken reliquary with a piece of flesh inside—all the way from my hip to the bottom of my rib cage. "It's okay, it's okay," I whispered over and over, as if I were attempting to quiet a troubled spirit not my own.

If I could, I would undo what I have done, I thought, though I knew that if I had to, I would do it again.

I wasn't new to survivor guilt. After all, I'd been living for a long time in the midst of the AIDS epidemic while so many of my close friends died: Larry, Ed, Darnell, Allen, Ricardo, Paul, George, Arcadio, Jaime, Wally, Billy, Victor, and David.

In this sense, it had been a relief to be diagnosed, to have a progressive disease that threatened my life, to be bivouacked with the others. "It's like you're one of us now," my friend Kenny had told me. "It's like you've got AIDS."

But I couldn't tell him it wasn't true, at least not after the transplant; it wasn't the same at all. I'd outlived everyone, even myself.

What did Lazarus want after he stumbled from the cave, tied hand and foot with graveclothes, his face bound about with a napkin? *Loose him*, Jesus said, and *Let him go.*

I survived. It's two years since the transplant. Here I am, in my new life.

I want to unfurl.

I want to become my gratitude.

I want to fly around the world.

I want to be a man with a suntan. The man in the Arrow shirt.

And above all, this: I want to complete what I've written here—these fragments, these sticky residues of trauma—by adding just one more line before the words *The End*: "It's a miracle."

It is a miracle, of course. I know that. Just the other day, for instance, stopping at a sidewalk fruit stand and buying a blood orange: *Oh*, I thought, *this will replace the blood I lost*. I carried the orange to the park, where I sat in the sun, lazily devouring its juicy flesh, its piercing wine-red tartness. *There's nothing more than this I need*, I thought. *I'm alive. I'm alive.*

But what happens after the miracle? What happens after the blinding light of change withdraws and the things of the earth resume their shadows?

What happened to Lazarus after his resurrection? On this, the Gospel According to St. John is silent. Did Lazarus speak after he was commanded from the grave and his shroud was loosed? Did he thank the One who was his Savior and then walk back into the house with his sisters Mary and Martha so they could wash him clean? Or did he turn in anger toward his Savior, demanding to know why He had tarried so long with His Apostles before coming? *If thou hadst been here, I had not died.*

Where did he go afterward? Did he live a long life? Did he forget his time in the grave?

Here is where I went after my resurrection: Miami Beach, Sarasota, Raleigh, Nashville, Peterborough, Madrid, Barcelona, New York City, and Provincetown.

And I went back as an inpatient to the hospital—five more times, at least to date. The hepatitis goes on, the doctor tells me. The transplant doesn't cure it. It gives the virus a new liver to infect and feast upon. (*Dear donor, forgive me, I can't save your life . . .*)

A year after the transplant, just after the anniversary the social worker called my "first birthday," these things happened: low-grade fever; weight gain; edema; jaundice; sudden and unwanted elevations in alkaline phosphatase, bilirabin, and liver enzymes. *This can't be happening*, I thought, *not again.*

"We need to biopsy the liver," the doctor said. He said we needed to measure the progression of the disease by assessing the extent of new cirrhotic scarring. I knew what that meant: it meant the story wasn't over, as I so badly wanted it to be. It meant that things were uncertain.

"Don't worry," the doctor said as he sorted through my file. "We can always discuss retransplantation."

No, I thought, I can't hear that word, not ever again, especially if it's applied to me. Where was the miracle now? I was supposed to have been restored. I was supposed to have been made whole. I wanted to loose the graveclothes; I wanted to unbind the napkin from my face; I wanted to be through with death forever.

Instead I was sitting in a windowless medical office, waiting for the phlebotomist to come and draw more blood. I wasn't sure I had the heart for more miracles.

Did Lazarus believe he was done with death after his resurrection? There's no record of whether Christ cured him of the sickness that had killed him in the first place, before he rose again; there's no record of the pain his body must have felt after having lain four days in its grave—long enough to have begun to decompose and (as the Gospel says) *to stinketh*.

As for me: For three weeks I got worse, then I slowly got better. A few months later the doctor said there'd be no need to discuss retransplantation, at least not yet, at least not in the immediate future.

It wasn't a miracle that pulled me back, at least not then: I was saved not by a sudden and divine intervention but by the persistent and real efforts of physicians, some with Cartier watches and others wearing scuffed shoes. The story didn't end with a tongue of flame or a blinding light. Each morning and evening I monitor myself for organ rejection, as I'll do for the rest of my life: blood pressure, temperature, weight. I go to the clinic for blood draws; I await faxes detailing test results.

Here is what happens after the resurrection:

Your body hurts, because it's hard to come to life again after lying so long in a grave, but you set goals and you labor to meet them, holding yourself up with your IV pole as you shuffle down the hospital corridor, slowly building back your strength. You learn your medications; you learn to pack your wounds with sterile gauze; you learn to piss into a bottle and shit into a pan. It's work, preparing yourself for sunlight.

Then the day comes when you are allowed to wash your hair and shower. A little while later you're walking down a street.

People you've not seen in ages stop to ask how you're doing; you say you're doing fine, you're doing great. It's life again, dear ordinary life! Life as you hungered for it, with its pleasures and its requirements.

Yes, it's life again, your life, but it's not the same, not quite. Or so it seems, because you can't forget how it felt to lie in the close darkness of that grave; you can't forget the acrid smell of the earth or the stink of the moldering graveclothes, especially now that you know, as you never did before, that you're headed back to the grave again, as is everyone, and you know this with a clarity you cherish and despise. The gift of life is saturated with the gift of *death*.

Sometimes, sleepless at night, I imagine I'm back in the hospital the night of my transplant, lying naked in a cubicle behind a thin curtain, waiting for a nurse to prep me for surgery. *This is how it feels to lie in a cold room*, I tell myself, because this might be my last night on earth and I want to feel everything, to feel once more how life feels, each breath in and each breath out.

The nurse comes in and instructs me to lie on my side. She administers an enema. *This is how it feels to be filled with warm water*. I go to the toilet and afterwards I look at myself for a moment in the bathroom mirror. When I return to the cubicle and lie down, the nurse says she must shave the hair from my abdomen, all the way from my groin to my chest. "I hope my hands are warm enough," she says, spreading the shaving soap across my stomach. She touches the cold razor to my belly, and I think, *This is how it feels to be alive*.

NO MO PO-MO
Lisa Zeidner

W e have adopted a baby.[1] It appears to be my sister's.[2] John is changing its diaper and notes, alarmed, that it is a hermaphrodite.[3] We bring the boy (officially it is a boy) to the doctor's, trying to hide the problem from Nicolas.[4] The doctor appears to be a veterinarian.[5] The vet takes one look and says, breezily, making her fingers into a pair of Churchill's-V scissors, "No problem. We'll just snip 'em off."[6] "Why," I demand, "do you make that decision? Why not stitch up the vagina?[7] Don't you want to, like, draw blood and check how much estrogen there is or something?"[8] The doctor agrees this is a good idea. I try to eat, but the ferry to Manhattan is late[9] and furthermore the food behind the deli counter[10] does not look particularly fresh or appetizing (fish-stick pasta salad?).[11] I have no idea where I left the baby.[12, 13]

Notes

1 When asked if I plan to have more children, my standard response is "I'd rather rip out my uterus with my bare hands." Just yesterday, my son Nicolas had a play date with an adopted Romanian orphan.
2 My sister made sixty thousand dollars on the stock market yesterday. I am not taking her windfall well. So severe was my reaction to her good fortune, and so embarrassed was I by it, that I spent yesterday online, researching the psychiatric literature on envy. I found wonderful articles like "The Roles of Invidious Comparisons and Deservingness in Sympathy and Schadenfreude" and "Cinderella and Her Sisters: The Envied and the Envying."* Needless to say, penis envy comes up a great deal in this context. My position on penis envy has always been fairly ambivalent.

 * This should really be "2a," but formatting that on Microsoft Word could take all afternoon. I only wanted to note that I am not going to stop to give the full citation for these articles, as David Foster Wallace would do. Of course stopping to say I am not going to stop to make the citations takes as long as stopping to make the citations.

My sister's stock is falling!

By the time you read this, NASDAQ will have collapsed. The "yester-day" above was accurate once. Dreams, like the stock market, always happen in the present tense.

3 My association with hermaphrodites is Fellini's *Satyricon*. I remember the parched lips of the hermaphrodite in the desert almost every time I'm thirsty, as I'm sure I was in my sleep (flu). The scene in *Satyricon* in which a slave is forced to have his arm amputated as part of a play unsettled my sleep for months in 1976, especially since I had read that this actor *really did have his arm cut off* on-screen—that he had bone cancer, was going to lose the arm anyway, and consented to have it done in this fashion, for his art. In real life, as opposed to in ancient Rome, he would have had an anesthetic. Still. My deep terror about loss of limbs would give some credence to a diagnosis of penis envy, unless that's castration anxiety (which Freud claims that women, too, can suffer from).

4 My son Nicolas qualifies as "all boy." Both my husband and I wept when we got the amnio results.

Because Nicolas has been having trouble falling asleep, it has become exceedingly difficult for John and me to have sex at night. Once or twice we have had to go into the master bathroom, lock the door, and turn on the fan. We are seriously considering my sister's offer to take our son to the beach this summer and give us a week to ourselves, but there has already been a great deal of worry about whether eight is old enough to board a plane alone.

5 The last thing we watched before going to sleep was the laugh-fest *Emergency Room Vets*, on the Animal Planet channel. We watched surgery on a pet rabbit to remove a hairball ("this one is a meticulous groomer," the surgeon noted) and the full-throttle efforts to save three corgis that were suffering from seizures, probably from strychnine poisoning.

6 The obvious reference here is John Colapinto's book, *As Nature Made Him: The Boy Who Was Raised As a Girl*. The circumcision got botched, and the arrogant doctor announced that they would simply change the boy into a girl. Except it didn't work. The child's essential boyness leaked through. This may be the single worst story I have ever heard, and I certainly remembered it scanning the psychiatric indexes on envy and seeing "The Bobbit Case and the Quest for a Good-Enough Penis" (Daniel Dervin, *Psychoanalytic Review*).

My other association with the vet's snippy fingers is how unpleasant it is to cut out the fabric-care tags from the back of my son's shirts while he is wearing them—pretty much how I always have to cut them out, because he always complains they're stabbing him when he's already late for school.

My association with the last association is Nicholson Baker's treasure trove of tiny impressions, *The Mezzanine*.

Let us pause to credit the real source of this digressive style of footnote. It is not Nicholson Baker. It is not David Foster Wallace. It is Sigmund Freud, whose *The Interpretation of Dreams* is, many contend, the seminal

book of the twentieth century—the book that demonstrates how the
detritus of daily life penetrates, and pollutes, consciousness.

7 Our adopted dog is "fixed." Does it bother her? It doesn't *seem* to bother her.
I have spent an unseemly amount of time staring at what passes, on our dog,
as "a vagina." It reminds me of the nose cone on an old-fashioned propeller. I
thought of her hysterectomy scar, barely visible through the white fur on her
tummy, as I watched the Animal Planet posse cut open the rabbit.

8 I am past childbearing age.
I have always hated having blood drawn.
This, too, is probably related to penis envy/castration anxiety.

9 We take the turnpike to Manhattan, not the ferry.
Bodies of water in dreams, of course, generally mean that you have to
pee. (Freud: "People who dream often, and with great enjoyment, of
swimming, of cleaving the waves, etc., have usually been bed-wetters, and
they now repeat in the dream a pleasure which they have long since
learned to forgo.")

10 John Belushi, *Saturday Night Live*, the Samurai Warrior delicatessen guy.
Belushi as malevolent mohel.

11 It was *shell* pasta. And fish sticks are phallic.
Tex-Mex dim sum. Bacon ice cream. Black bean soup with chocolate
croutons. For some time, I have wanted to disgorge myself of a piece of
criticism called "No Mo Po-Mo," in which I deride the pathetic state of
what passes for postmodernism in contemporary culture. The typical po-
mo gesture now consists merely of shoving together two seeming absurd,
mismatched, contradictory entities. It is the impulse mocked in the pitches
in Robert Altman's *The Player* (*The Bride of Frankenstein* meets *Pretty
Woman*). In *Vogue* it shows up as leather and lace, or cowboy boots with
your evening gown. The once-challenging modern dancer Twyla Tharp
now pleases crowds with Frank Sinatra tunes. I actually heard some
Quentin Tarantino wanna-be gravely revealing his approach to filmmaking: "I pick a genre, make a parody of it, that sorta thing."

Dave Eggers mocks this approach in *A Heartbreaking Work of Staggering Genius*, the genius of which I find underwhelming, in a list of
prospective names for rock bands: Van Go Dog Go, Jerry Farrakhan, etc.
"Most of the names are like this, the melding of two or more cultural
elements, ideally one high and one low, the smugly clever, utterly meaningless result." But of course Eggers wants us to laugh knowingly. And if
we don't, he preempts our disapprobation, and if we disapprove of the
preempting, he beats us to the disapproval. About the hip young magazine
he edited, he admits:

> We begin a program of almost immediate opinion-reversal and self-
> devouring. Whatever the prevailing thinking, especially our own, we
> contradict it, reflexively. We need to make clear that . . . if you look
> closely, we are winking, smirking ever so slightly . . . We can play it
> both ways, all ways.

Does Eggers's self-consciousness constitute an insight? Not. Or maybe an
itsy-bitsy, adolescent perception—the equivalent of "Am I a man dream-

ing I am a butterfly, or a butterfly dreaming I am a man?" It is to real
writing as Escher is to real art.

Meaninglessness is not clever. Arbitrariness is not clever. Dreams—
which seem, at first glance, to be arbitrary—turn out to be not arbitrary at
all, but deeply moored. And art should be more artful than your average
slapdash dream. Compare the shocking but deeply revealing juxtaposi-
tions in a Buñuel film with MTV.

Art requires commitment.

You can't be a girl *and* a boy. You have to choose.

12 Last night's eleven o'clock news featured a mother who was charged with
child abandonment, because her five-year-old daughter woke up in the
middle of the night and sleepwalked out of the house down the street. The
munchkin somnambulized for half a mile before a trucker picked her up
and deposited her at the police station.

The review of Eggers's book in the *New York Times* was titled "Home
Alone."

When is a child old enough to board a plane by himself, leaving his
parents free to make love whenever they want, making however much
noise they want?

13 The dream is over, but Microsoft Word still insists on skipping down to
the very bottom of the page to record the footnotes. I have spent a full half
hour failing to solve this problem. Often I fret that all the channel-surfing,
mouse-clicking technology, the distraction of fonts, the splatter art of
Nintendo graphics, have significantly reduced my ability to write. Formatting is not thought. I miss the purity of an old-fashioned blank page—
or even the uncluttered blue page of WordPerfect 5.1. (Yes. I know. You
can make Word's screen blue. I have done so. Have even done the Full
Screen Zoom. Still, it's not the same. The blue's too dark, and you've still
got that "Full Screen/Close Full Screen" box in the upper right-hand
corner, annoying as the channel logos now superimposed over all television shows.)

In his story "The Babysitter" (1969), Robert Coover composes a manic
set piece about how television has rewritten the narrative of our dream
lives. It rankles me that Dave Eggers, for all his tics of reference, doesn't
acknowledge how derivative his work is of seventies postmodernism, of
Coover and Barth and Barthelme. But then I wonder whether the children
even *know* their forebears, or just pick up po-mo secondhand, from
David Foster Wallace or David Letterman—or even thirdhand, from
MTV.

There's no anxiety of influence. Do they worry that the last famous
person to wear the eyeglasses currently in fashion was Lee Harvey
Oswald? They don't care if it's been done, or by whom. They are young,
and get to do it all again.

Am I Just Jealous—the charge always leveled against surly critics?
Partly. Why them and not me for the big-dick advances, the splitting
stocks? More than the money, I begrudge the youth itself—the sheer
freedom from the debt of Been There, Done That. The Daves are *boy*-
writers, too, virile and swaggering, the kind who always get the literary

kudos—belonging to what the novelist Dawn Powell liked to call "the PENis Club."

(Forgot to mention that my son got a haircut yesterday. "Snip-snip." When a middle-aged friend heard that Dave Eggers was giving free haircuts as a party publicity stunt, he sighed, "I'm too old for this shit.")

The drive for success, as anyone who has passed Psych 101 knows, is only a secondary need. We want status and success so we can get laid. The endless humping on Animal Planet is a useful reminder that technology changes nothing, that there are no new tricks, that mammal nature is fixed.

We dream what we've always dreamed. Thus mine. Sex, and the guilt that I wish my son would just go away, so I can have it. Even if I am really, really old.

WEBB PIERCE'S
"THERE STANDS THE GLASS"
Ken Tucker

I t i s a perfect song—not just a perfect *country* song—one whose
pleasure is only intensified by the way its impeccably controlled
construction and performance courts imperfection: loss of control of
one's life. Recorded and released in 1953, "There Stands the Glass" is
the starkly sketched story of a man who walks into a bar and orders a
drink, ponders its curative powers and its curse, and immediately falls
into a reverie of regret and self-pity. After stating the title, the singer,
Webb Pierce, avers that the glass's contents "will ease all my pain" and
"will settle my brain," even as the quaver in his voice lets you know *he*
knows he's deluding himself. He ends the first verse with an avowal
suffused with a shame highly unusual for pre recovery-era country
music: "It's my first one today."

I've long thought that "There Stands the Glass" would make an ideal
anthem for Alcoholics Anonymous, for the way it makes drinking sound
so utterly dreary, and for the way "It's my first one today" contains an
echo of the AA abstinence mantra "One day at a time." Instead, the song
upon its release was interpreted as an unabashed hymn to getting shit-
faced—was, indeed, banned by a number of country music stations. Fred
Rose, one of the most influential figures in country music history as co-
owner of the all-powerful Acuff-Rose Music Publishing company and by
a number of accounts himself a reformed alcoholic, understood the
allure of the song, and is said to have tried to dissuade Pierce from
releasing it, protesting, "It hasn't even got a moral!" Instead, Pierce
reveled in the song's success, referring to it as "the national anthem of
barroom songs," one that quickly inspired a temperance answer record
called "Throw the Glass Away."

The bridge of "There Stands the Glass" occurs two verses in—when, in metaphoric time, the contents of the glass's first couple of gulps have warmed the singer's throat and soul and loosened his tongue. It's a four-line marvel of condensed mixed-emotionalism. It begins, "I'm wond'ring where you are tonight / I wonder if you are alright," the singer expressing concern for a lost love before moving onto the real purpose of his sodden lament—utter, unearned self-absorption: "I wonder if you think of me / In my misery." No one who has ever listened closely to "There Stands the Glass" could possibly believe that the vocalist's long-gone honey is now thinking of him, or indeed, gives two hoots about him. Instead, it's more likely that this fellow's line of palaver (ostensible concern for another person, immediately giving way to feeling sorry for oneself) is one big reason the girl left him in the first place. Settling more seriously into his funk as a keening steel guitar—the signature honky-tonk instrument—wafts up and around his vocal, the narrator resumes the previous metrical form, and tells the bartender to fill his now-empty glass "up to the brim / Till my troubles grow dim." That last line would seem an unlikely occurrence anytime soon: The only time this guy's troubles will dim is when he passes out later in his lonely hotel room, or, more likely, right there on the bar stool.

When he released "There Stands the Glass," Webb Pierce was twenty-six years old, a Louisiana-born former clothing salesman for Sears Roebuck with four number-one country hit singles under his belt. It's almost miraculous, really, that Pierce—who'd never specialized in fifties country music's perennial topics, drinking heavily and fornicating beyond the bounds of marriage—found it within himself to summon up the abject, insidious, grandly beautiful despair that suffuses his recording of "There Stands the Glass." Pierce, who died in 1991, had a soft, doughy face and brilliantined hair, a nice pair of jug ears, and a fondness for the garish suits designed by the Nashville custom clothier Nudie Cohen: a typical Nudie suit was lime green or pink or orange, appliquéd with swirling musical notes or flowery vines. After he became a star, Pierce drove a car whose steering wheel and interior was studded with silver dollars and had pistols as door handles; the singer installed a guitar-shaped swimming pool in his backyard. (In the seventies, long after he'd placed no fewer than fifty songs in the Top 10 of the country music charts and the hits had stopped coming, he charged tourists to troop through his property and admire these artifacts.) Pierce was a dependable, upbeat guy, one who caught his biggest break in 1952, when he replaced his genre's greatest star, Hank Williams, on the all-important Nashville Saturday-night industry showcase and radio show, *The Grand Ole Opry*, at a point when Williams was doing real-life variations on filling glasses up to the brim—doing speed, missing tour and *Opry* dates.

Unlike Williams, a gaunt genius of ceaseless creativity, the pudgy Pierce wrote few of his own hits. The authorship of "There Stands the Glass" is credited to Russ Hull, Mary Jean Shurtz, and Audrey Grisham, but was written only by Hull and Shurtz. Grisham was Pierce's wife; in a practice common in that era, a popular artist could demand an additional profit by securing a songwriting credit, either to himself (Pierce is listed as co-writer on any number of songs he did little more than agree to carry into the recording studio) or, as in this case, a relative. And it was a relative of my own—my father—who inspired me to think about this song as much as I have. "There Stands the Glass" was one song among many that were playing the night my father, drunk, took a rifle out of our living room closet and held it to my mother's throat. "You want me to use this?" he yelled, his usually deep voice cracking into a shattered-glass scream on the word "use." "You want me to *use* this?" he yelled again. "No, Doug," my mother said quietly. "Stop it. For Jesus' sake, go to bed."

When I asked my mother about this old scene recently, she said I had the music wrong. "Your father was listening only to Willie Nelson by then," she said, as if she'd kept track of the progress of his alcoholism by the singers he favored—not a bad measure, when I thought about it later. After all, people do go on music jags as much as they do on booze, movie, or ice cream jags, and my father did tend to obsess on favorites for defined periods. For a few years, George Jones was the best singer on earth. Then it was the syrupy country crooner Ray Price. Then Willie Nelson, with whose "outlaw" period my father nurtured a pathetic identification. Each shift in taste signaled a different phase of his obnoxiousness (as far as I and my siblings were concerned) or his sinning (as he would eventually, in thrall to AA and the church, more loftily consider it).

My mother and I had the Pierce vs. Nelson discussion shortly after my father died a few years ago, after the inside of his own throat had closed over with cancer. I went down to Florida to go through his possessions with my brother and sister. When my sister asked my mother if she could have a particular Ray Price album, Mom said quickly, "Take it; it gives me the creeps. It has that song he used to play over and over again when he was with that woman"—and that was how I found out that, when I was a dull, self-absorbed teenager, my father had had an affair with the wife of one of his best friends; that my mother knew about it and did nothing to stop it; and that in her mind it had all played out to repeated playings of Price's maudlin hit "For the Good Times": my father dancing to the song with this other woman, both of them drunk, his huge hand damp against the back of her thin cotton dress.

But I remain convinced that there was a Webb Pierce greatest-hits collection in the pile of vinyl albums stacked on the record changer of the big living room stereo the night the rifle came out of the closet. Maybe, as my mother believes, "There Stands the Glass" wasn't playing at the exact moment the gunmetal found the pulse in her neck as swiftly as if its throb was a magnet. When my father's voice broke into the high-pitched yowl of "You want me to *use* this?," whatever song may have actually been on the turntable, it was the dolorous agony that pours forth from "There Stands the Glass" that filled up our living room like whiskey filled to a tumbler's rim, leaving the room—like that glass, like his throat—airless.

DRINKING MY INHERITANCE
Sara Roahen

My earliest memory of winter evenings in Wisconsin is of being in a canoe-size toboggan shuttling down the slalom course of Aunt Nancy and Uncle Larry's front yard toward a congregation of evergreens. The grownups would pile on the toboggan with me, their warm-sour brandy breath visible in the pinching cold as they talked incessantly about all the fun we were having. Hours later, my younger sister, Stephanie, and I curled up on a makeshift bed in the living room, listening to faraway yelps and squeals of the grownups as they sprinted, nude, from Uncle Larry's incendiary sauna to a snowbank outside and back again, pausing only to refresh a cocktail. Stephanie dozed off effortlessly, but I lay awake, petrified that a cold-induced heart attack would orphan me at any moment.

Their choice of cocktail was seasonless, but activities at the weekend-long parties changed with the weather. Come summer, the snow melted to reveal a swimming pool surrounded on all sides by overgrown Christmas trees and rented plots of feed corn. The men shot at clay pigeons all day as their women pretended to watch, but Stephanie and I stayed poolside. While she perfected her back dive, I dripped dry beneath the porch with plates of sour cream cucumbers and a prickling sunburn. It was impossible to gauge back then—or now—which was more to blame for my bouts of summer insomnia: the green shag carpeting that poked through Aunt Nancy's satin sheets against my blistered skin; the orchestra of moths searing in the bug light outside; Jefferson County cops triaging drunk drivers over Uncle Larry's radio scanner; or the grownups' howling as they drained the swimming pool in a cannonball contest. Heart attacks didn't worry me in the summertime. Instead, I was sure one of them would crack open a skull on the pool's cement lip.

Occasionally these weekends terminated at Sunday Mass, where we thanked the Lord in person for so much fun. But mostly Stephanie and I feigned sleep when Aunt Nancy woke up on Sunday mornings, praying that instead of rousing us for church she would switch on the Christian radio station she claimed would save our souls. It was a weak substitute for church, she admitted as she shuffled back to bed, but at least it would keep us out of hell for another seven days. If you had asked me at the time to what we owed this stroke of heathen fortune, I would have answered: Uncle Larry's brandy old-fashioned sweets.

These were not the gentlemanly whiskey old-fashioneds of water splashes and sugar cubes and *absolutely nothing carbonated* that cocktail academics believe was invented in the mid-1800s in Kentucky. These old-fashioneds were big and stiff, as generous as the beers sold at Lambeau Field, with a pitch-perfect balance of sweet and bitter, alcoholic warmth and ice cube chill. And they were apparently refreshing enough to drink all night long. Uncle Larry still measures his old-fashioneds in brandy glugs and shakes of bitters and finishes them with 7Up. He stirs them with cinnamon sticks and garnishes them with maraschino cherries. While he is considered the authority on old-fashioneds in our family—his heavily researched recipe is still the platonic ideal for us all—his typically Wisconsin version of the drink is to the original highbrow cocktail what a double espresso latte with whipped cream and cinnamon is to a cup of joe. It's bigger, it's sweeter, it's got more spice. Its smooth base, brandy, is at least as different from whiskey as an espresso shot is from a straight-up French roast. Except around the pool, where only plastic UW-Wisconsin Badger football cups were allowed, these old-fashioneds always came in ice-packed glasses painted with pheasants soaring over marshes and spaniels pointing at flocks of plump, deaf quail.

The garnishes were the greatest thrill for little girls. Phosphorescent, brandy-marinated cherries shimmered under the melting ice in sweating glasses like brightly painted fishing lures. But, like Mom's holiday bourbon balls—which always ended up spit into a poinsettia napkin—the cherries were deceptively harsh. So we gnawed on the cinnamon sticks, which were never alcoholic, just spicy and wet. To this day, when throwing a cinnamon stick into a pot of black beans, I find myself back in the campfire air of Aunt Nancy and Uncle Larry's wood-heated home.

While I grew up around brandy old-fashioneds, my father's parents hadn't even heard of brandy before eloping from Ohio to Wisconsin in 1939. It became their drink of choice when they found that their new friends kept no other liquor in the house. Brandy consumption in Wisconsin has always been higher per capita than in any other state, but a growing taste for spiced rum, flavored vodka, and specialty martinis among the younger Wisconsin social-drinking circles has led to a sharp decline in statewide brandy sales. This drop is causing panic among brandy producers. Since Wisconsin's bordering states have such similar geographical, socioeconomic and ethnic breakdowns, they have never figured out what originally drove Wisconsinites to covet it. Therefore, they don't know how to ensure that our passion doesn't fizzle out. Says Gary Heck, owner of Korbel Brandy: "It must have been what the wagon had on it when it first got there."

It appears that the wagon was brimming. Generations of Wisconsinites have ensured that brandy's uses are boundless. Especially in rural areas, bartenders often use brandy in place of other brown liquors without warning. Natives expect it, but out-of-state customers learn to specify brands when ordering a bourbon and water or a whiskey sour. Most brandy old-fashioned drinkers I know drink them sweet, made with 7Up, but you can also order them made with sour mix (a brandy old-fashioned sour), with water, with seltzer, or with half 7Up, half seltzer. This half-and-half version is called a brandy old-fashioned Press, short for Presbyterian—though no one seems to know the connection between Presbyterians and brandy old-fashioneds.

By the time I landed my first job, brandy old-fashioneds were as embedded in my consciousness as frostbite and fried cheese curds. Most bars wouldn't let kids my age onto the premises to use the pay phone, much less to work, but since the management at private golf clubs in Wisconsin didn't believe in age discrimination, I brought in more cash cocktail-waitressing the summer I turned eighteen than I've made during any three-month period since. I also became unusually attached to the smell of sticky brandy and bitters drying on a cork-lined cocktail tray. I still didn't drink old-fashioneds, preferring Mogan David at the time, but it became clear that a fanatical allegiance to the cocktail was not particular to my family. Thursday's men's nights at the golf club were the rowdiest and most lucrative for me, but it was during Friday night fish fries that my fellow statesmen and -women most openly indulged their affections for our regional cherry-brown drink. Friday night fish fries in Wisconsin are as ubiquitous as brats at a Brewers game, and everyone knows the protocol. You always take as much of the family as you can, you always take the good car, and you always show up early for a drink in the bar. Club members whose aperitif preference wasn't a brandy old-fashioned were such a minority that more than a decade later I still remember these anomalies: the retired couple with a powder-blue golf cart who only drank vodka tonics; the Miller Genuine Draft–swilling lout who was an ass pincher on Thursdays and a family man on Fridays; and the leather-skinned golf pro who separated himself from the hacks by drinking whiskey old-fashioneds with olives.

Today there's a very new-millennium martini menu at Club 26, a supper club just south of Fort Atkinson where my parents found the fried cod so superior that they held their wedding reception there on a Friday evening in 1970. Yet the club's bartenders still make so many brandy old-fashioneds that they prepare for Friday evenings by mixing gallons of simple syrup and bitters (not to be confused with the appalling old-fashioned blends sold in Wisconsin liquor stores next to the piña colada, Bloody Mary, and margarita mixes). I doubt a Club 26 bartender has ever made an old-fashioned in that sodaless manner that characterized them in nineteenth-century Kentucky, and that still characterizes them in forty-nine states. If a customer requested one, the staff would probably react with the same confusion that strikes bartenders outside the borders of Wisconsin when you ask for an old-fashioned made with brandy and 7Up even as they're reaching for the whiskey and the sugar cubes. At Club 26, you get an above-average if weak version of Uncle Larry's old-fashioned, minus the wildfowl glasses and the cinnamon stick (both homemade touches). The first one goes down like a Shirley Temple while we pretend to consider Club 26's newer menu items—chicken schnitzel, salmon with sauerkraut—and then agree on the cod.

I've heard it said that a Wisconsin fish fry isn't genuine if it doesn't come with a relish tray of raw vegetables, sour cherry peppers, olives, and little pickles. Club 26 ditched the relish tray for deep-fried dinner rolls long ago, but the centerpiece is still nuggets of firm, bleach-white cod fished from oceans far from the Great Lakes and wrapped in clingy sheaths of brown batter that are more chewy than crisp, but never greasy. A brandy old-fashioned remains the natural accompaniment to fried fish for many of us, but now that Kendall Jackson and his California friends have infiltrated nearly every wood-paneled supper club across the state, even my grandparents occasionally fall for research suggesting that wine will conquer the wicked effects of fried foods.

Nevertheless, there's little other sign of a brandy recession in any generation of my family. The moment we enter the house on a visit, before Mom can set the table with cheddar cheese soup and macaroni salad, Dad asks, "Regular 7Up or diet?" (Some Wisconsinites do count calories.) My cousin's husband, Doug, Uncle Larry's nephew by marriage, is another artisan of the regional cocktail. His patent-worthy technique, the results of which we taste every Christmas Eve before presents, involves holding the glass up to the stained woodwork in the bar he built himself. If the woodwork is darker than the drink, he adds more brandy.

Those panicking brandy makers might also take heart if they saw the solid wall of brandy displayed at a certain truck stop just outside Wisconsin Dells. It's the last place I know of to buy a bottle on the way up to the home where Aunt Nancy and Uncle Larry retired among the osprey and eagles of Lake Castle Rock. Their weekend-long parties have gone the way of Badger football victories, but I have noticed a sauna built suspiciously close to a sliding glass door in the basement. Still the barrel-chested, baritone-voiced man of my youth, Uncle Larry mixes everyone two old-fashioneds before we head out to their favorite local fish fry. I'm the only one who can't finish both. When I was younger, my dad used to stabilize his Friday night old-fashioned-for-the-road between his thighs as he drove; I would fret in the backseat, longing for the day when I could take the wheel. He still protests when I offer to drive—the restaurant is just a few miles down the road, after all, and cars have cup holders now. During dinner I pour my fourth old-fashioned into Aunt Nancy's empty glass, completely undetected. It has always been a combination of thrill and dread trying to keep pace with the grownups.

Most of the family in the generation older than mine is still fairly young, settling down but not nearly ready to give up. They aren't sure yet what part of our family they would pass on if I asked them to. There are no cows to milk, no taffy to make, no shoes to repair in our clan. No law firm. No corner store. But I'm older now than they were when we used to pile on that toboggan, and I have reached an age when finding something to claim as ours before it becomes just me feels crucial. It's a primal impulse, a nostalgic ache for things that aren't gone quite yet—something like the urge to procreate, only in reverse. So I thought about my inheritance options and came to a conclusion that surprises even me: I'm taking the old-fashioned. Taking the garnishes and everything else that comes with it. It was there from the beginning anyhow. I just needed the recipe.

UNCLE LARRY'S BRANDY OLD-FASHIONED SWEET

Most brandy old-fashioned makers I know are partial to a particular brand (Uncle Larry likes Christian Brothers), but any inexpensive brandy will do. It's essential to make ice in the largest cubes possible; the balance of bitters, brandy, and sweetness is easily diluted, and the kind of nubby ice sold by the bag melts too quickly. Lastly, most store-bought bar syrups are either saccharine-sweet or have a plasticky flavor. After years of empirical research Uncle Larry found one to fit his taste, Sweet 10, but you can also make your own simple syrup by heating equal parts water and sugar on the stovetop and stirring just until the sugar dissolves. For easy access, store the syrup in a squirt bottle or other covered vessel with a pour spout.

liberal 2 jiggers (3 ounces) brandy
4 or 5 strong dashes Angostura bitters
1 teaspoon simple syrup
½ of one 2-inch cinnamon stick (split it lengthwise)
6 ounces (half a can) cold 7Up
maraschino cherries to taste

Fill a 12-ounce tumbler to the top with ice cubes and pour in brandy. Add bitters and simple syrup; stir with cinnamon stick, leaving the stick in the glass. Top off the drink with 7Up and stir again with a long-handled bar spoon. Garnish with maraschino cherries, either floating or skewered on a toothpick.

AFTER YOU
Christopher Merrill

A gha Shahid Ali liked to white out his birth date on the copyright pages of his books, determined to hide his age even from his closest friends. Indeed there was something timeless about his presence and his poems. But here are the facts: he was born on February 4, 1949, in New Delhi, two years after the partition between India and Pakistan that left his homeland of Kashmir in a geopolitical limbo from which it has yet to emerge, and he died in Amherst on December 8, 2001, the anniversary of his mother's first seizure from the same form of brain cancer that afflicted him. Massachusetts law prevented his family from following the Muslim custom of burying him within twenty-four hours of his death, on a Sunday, and so he was interred on Emily Dickinson's birthday, just down the road from the poet who wrote:

> If I could bribe them by a Rose
> I'd bring them every flower that grows
> From Amherst to Cashmere!

These were the lines Shahid used as an epigraph to his Dickinsonian poem "Some Vision of the World Cashmere." What he gave to his friends and readers, who would surely trade every flower for another day with him, another poem, was an enduring vision of Kashmir—the land of "doomed addresses" evoked in such haunting terms in his later work. And with one phrase—"A route of Evanescence"—the anchorite of Amherst not only inspired Shahid's finest pages in *A Nostalgist's Map of America* but also described his journey through our literary landscape.

*　　*　　*

He perfected his English watching American television. At the age of twelve he moved with his family to Indiana, where his father took a doctorate, and in the heartland his vision of America took shape, fueled by his parodies of TV commercials. Which is to say, he was conversant with everything this culture had to offer. He knew the dialogue of *Mommie Dearest* by heart. Also *The Lion King*. And poetry, his own and others. He recited his own poems until his final days, even after much of his memory had been destroyed. Milton's "Lycidas" was the last poem he attempted to memorize, and toward the end he believed, wrongly, that he used to have the whole of *Paradise Lost* by heart. But for Shahid paradise lay all around him—in poetry, in the spicy meals he cooked for his friends, on the dance floor, with the people he loved.

For his sixteenth birthday he received from his father a beautiful leather-bound notebook with this inscription: "Another notebook for the same game. Spontaneous self-expression must now turn into studied attempts at conciseness and discipline." He spent the next thirty-five years obeying that imperative. He earned degrees from universities in Srinigar and New Delhi, at State College, Pennsylvania, and Tucson, Arizona; his academic career took him from Hamilton College to the universities of Massachusetts and Utah; he held visiting professorships and taught at several writers' conferences. In the class-room he was at once witty and rigorous. In a poorly executed exercise he could spot the seed of a poem; his students were thrilled to watch him turn a work inside out, in the hope of discovering its secret heart. Nor did he tolerate bad writing. He quipped that one line should be put up against a wall and shot—a joke that takes on more weight when you consider the tens of thousands of people killed over the last decade in his war-torn homeland; the relationship between poetry and politics was uppermost in his mind. And his playfulness served a larger purpose. Once, when a student asked him to raise his grade, Shahid agreed, on condition that he sing for him every verse of "Achy Breaky Heart." Which the student did, in a cracking voice. Shahid gave him a better grade—and a lesson in humility.

*　　*　　*

His readings were, in the memorable words of the late poet William Matthews, a kind of stand-up tragedy. He would stop in the middle of a poem to pose for a photograph or to castigate someone for leaving the auditorium. More than one person returned to his or her seat when Shahid asked, "Are you leaving me?" Once, when an overflowing crowd forced some members of the audience to sit on the floor by the lectern, he exclaimed, "I love to have white people sitting at my feet!"

What stayed with his listeners, though, was the tension between his casual asides and the seriousness of his work, even his light verse. Shahid was a darkly humorous poet. As he wrote in the conclusion of "An Interview with Red Riding Hood, Now No Longer Little":

Q. Do you have any regrets?
A. Yes.
    I lied when I said it was dark.
    Now I drive through the city,
    hearing wolves at every turn.
    How warm it was inside the wolf!

Shahid wanted to publish poems in journals beginning with all the letters of the alphabet; he even tried to convince the editor of *Zyzzyva* (a magazine that only publishes California-based writers) that he came from a Pacific Rim nation and thus belonged in its pages; his only reservation about *Tin House* was its name—he already had a T.

He signed books—his own and others—with lavish inscriptions. At lunch in Venice, California, for example, he presented me with a book containing Xavier Villaurautia's poems and an essay by Octavio Paz, *Hieroglyphs of Desire*. On the title page, inspired by the sight of all the sleek women in bikinis Rollerblading by, he wrote: "We again learn, on the boardwalk, that some hieroglyphs of desire move on wheels." And once, in a used-book store in Syracuse, when he discovered a signed copy of his *Walk Through the Yellow Pages*, which he had given to a married couple, he bought the chapbook and sent it back to them with instructions never to sell it again!

How happy he was to buy a converted flat in the former Northampton jail. He even considered writing a book of poems titled *Jail*. Which goes to the heart of his genius: in his personal life and in his poetry he escaped the bonds of conventional practice and thinking. A triple exile, from Kashmir, from India, and from his mother tongue, Urdu, he refused to play the role of victim; as he wrote in one poem, "for whose world is not in ruins? whose?" A student at Reed College in Portland, Oregon, complained to him that as an Indian he felt alienated from his fellow students, because he was different. Of course you're different, Shahid told him. Celebrate that difference. The poetics he fashioned out of celebrations of difference, the liberation he secured from the shackles of staid thinking, inspired devotion from his friends and readers.

He was my daughter's godfather, a role he took seriously. He bought Hannah gifts from the silver emporium in New Delhi, he asked after her in every phone call, he drove through the snow from his home in Massachusetts to Pennsylvania for her christening, even colliding with another car en route. After the Episcopal service, my wife asked him if, as a Shiite Muslim, he felt uncomfortable assenting to the Christian creeds.

"Not at all," he replied. "I take it all very metaphorically."

Which is not to say he had a cavalier attitude about religion. His work is sprinkled with references to the Koran; his respect for religious ritual, in any denomination, was profound. Poetry was for him a form of prayer and petition to the gods of desire, of love, and of loss.

I used to think that when my daughter grew up she would realize how fortunate she was to have him as her guardian angel. But she seemed to know that even at the age of six. On the day he died, before I gave her the news, she covered the walls of my office with her drawings. When I told her that Shahid had died she asked me how long it would take for his soul to get to heaven. Faster than a car? A plane? She said she would talk to him, in the same way that she talked to her late grandfather. And he would ask her what all of the dead ask: "Are you happy, Hannah?"

A crucial development in his poetic evolution was his friendship with James Merrill. If the publication of *The Half-Inch Himalayas* introduced a new voice into American poetry, combining wit, seemingly exotic imagery, and an astute political conscience, under Merrill's sway Shahid grew into a sophisticated formalist. In *A Nostalgist's Map of America, The Country Without a Post Office*, and *Rooms Are Never Finished*, he wrote in a bewildering variety of forms. Syllabics were his favorite pattern, and while he did not really hear stresses in English it may be argued that he created a new jangled music akin to the syllabics of Marianne Moore and Thom Gunn. Sapphics were thus congenial to him; he even translated Faiz and Pushkin into Sapphics. Likewise the three canzones he wrote, a feat that prompted Anthony Hecht to remark that he deserved a place in the *Guinness Book of World Records*. The third one, "The Veil Suite," was completed even as he learned that he had lost his battle with cancer. Its origins lay in a dream he had the night before his first biopsy, in which he was visited by Death. The last lines: "I'm still alive, alive to learn from your eyes / that I am become your veil and I am all you see."

Kashmir was his poetic lodestar. *The Country Without a Post Office*, his most overtly political work, is a meditation on the tragic history of his land, the fate of which is linked to his mother's death in *Rooms Are Never Finished*, a National Book Award finalist. Before his mother fell ill, Shahid liked to say he refused to suffer for more than thirty seconds over anything; with her death, however, came a more complex vision of the human condition, which corresponded to the deepening of his engagement with English and Urdu literary traditions, politics, and religion. In his trio of canzones, "After the August Wedding, Lahore, Pakistan," "Lenox Hill," and "The Veil Suite," we see his poetry turned into prayers, first for his homeland, then for his mother, and finally for his own soul: "On the farthest side of prophecy, I still need a veil."

The ghazal, Shahid liked to say, is pronounced "ghuzzle." The average American poet's inability to say the word correctly upset him no less than the widespread belief that poems could be called ghazals when they were nothing of the sort. And so he took it upon himself to properly introduce the form into American literature, cajoling more than one hundred poets to write, as he said, "real ghazals in English"; his own collection of ghazals, *Call Me Ishmael Tonight*, is forthcoming.

It is not often we can trace change in the poetic landscape, but here we can. Imagine when the Italian sonnet washed up on the shores of English literature: how in the hands of Sir Thomas Wyatt, Edmund Spenser, Philip Sidney, William Shakespeare, John Donne, and many others the form reshaped our literature. It is too soon to say if the ghazal will have a similar effect on American poetry, but if it does literary historians will credit Shahid's pioneering work.

The poet traditionally names himself in the ghazal's signature couplet—the last or *mukta* couplet. The lines that will be inscribed on Shahid's gravestone in Northampton, Massachusetts, come from his most famous ghazal:

They ask me to tell them what *Shahid* means—
Listen: It means "The Beloved" in Persian, "witness" in Arabic.

Shahid was the Beloved of so many people. His witness? A body of poetic work destined to shape the language in a new image of desire.

VIOLATION
Sallie Tisdale

My sister writes to me often these days, though most of our communication is business. Our father died several months ago and she is his executor. Back and forth my brother and sister and I go about annuities and armchairs, social security numbers and thank-you notes, the debris of death. This kind of business, weighing the heft of memory, is never indifferent. The armchairs, the thank-you notes— each leads us back to something else, things of vaguer shape and sharper meaning.

She is angry. She is especially angry about my newest book, and she is also just angry. A river of old pain long staunched slides out easily now, in brief fragments, disjointed rambles, long commentaries. In the dismantling of houses and bank accounts, we dismantle long decades of false courtesy, too.

Almost all this talk, these complaints and sorrows, come to me by e-mail. E-mail is a strange construct for such strong feelings, but these odd missives are what I have. In the midst of her coded address at the top of my screen, I see the time she sent me each note. Often she writes to me after midnight. I imagine her alone at the desk in her dining room in the poised silence of the night, her eyes intent, while her teenage daughter sleeps and the jittery dog shifts at her feet. I imagine the pool of light reflected on the French doors behind her, blanking the empty yard, shading the day's dishes, the dog's bowl, the emptiness. I imagine this, knowing the room, the dog. The night. Knowing her.

She has no idea, I think, how artless her words are, how revealing, and so she sends them into the ether assuming they will never return. They slip in a series of resentful taps onto the screen shimmering before her. That screen, that dim room, seems to be such a private and solitary place. It is exactly this privacy, this solitude, I violate.

She hates my "nasty little book," she writes one night. "You are airing family business in public—like it is the truth, when it is your opinion." Later: "That book really hurt. Those were your thoughts, not necessarily truths." Another day: "I have to live in this town, not you. I don't think a lot should have been said, whether true or not." A few days later: "Don't use my name in a book again without my permission."

She is sixteen months younger than me, truly my little sister, still half a head shorter than me. When she is angry, she moves, and her words roll across a room or the page in one long, unpunctuated injury. They arrive in my study heavy and solid, as all words are. With what she believes to be vapor, she protests the permanence of what I say.

Families are dreadlocked worlds; they tangle together so finely one cannot always get through. It is not easy to have a writer in the family; I understand this. Nor is it easy to be the writer in the family; writers charge themselves with the burden of a family's unspoken story. We can bury it in fiction or parse it into poetry, but form doesn't hide as much as we might like. No matter how plain or muted the source of our material appears to be, the people in our lives know themselves to be material. We who write know them to be, and knowing can make a writer shake with terror. If we aren't careful, it can make us into monsters.

For the memoirist, for those of us doomed to the first person by our cracked talents, the obvious questions of disguising characters and shifting locations shouldn't arise. Our questions are simpler, perhaps harder. The territory of what we have experienced is a restricted one for a writer—but so full, so rich, so slippery and unclear. The intimate and hidden interest me; the ordinary interests me, because it is so strange. I've never wanted to write anything else, never begun to mine the vein of what just happens each day. But being bound to experience as a source of material doesn't save me from betrayal. Writing about myself, I betray my past and everyone in it; I am betrayed in turn by the limit of my memory, my small, human needs.

Like many others, the chorus of my family has several interlocking lines: *How could you?* (whispered as quietly as thought). *That's not fair*, intoned in a young and injured voice. *That's not true.* For how little we talk to each other about what really *did* happen, or about what is happening now, our arguments seem always to be about exactly those things.

When I have allowed myself to consider, even a little, what I do from the point of view of my characters (that is, portions of manuscript, narrative devices, people I love), I am wrapped in worry. Is it true? For a long time, this was my rigid concern. Every word, the tone, an adjective: is it true? But simple truth can be a terrible harm. I began asking: Is it fair? And fair to whom?

I sometimes hesitate even to say I write memoir these days. The current fashion in the genre is for extraordinary detail in a distinctly fictional voice, and what I write is nothing like that. Looking backward, it seems to me that I've written very little about my family— either family, the one I came from or the one I made. I've crept so cautiously around them that several people—including my sister— have complained that I left them out of stories where they belonged. Several readers have assumed I was a recluse of some kind. There are many kinds of recluses, of course. Part of me is a plain coward. Part of me is constrained by notions of duty and integrity. But I am also constrained by my own reserve, which comes partly from the knowledge of exactly how untrue and unfair all writing is. The book is not the life; the writer is not the person. The mask is not the self. So who are the characters?

My sister's anger now is rooted less in my recent book than in the vignettes themselves, and all they imply. My few, carefully shaded words loom large to her: a passing reference to my father drinking his "hair of the dog" each morning, how he irritably waved the carving knife at me during dinner. Clues, hidden—but, like me, she knows where the bodies are buried. There is nothing oblique to her here. My brother, the eldest and most likely to remember what I remember, has never said a word to me about my work. Craven, I haven't asked.

In 1995 I wrote an essay called "The Basement," for the anthology

Home. I sent my sister a copy last year after long consideration, and she has been coming slowly to the boil ever since. In that story, I describe her at age six as "squeamish, chubby, pale and black-haired—she's the one left out, the baby." She is aggrieved over this line; she has been wronged. Every word chosen creates a world. Selection is all and only what writers do; nothing is neutral. Objectivity is the biggest lie a writer tells. My sister's anguish is that of the silenced defendant, listening to the eyewitness tell lies. We all know how unreliable eyewitnesses are, but we listen anyway. We believe—we condemn. "I was *not,*" she says now. *"Not like that."*

The real betrayal of all nonfiction writers is that we forget. Days pile atop each other, knocking things out of the way—and we forget. In the end, it's not our parents' criticisms or our siblings' anger that breaks us, but our own—our own endless punishment of ourselves, the grand and self-absorbed masochism of people who struggle to say it just right. We will inevitably fall into the cracks between every possible solution—every safe place. We fall between cowardice and kindness in our desire to be fair; between courage and cruelty in our need to tell the story. We are betrayed by our own amnesia, by the fact that one can never be sure. I don't believe, though, that our greatest fear is being wrong. We're afraid of speaking at all. We are more afraid of what others will think, whether they will still love us after we speak, than we are of being wrong when we do.

For years, students in my writing classes have asked me the same questions I continue to ask myself.

In an elementary school classroom on the Oregon coast, the small desks shoved to the side in the cool, sweet air of a summer morning—in a basement meeting room of the Unitarian church, the walls covered with cheerful slogans about kindness and honesty—in a humid conference room in upstate New York where the heat lies upon us like wool—I am asked the same questions: "What if I don't remember exactly?" "What if people disagree about what happened?" They have begun to worry about fragments and dangling plotlines, the gaps like broken typewriter teeth in the stories they want to write. A few already have the nagging suspicion that the fragments aren't in the writing, but in themselves. When the conversation gets rolling, there are other questions: "Isn't it okay to make up the details?" "Isn't memoir better with dialogue?" "Why not fill out a little?" Why not?

Nonfiction—not false. But nonfiction is never exactly true—the writer's own perfume lingers on every word, gently and insistently filling the reader's head with one person's singular world, shared by no one else. Easy enough to take what we do remember and fill it out, fill it in, with period detail and nicely timed entrances and inner monologues. This is the stuff of good drama—exactly the kind of drama my students want to write into their own memoirs, the kind they hope to get past me. They admit that they don't really remember things in great detail. The details they add just *feel* true, and therefore must be.

I say no. I always say no. Essay and memoir writers don't mess with plot or chronology, don't invent dialogue or combine characters. One wrestles with words, molds language, atmosphere, tone, suspense— not history. The bones of the story are already there, laid across the table, and to bare it exactly is the writer's role. Nonfiction is supposed to tell the truth—and telling the truth is what people *suppose* us to do. I have been more strict, even puritanical, about this than many writers I admire. (It does not escape me that obsessive concern with facts is an antidote to chaotic childhoods. Finding one's secret turmoil to be the mundane anecdotes of psychology textbooks isn't quite a cure.)

My students are disappointed when I answer their questions. Many clearly not only want me to say yes, they expect me to say it: yes, you can create, invent, conflate; yes, you can fill in the details. They are surprised when I say no.

Instead, I tell my students to write down all they *can* remember, all of it, to put everything in, all the chaff, all the crap, all the garbage. Only then do you find the wheat, the treasures. Wheat and chaff are entwined and must be thrown to the wind in order to separate. Put it all in because you may be wrong about which is which. Figure out your agendas, your vengeance, your grief and desire. Use the confusion and forgetfulness, the sound of crickets in August twilight, the thud of a heavy shoe stopping outside your bedroom door. So goes my lecture, and my students nod and write it down. Wheat, they carefully note. Chaff. Sound of shoes.

Our lives are uncertain, I tell them. Make that uncertainty part of what you tell. Believing that, taking it as my own measure, I am a liar, too.

A few months after my father died, my brother and sister and I were cleaning out his house. My father had lived alone for the last twelve years of his life, shrinking in on his grief at my mother's death and his fifth decade of alcoholism. His house was not dirty, thanks in part to my sister's regular visits, but it was as untouched as a crypt. A layer of dust covered almost everything—my mother's books, his record albums, the cans of soup in the pantry, all gray with a fine, silky silt. His suits were wrapped in dry-cleaning plastic years old, and his bedroom was piled high with mail-order travel and history books still in their cardboard packages, books he couldn't be bothered to refuse. When we began cleaning his house, we were literally dismantling it. I gathered up an armload of books from the position they'd been in as long as I can recall, and I half expected the house to come down around me, its structural integrity suddenly gone.

I bought my siblings lunch at the brew pub where the Sambo's used to be. Perched up on teetery bar stools, we finally began talking about the furniture, the old dusty house, and what to do with it all. On the rare days when we are all together we are in a web made more of the tension between us than the tensile strengths of our bonds. I hold each of our quiet conversations or pleasant hours as though they were ancient papyrus about to dissolve; I hold them with great care because they are so few. I was glad to be there, to be doing this, eating bar food next to the shiny vats of ale in the building that once upon a time had been the orange diner we hung out in after high school. The change from then to now measured the arc of my life. I was more than ready to tackle a project that had begun to seem more like archaeology than grief. Do you want the green chair? one of us asked, and the mood was generous, without rancor. Do you want the kitchen table, the circular saw, the car?

Then this happened. We go back to the house and into the kitchen. I lean over the tiny kitchen table with its uncomfortable wrought-iron chairs, and ask my sister, "Do you want this table?" And she loses her hold all at once, flaring like a gas main, and stomps past me as heavy and hard as my father had stomped, knocking the chairs aside. I feel a strange peace. I am standing at last in the DMZ of my own history, the small neutral territory where enemies meet and no one is right and no one is wrong.

"I already *told* her!" she shouts to my brother. "No one ever listens to me!" Together they run out to the yard. I'm standing in the kitchen door watching through the window as they yell at each other. I can't hear the words. Then my sister peels out of the driveway in her Ford Explorer, almost taking my brother's foot off where he stands, broad-shouldered, hands clenched, watching her go.

How can I tell my sister that I'm not writing about her at all? I'm writing about me—who she is in my life and work is not who she is in hers. The me you see is not the me who sees you. My students ask over and over again. I answer them. But I don't believe what I say. My sister would tell a different story about that day; a story with a different moral, a different wound. How can I blame her? (Do I pretend that I am above blaming? What a comfortable place to be.) Alexander Smith called the essayist "a law unto himself." We've heard it all before—we've *said* it all more than once, to each other, to our angry sources. Grist to the mill.

When it is my turn, I am like a pitcher facing a hard drive straight back to the mound; the ball so assuredly flying away shoots back, with no time to prepare. I have carefully avoided reviews of my new book, delicately stepping past them, whatever they may say. I've learned to shield my writing, when I can, from the work of being published; they are sometimes quite different things. But by accident I come across a brief review in the back of an influential national magazine. A bad review—mean. I flinch, read sideways, don't finish. I call my editor, a friend, other writers. They commiserate—it's really not fair. I have long conversations with my bedroom ceiling: defense, summation, resounding acquittal—and no one to tell. I can't resist, and go back to count up: four or five short reviews in this magazine every week, and for months all are kind, a growing mound of genteel enthusiasm. Except for one review. Except for mine. It is so not fair.

"Writing, I explained, was mainly an attempt to out-argue one's past," wrote Jules Feiffer in his novel about identity, *Ackroyd*. One tried "to present events in such a light that battles lost in life were either won on paper or held to a draw." I don't get to talk back. No one ever does. But I write, and own the truth of every story I write because I write it. In writing it, I make it the truth. Complaints are impotent—competing versions of the story I've already told, and much less likely to be believed.

My friend Maria Dolan has been working for years on an essay about her relationship with her parents during their divorce in her childhood. She has long been stuck somewhere in this tragic, funny memory of her girlhood. This particular block is partly my fault; I once told Maria not to think so much about whether the story was true, but whether it was fair, and now she can't write at all.

"My desire to be fair means I never think it's finished," she tells me. "Since I keep interacting with my parents, I don't want to freeze them in the way they used to be. I struggle to tell the story in a way that reveals them as people who can and will change."

In the last few years, I've begun to tell my students that we can say only so much about the truth, and the facts, vital as they are, are not exactly the point. What we really want to write down are the unprovable facts, the experiences that can never be defined but which demand to be considered, truths which seem to contradict each other and therefore can't be true. One wants what I call the felt truth most of all. How easy to rationalize hurting people. How easy to say that our feelings count more than the facts.

My friend Deborah asks what I'm working on, and I describe this story I am writing now, and she tells me about something that happened when she was eighteen. It was the late 1960s in Los Angeles, and she was about to move into an apartment with her boyfriend. Her father often wrote her long letters of advice, and he did so then, carefully explaining why he thought this was a mistake. But her father also happened to be an editor at the *Los Angeles Times*, and after mailing Deborah her letter, he printed it on the editorial page.

He meant well, she added. She has not quite forgiven him.

Are we foolish enough to think others can rely upon our goodness of heart? Let us trust each other, our hope of redemption, our best use of words. But most of us don't know ourselves well enough to know how good we really are—else we wouldn't be writing so many words about what's happened to us and what we've done, and how it felt and what it might mean in the end.

I remember my childhood as though it were a silent movie with the subtitles removed—made out of black-and-white snapshots and the jerky 8mm whirring in the background. Bend and pick up an Easter egg and hold it up for the camera. Pose on the sled in the soft snow falling like a fog across the lens. The most vivid moments are recorded nowhere but in me, and yet they have the same quality, this mute and almost self-conscious quality of being recorded somehow. I am swimming across a silent lake through a dawn mist in the shadow of a white mountain, at first fearful and then exultant as I've never been before. I am sitting in the crotch of my grandmother's black walnut tree, listening to the ratcheting of the blue jays above me, and there is nothing in the world but blue jays and walnut bark and nothing else needed at all. I am sitting at the dinner table when my father explodes and grabs my sister and begins spanking her, and she is yelling and my mother is crying and I leap from my own chair and shout at him to stop, to leave her alone, to leave us all alone. And the film fades out into black and the rest is unknown—after the lake, after the tree, the shouting, what?

For a long time after I left my parents' home, I was drawn to simple stories—ones with obvious narrative devices and clear morals. That was how I told my own story, explained myself to me—in starkly defined characters with set roles and explicable motives. As time passed, these stories were less satisfying—less true. But the conventions of storytelling have a strong pull. We want neat endings and known winners. We want to answer that question—what happened next, what did it mean?—with all our hearts. We want to answer it so much we make out of the fragments a kind of whole cloth.

Memory is terribly uncertain, made as it is out of callow ignorance and youth. We invert the chronology, combine characters, reorient the compass of our lives, until it is like a vaguely remembered dream with potent and cryptic elements in random order. It is up to the dreamer to decide what each element means. We can only know this moment and try to see it clearly, this moment of remembering those moments then, a world long gone in which someone I used to be used to live. The very best we can hope for is the ability to tell *a* truth, some truth or other, some portion of it, and tell it as close as possible to the moment of its being true, before it changes into something else again.

I find now that a lot of my questions can't be answered at all. Not being able to remember exactly is a story, too. And the story doesn't end, doesn't really have a moral, sometimes the crooks have good hearts and the heroes are corrupt and sometimes I can't tell which is which, and that has to be the story I tell.

Cleaning out my father's closet this spring, I found a grocery bag filled with color slides dating from the 1940s. In among the weddings of strangers and blurry backyard luaus are hundreds of pictures of my brother and my sister and me when we were young that I have never seen before.

We are often together here, if nowhere else. From year to year, in summer and winter, by the riverbank and beside the Christmas tree, we stand beside each other—the kids, only a few years apart, bound together.

My brother leans toward the camera, grinning, perfecting self-confidence. By the age of five, he is a sturdy and seemingly fearless boy. At three, I am hardy and strong. He and I almost look like twins, except he smiles widely and I face the camera with composure—a rugged girl in jeans, giving nothing away. My little sister is pretty and dark with charming bee-stung lips and black hair falling in big, natural curls.

Photographs are false truths, too. My brother's confidence is shallow, brittle. My composure is deeply cracked. And my sister, who is almost dainty, is crying or beginning to cry or has just finishing crying. She sits on our mother's lap, with big eyes, because we have left her behind, forever ditched in the backyard when we want to climb trees. She isn't plump; I was wrong; how could I have remembered it that way? I was wrong and I was right, for this is what I meant by that word—this fragility, this girlish weakness in a world where weakness was lethal. These are the chorus lines beneath the singers. Beneath *it's not fair* and *that's not true* runs this river: *I was strong. You were weak. You walked away and left me behind. You stayed behind, and I survived. You—we're not sure about you yet.*

Most writers approach a new story like a boxer circling the ring—with a certain reluctance to engage and break the spell of *what might be*. To write memoir is to live in *what is*—not only the truth, but the story one is capable of writing and not the great story of which we dream.

I was excited when I began to write "The Basement." The anthology was a good project—a dozen or so writers were each assigned a room; we had only to write a true story about something that happened in that room. I wanted to write about my grandmother's basement, where we spent a lot of time as children. I could revisit that world where my brother and sister and I were together, a gang of three. I would write about driving to Grandma's house in the old station wagon, how we would run through the living room and down the basement stairs and play all day long in a child-driven world while our boring relatives visited upstairs. I began there, and then I was paralyzed for two months. I could write nothing at all. I played solitaire for hours, read mysteries, took naps.

Toward the end of my writing workshops, when everyone's guard is down and little secrets have slipped out, when the room is as safe as rooms of nascent writers can be, I sometimes ask students to fill in the blanks of this sentence: "I can't write about _____ because _____." I give them only a few minutes, time for a few words.

Then I make two columns on the blackboard. On the left, I list the first words they wrote: *A car accident. Sex. Parents' divorce. A crime I committed.* This is hard for the students, to say out loud what can't be written. Then, on the right, I list the reasons: *I feel guilty. Feelings will get hurt. It's embarrassing. No one cares.*

Finally, I erase the column on the left—the events, the memories, the ideas. The stories. All that matters is the reasons. Those are the stories—this is what you write: how it feels to commit a crime, to be afraid, to not know how it ends. This is what all good stories are about. Start there, I tell them. Start there.

I sank for two months into the lassitude of unspent words until I started to ask myself that question. "I can't write about Grandma's basement because—" Because—Because. Because I was so lonely there it was as though I'd already died. Because childhood is a dangerous place. Because we were ordered into that basement and it seemed to me that we might never be allowed to come out, that the whole world was filled with sunlight I would never see. Because I hated my grandmother, and you are not allowed to hate your grandmother. Right before me like a ghost in the room was that poor little girl with her solemn face and her jeans and dirty T-shirt—right before me stood that poor thing who is not me and has not been me for a long, long time, and I started writing like crazy.

So I wrote the truth no one but me knows and no one but me can tell. I rewrote history: down, down to the basement we go in the story, again and again, and at the end of the story, up I come, and fly away. That is the moral of my true story, that I did fly away, on wings light as the summer, wings I made out of words like these.

My friend Maria says she is unwilling to freeze her parents in their mutual past. I tell her that the story will also freeze her, in its telling. We fear getting stuck with the claims we make, with any day's untidy thoughts. It isn't just the people who live on; the story also lives on, its narrator lives on—forever the same, saying the same things, the writer's ghost. When I look over books and essays I've written, they were clearly written by someone else. I could not have written these stories—that is not my point of view, those are not my beliefs, that is not my voice. It is not me, they are not true, and it is not fair.

One of the few things I wrote about my father in the new book is that my mother brought him a Bloody Mary in the morning. It was part of her ritual day, and meant to say as much about her as him. What I didn't say, what my sister called family business, was known by the whole small town: his decades of drunkenness, just keeping his job, sleeping much of the rest of the day away, the sudden snapping of temper like a hurt dog, the kind of drunkenness that makes morning such a trial my mother had to bring him a drink while he still lay beneath the covers, and after he'd taken it he'd totter slowly into the kitchen where we were eating our Frosted Flakes and reach behind me into the cupboard to pull out the whiskey and pour himself a neat two fingers, his hair uncombed and his crumpled pajamas sour with the night, and then shuffle back, like an old, old man, to dress for the day.

I didn't write that. I didn't use the bare words. I told myself it was tangential to the story. I told myself there were too many musty confessions of alcoholic childhoods out there, it was a too-familiar territory. In fact, I could see my brother's face, my sister's face, wanting it not to be true. Most of all, I could see the composed face of that plain little girl, who was such a tough cookie and loved her daddy after all.

"Please don't use my name without my permission again," my sister adds, late at night, alone in her room. And the *please* makes my heart flip over. It is so plaintive. But I don't stop. I don't have the right to tell these stories. How could I have the right to the lives of others, to their former selves and hard losses? These stories are like slamming doors. No right to speak unprovable truths. Life's not fair. It's all so not fair.

LITTLE BROWN SHACK
GARY GREENBERG

S ome parental odysseys originate in strange and tawdry circumstances, and mine is one of them. It begins on a cold morning
in early March. My wife, Susan, and I are walking through the slushy
driveway of the Little Brown Shack, a ramshackle roadhouse hard by
the interstate. The air outside is heavy with the exhaust of idling
trucks, and inside it's little better: a thick roux of fry grease and
cigarette smoke. We're braving all these foul atmospherics because
we're on a mission. We're here to talk a woman into giving us her just-
born son.

It's more on the up-and-up than it sounds. Social workers will be
overseeing these negotiations. Members of their profession have been
protecting the desperate from the unscrupulous, facilitating what they
like to call family building since the mid-nineteenth century, when
states, hoping to straighten out the knotty legal problems arising when
children were unrelated to their parents by blood, first took upon
themselves the regulation of the baby trade. Lawmakers found ways to
manufacture blood ties, to provide adoptive parents with clear title to
their children (and children clear claim to their inheritances), to
expunge the birth parents from the historical record, to create a
genealogy whose fiction was a secret. Only the social workers would
know everything: birth parents, adoptive parents, the reasons the child
was given up and that certain parents were chosen over certain others
to receive it—a public trust that demanded they become experts in
figuring out who would be fit to bring up a baby, that they develop an
algorithm of difficult questions to winnow the applicants.

Questions that, I must admit, we never answered. The social worker
assigned to do our home study was so intimidated by our advanced

degrees and even more advanced ages and our totally self-actualized lives that she just blurted it out in our first meeting—"I'm looking over your application and I just wanted to say that you're obviously qualified, but we have to go through these interviews anyway"— and proceeded to do us a whale of a professional courtesy: immunity from the interrogation about motives and intentions, about how we would raise and discipline a child, about our sex lives and the ghosts of our own childhoods. Three easy interviews and fifteen hundred dollars later, by the power vested in her by the State of Connecticut, her agency bestowed upon us a license to be parents. We never got the wallet copy.

So we are officially sanctioned to be sitting here in the Little Brown Shack, among the truck drivers and bustling waitresses with their perms and little aprons, watching the door for the woman the social workers have been telling us about for the last ten days. And here she is—a slight blonde in jeans crowded between two middle-aged, over-weight matrons, standing hesitantly in the entry, nervous pale eyes looking for us, maybe wanting to catch a glance before we know she's there, to size us up before we can put on the good-parent act.

Which is exactly the same thing that we are doing to her. Because you could be sitting in your hot tub on a Friday afternoon, leaning back into a friendly cannabis fog, looking out the window and counting your blessings, literally enumerating them—the peace and quiet of the house you built in this forested sanctuary with your own hands, the comfort of a good marriage to a better woman, the ease of an interesting and not terribly demanding job, the freedom to be here while the rest of the world toils away, a life, in short, worth living— and the next thing you know you could be on the phone listening to a social worker delivering incomprehensible facts with practiced cool-ness—a baby boy and a mother gone, an incubator, an Apgar this and a gestational that—and asking questions about what you want to do, questions that must be answered indecently soon, and even as you tell her you have to wait for your wife to get home, you know that this is only stalling because she won't know either. And you could realize that it doesn't matter, because the view through the window has been replaced by a stained-glass tableau: an infant lying in the harsh light of a hospital room, alone in a crib, his arms reaching up, and you feel them around your neck. All of this could happen and no matter how long you've been waiting for it, no matter how strongly you feel his pull, you will still really want to know what you are getting yourself into. I mean, you wouldn't want to go off into parenthood half cocked.

You fix your stare on the woman. You take in her bright nylon jacket with the truck-repair-shop logo, her country-and-western good looks. You see the fear painted on her china-doll face. But you want to get a closer view, maybe count her teeth or read her palm, crack her open and get at her source code. Because you have to make a decision and she is all you have to go by. And even if you're a psychotherapist and spend your days working the premise of the human being's infinite malleability, you are searching for your still provisional son in his mother's DNA. Which means, you realize as she moves toward the table, that you are still shopping.

Because this is a commercial transaction. Money is changing hands, a lot of it. I don't know where it is all going. I've asked the social workers about this, and they've told me some things that I don't quite grasp: counseling for the birth mother, paperwork, legal fees, rent, salaries (like they'd never been asked, like nonprofit status and trafficking in desperate dreams provide double indemnity against such probing). Of course, the free market rules here as everywhere: The price comes down if you want to adopt a "hard-to-place" child— sick or crippled or multiracial or just plain too old to satisfy the desire for a baby. We've gone down the list and specified our options: this race or illness or deformity or age or gender preferable, that one not. We've tried, that is, to hedge our twenty-five-thousand-dollar bet. So who could blame us now for our caveat emptoring?

Especially with what we already know—and don't know—about this boy and his mother. After I hung up the phone, I realized I'd failed to find out much of anything at all. Was he okay? All his fingers and toes? Why didn't she want him? What was *she* like? And for a moment, I considered not telling Susan about the phone call. I could just pretend it had never happened. Or I could spin it hard the wrong way: "The agency called with a kid, he's got some serious problems, but if you really want to go ahead . . ." I was deciding to just play it cool, let her come in and get settled and then, in the chatter of the day's recounting, let it slip out in an oh-and-by-the-way, when I heard her car, and even though it was February, I was out in a bound, dripping naked on the porch. "They called. There's a kid, born yesterday. A boy. Seven weeks premature. He'll be in the hospital for a month. We'd have to be able to visit him in the hospital lots, if not every day. They want to know if we want to be considered by the birth mother."

That's how it works in these supply-side days. No longer are children whisked away from their birth mothers by nuns, who pick the parents who have risen to the top of the list by dint of time or connections or well-timed contributions. Instead, an adoption agency assembles dossiers of the bidding parents, little ad campaigns in a manila folder, complete with photos of you and your dog and flowers, and a heartfelt and completely honest "Dear Birth Mother" letter in which you tell her all the reasons you'd be the perfect parents for her unborn child, and the woman—picture her young and in her maternity clothes, photos and letters spread out on her bed—chooses who will get the child kicking in her belly. In the seven months during which we'd been actively listed, we'd been rejected by three of these women, and we were beginning to think we'd have to adopt some new tactics, maybe make a video with some real production values.

Susan followed me into the house. "What else do you know?" she finally asked.

"Not much. The mother smoked while she was pregnant. She didn't tell anyone about it. She's thirty. She has two other kids. She's on welfare."

"The other kids didn't know?"

"I guess not."

"He's healthy?"

"I guess."

"Then why's he in the hospital for a month?"

"I don't know."

"And what hospital?"

"I don't know. I can call and find out."

"I hear you," said the social worker on the phone, "and I know you're wanting to know more. But we just don't have any more information than that."

"Well, can I call the hospital and find out more?"

"No. All the information has to go through their social worker to us and then we relay it to you."

"Well, I suppose if we have more questions over the weekend, someone will be on call to talk to us."

"I'm afraid not. If you're really overwhelmed and needing to talk, you can call the service and someone will get back to you. But that person won't know any more than we do now."

"Okay. But can you at least tell me what hospital he's in?"

Now, I don't really believe in all that universe-is-your-friend, it-all-happens-for-a-reason woo-woo jive. (And if I did, I'd want to know why I had to go on the open market to get a kid, couldn't have one like everyone else, by making love with my wife. Why, I would ask, had we had to suffer six or seven—but who's counting?—miscarriages, what Great Plan was that?) Still, I'd be lying if I didn't tell you the hair on my arms stood straight up when she named the hospital in which I was born.

But my wife, the stalwart, the one who had insisted and cajoled and looked on the bright side through all the treatments and procedures, the poking and the bleeding, who, when all her considerable hope was finally gone, had ridden the other horn of the adoption dilemma, offering a counter to my every point about why this was not a good idea, and who had never, not for a moment, indulged in my own whining pessimism, not even when we spent the money earmarked for adoption on a car—Susan wasn't feeling plugged into the great unity of it all. "How much did you say he weighed?"

"Three and a half pounds."

"That doesn't sound like much."

"Kids are born like this all the time now."

"She smoked."

"My mother smoked."

"What if he's sick, what if he doesn't . . ."

"He'll be fine."

The true sign of long marriage may be when you realize that you have unwittingly divided the labor of ambivalence. For years, she had carried the light and the hope and I the dark and the fear, and now, suddenly, after the real thing came into view for the first time, into the light of a stained-glass epiphany, the burdens were reversed.

So we threw our hats in the ring, and now we are sitting here talking to this woman. The social workers introduce us; we already know each other's first names (and I'll call her Carrie here), and they keep it that way, presumably so we can't track each other down if one of us changes our mind. She takes off her jacket. She's wearing a Connecticut State Police sweatshirt.

The waitress arrives. The social workers and Susan order tea, Carrie gets coffee. Ten days postpartum, she can't weigh more than ninety-five pounds. I want to tell her that breakfast is on me and go ahead and eat hearty, but then I wonder if that's appropriate. After all, great care has been put into arranging this tableau. The half anonymity. The neutral setting. The state-licensed third parties. Their gentle arm-twisting helping her to see for herself (not that they had any opinion, of course) that it's really the best thing for all concerned, so that when she finally got in the social worker's car and set out for the Little Brown Shack, it was of her own free will. So much care has gone into making this scene precisely not what it was that it would be a shame to wreck it by offering even this minor bribe, or for that matter by reaching across the table and picking her up by her State Police sweatshirt and yelling, "Give me your fucking baby!"

I order an English muffin and a decaf, and after the waitress leaves, I fidget with my silverware and say something about the Shack bringing back memories of when I lived just across the road, but stop short of the memory itself—of the brief and unhappy flirtation with condo living that came on the heels of living in a cabin I'd built on my grandfather's farm, three years of the postapocalyptic lifestyle brought to a sudden end when a family coup relieved my grandfather of his deed and me of my home, and I fled like a refugee to my future ex-wife's town house—stop right in the middle of a sentence when I remember that I wanted to kill the cousin who came to tell me that I was homeless, that I looked over his shoulder to my loaded shotgun in the corner and for a brief, clear moment contemplated the deed, the logistics of hiding his car, of burying him. I stop short now as I did then, because this is an audition, not the place to impress a stranger with my colorful past and my penchant for confessions about the blackness of my heart.

I look at the social workers. One of them looks like she has just had some terrible news. Her eyes are sunk in her head, her chin on her chest as she sits inert and unresponsive, and I think she is going to break down and sob, or simply stop breathing, at any second. But the other, Lil, the head of the agency, has an idea. "Carrie, I thought you might tell Susan and Gary why you chose them."

Of course! They brought the icebreakers. They think of everything.

Except this. I know what we put in that manila folder: a picture of Susan and me sitting on the porch trying to look just exactly happy enough to love a kid but not too happy to need one; an interior scene of our light, airy house, full of warmth and good feeling, but just missing that one thing; a letter, carefully modulated in tone ("don't make it too sophisticated," the social workers said), neither desperate nor smug about how we would of course be the best parents in the world for your little bundle of joy. I know what we put in, and I know what we didn't put in, just how cleverly we committed and omitted our way into position, and I'm sure I don't want to catch my own sales pitch coming back at me from its life-bedraggled target.

Because the truth is, the car was my idea.

We decided, finally decided, on our fifth wedding anniversary, sitting in the same spot where we were married, a promontory looking out over a river valley. While the hawks rode the thermals out of the ravine and wheeled away into the fall air, we resolved to suffer this blow together, to be humble in the face of what we could not control, to live out our days without children, and really there are far, far worse things. Like illness and poverty and marital strife. Like giving up all your freedom and flexibility and having to hustle for a buck and save for college and go to Little League games and socialize with other parents and finally buy the whole boatload of crap that you've been successfully avoiding all your life.

I did need a car, really. My fleet—a '62 Ford and a '66 VW and a rusted-out pickup truck—wasn't getting any younger and cold mornings were coming. Approaching forty, I had lost the desire to lie under a car, poke around in its nether parts and wipe rust out of my eyes. So it seemed like fate when I just happened to be looking at the car ads in the very next morning's paper and saw a nine-year-old Audi, low miles, all the mod cons, a steal at five thousand dollars. Which we had and now could be spent, not only because I wouldn't be giving it to an adoption agency, but also because I had no more need to worry about money. After all, I was joining the ranks of the child-free.

When I brought the car home, it sat in the driveway, four doors of gray remonstrance. I even tried to sell it right away, but then the transmission case on the Falcon broke, and the VW didn't have heat, and salt and icy slush sprayed through the floor and bathed my crotch every time I drove the pickup through a puddle. So slowly I got used to the heated seats and reliable brakes and the quiet so deep you could carry on a normal conversation as you drove. I even learned to look at it as a car and not the thing that I bought with the baby money.

That's how bad infertility will flick with your head. It turns a routine case of buyer's remorse—that most banal affliction of affluence, the bad faith of buying and selling masquerading as the conviction that you bought the wrong thing—into heavy symbolism. Because you'd known since the beginning, when you threw away the pills and the rubbers, that you just weren't sure. And since the beginning came pretty late—you were thirty-five when you were first capable of forming even the glimmer of the thought, you'd been living in a state of grief most of your life, you really just wanted to figure out a way to go back to the autistic bliss of your cabin in the woods— you'd gathered at least one piece of wisdom: that all the agonizing in the world over pros and cons would not bring an answer into clear view. Because one thing was obvious: children will ruin your life. (Later on, when we told other parents we'd joined their ranks, they often rolled their eyes and said, "Well, your life is over now," commiseration like some kind of secret handshake. And it wasn't just the interrupted sleep, the enforced celibacy, the endless round of feeding and burping and wiping and worrying, that made them say so. It was the way that freedom had deserted them and the pursuit of happiness, to the extent that it hinged on autonomy and self-realization and getting in the car on a minute's notice to go to a movie or to Mexico, had come to a crashing halt.) Presumably, a new life arises from the ashes, in which the losses won't mean so much, and you'll look back on all that independence as hardly worth the candle. Best not to think too hard on this, though, because the bet is too big for a sane person to take. Best to let biology trump psychology, introduce Mr. Sperm to Ms. Egg, take the ride wherever it goes and don't look back.

But sometimes biology trumps itself. Susan got pregnant the first month out, six years before we bought the car. She was visiting an out-of-town friend. Just before leaving, she'd seen a gynecologist, figuring that if she was going to try for this, she ought to make sure all was well with her. He called with news about this "very big coincidence." She'd arrived for her exam pregnant. But he was ordering a blood test.

"Is there a problem?"

"No, it's just that with an older patient we want to be sure. No need to worry."

So began our pilgrimage to the land of the elderly primigravida, which is what the medical texts call a woman of a certain age pregnant for the first time, the daily bloodletting and breath-bated waiting to find out if the levels had doubled overnight, if the embryo was making its requisite demands on the hormone factories. This first time, Susan got into the thousands before the numbers trailed off. But it was, the doctor told us, still not such bad news. Happens all the time, usually without a woman even knowing it. No need to worry.

And we didn't, at least not for another year or so, after a succession of regular periods sent us to books and friends for advice. So we learned about basal thermometers and in-home ovulation kits, about cervical mucus and breast tenderness and urinary prolactin—all the preparatory swellings and flowings that generally have the decency to pass unremarked. And we learned to fuck on command, to fuck for God and country, to fuck without desire, to fuck because a drop of piss turned blue, to fuck the way you sometimes go to work—because you have to if you want to get what you want.

And that's not all you have to do.

There are all sorts of theories about why women don't get pregnant or stay that way once they do. And to see which one might fit your particular case, doctors will happily inflict on you the best that medical science has to offer—biopsies and laparoscopies and hysterosalpingograms, and other ways of extending the reach of fingers and eyes into the darkness of the human body. And you will get used to it, to all the things they do to your wife, to the puniness of your own sympathy in the face of her stoical submission. After all, if you can get used to fucking on command, you can get used to anything.

Well, almost anything. I never did get used to handing over a cup of freshly produced semen to the medical lab. You'd think this wouldn't be so bad, but I am firmly of the belief that onanism is one of those minor vices like watching TV or playing computer games: no use denying you do it, but most fun when kept to yourself.

And no fun at all when Susan's doctor called with the results. When he first asked if I'd ever had a sperm count done, I said no and added, "But potency runs in my family." I thought it was a funny line, a little in-joke for those of us educated enough to understand how natural selection works.

The doctor did not laugh, but I know he heard me because he used my joke to break the news. "It seems that the family legacy has skipped you," he said, and I wondered if this somehow satisfied him. A sperm count of seventeen million, he told me, and anything under twenty is considered low. Not sterile, he said, but still a cause for concern, especially given how hard it is for her to stay pregnant. "This may be the problem," he concluded.

"But she gets pregnant."

"Yes, but not as easily as you would like. And defective sperm can make a defective embryo. You need to go see a urologist."

Suddenly I was scrambling for my maleness. When the *New York Times* published a story the next week about the drop in sperm count in industrialized societies (one that made my seventeen million look much closer to adequate), I wanted to call the gynecologist and read it to him.

Until I talked to my urologist. "Small testicles," he said. "You have small testicles."

You'd think that would have been something I'd have already known. I wanted proof. I wanted to see his, cup them and roll them around between my fingers as he had mine, get out the caliper and plot the numbers and send them to the *Times* and ask them about average testicle size in industrial societies. I wanted to call my wife, my ex-wife, my ex-lovers and ask: Did you know and want to spare me? Or is this just something that urologists, with their ball-practiced hands, can assay with such certainty? I wanted, as he rambled on about sperm production and viruses and really everything else is quite normal, for it not to be true. I wanted to disappear into the shame of my newly diminished gonads.

My wife never, not once, said the obvious thing: "Well, we've been going along here thinking it was me. I've been prodded and snipped and stared at by men in search of my flaws; I've cramped and spotted and bled out my hope, hated myself for not being able to capture these little sparks of life, wept over their not wanting me enough to stick around. All that sorrow and rejection and self-recrimination, and it turns out it might have been you all along!" That's probably what I would have said. Instead she told me not to worry. She volunteered to help me with future sperm tests (for such there would be, after a course of antibiotics taken on the possibility that infection impaired my too necessary efficiency). And she told me she had no idea what the urologist was talking about.

Because in the country of infertility, blame lurks around every corner. Here you are, and you've always been able to set nose to grindstone and do whatever you set your mind to, just like your parents said you could, and the things you haven't done you've been able to say you decided not to do. Life has never just stopped you stone cold before, certainly not with this kind of bare, binary predicament: one of you must be responsible. But you avoid recrimination like the plague, because you are on a desert island with this person and you must stay true to one another or you will surely not survive.

And at some point, you have to begin to give up. The doctors won't tell you this. They'll offer you another test, maybe the one where she goes into the office just after you've had sex so they can inspect the sperm's progress, see what happens next. They'll tell you about intrauterine insemination, in which you go in bright and early on the day that the test kit says is the right one, get friendly once again with a sterile cup and hand it to the doctor, who puts it right into a centrifuge that separates the sperm from the spooge, gets the pure stuff into a syringe, injects it directly into her uterus, an affirmative action plan for the sperm-disadvantaged. They'll send you to a university hospital, where important doctors with fresh-faced residents in tow will perform their lecture on your wife's body, who will nod and cluck and promise to get to the bottom of things and then never even call you on the phone to let you know that they haven't the slightest idea why you can't have a baby, will make you call and leave five decreasingly polite messages on their answering machine, until a nurse finally plays the tape to a doctor, shames him into calling you back and telling you the truth. They'll remind you about in vitro fertilization, a drop of you and a drop of her in a petri dish, and when you recall for them that she can't seem to hold onto embryos, they'll give you the names of lawyers who round up women willing to be implanted with the zygote, willing to rent out the space in their wombs, to court stretch marks and varicose veins and labor pains and episiotomies, who will sign legal documents that swear this is not white slavery. But they won't tell you, unless you ask, that if you divide the cases of infertility caused by the conditions they can look for by the all the cases in the world, you come up with a small fraction, maybe one fourth. They won't tell you, that is, that medicine searches for the cause of infertility in the same way that the proverbial man who has lost his keys searches for them: under the streetlamp, even if he lost them elsewhere, because that's where the light is.

Not that that's their job. Their job is to work a miracle, to make a baby where there was none. Sometimes they find the kind of malfunction—the hormone that doesn't get delivered to the uterine wall in quite enough quantity to create a foothold for the fetus, or the scarring that prevents ovulation, or the faulty valves in the spermatic vein that impair the production of sperm—that they can fix. Sometimes they succeed, and in return for all the time and money and indignity, for surgical and pharmaceutical risks, for turning yourselves into a science project, you get a baby. And no one who has held his own tiny child in his own hands, who has felt an infant's head against his chest, a warm shot of ambrosia penetrating through gristle and rib, right to the heart—no one will deny that it was all worth it (although you might always grieve over having had to make the calculation).

And one day, another cold February day three years after the first miscarriage and four years before the meeting at the Shack, the phone rings and it's the doctor's office and you're standing on top of the house you are building with redemptive fury—proving that you can bring something into being—and scrawling the latest lab results and doctor's orders on a two-by-six with a carpenter's pencil. The numbers aren't good, the drugs are strong, and you can't wait to nail that lumber into a wall, bury it under Sheetrock and paint. A few days later, on a Saturday morning, you find your wife on the border of refusal, almost unable to drive to the lab for another blood test, and yourself unable to push her out the door. You both know, after all, that the levels are either going up or they're not, and there is nothing to be done either way. The recalcitrance in your bodies tips you off to the decision that you've made without knowing it. That you are done. That there will be no jerking off in the doctor's bathroom, no more lying on cold tables under harsh lights pretending to be brave, no more trips to the lab or needles to the cervix, no more fucking on command, no more, no more.

We hadn't put any of this in the folder that Carrie read. We didn't tell her that the last few times Susan got pregnant, we were so fully sickened at having to care about something that would inevitably disappoint that we skipped the doctor and just waited to see if she would swell up with child or bleed. We'd left out the crying and the fist-shaking rage and the panic that set in as the days passed and the periods came and we stopped counting the miscarriages. We'd left out the way that it became impossible to distinguish between wanting a child and not wanting to be foiled by something so arbitrary, the way that life without a child began to gather its own steam and relief began to mix in with anguish—relief at not having to make room in hearts that time and circumstance were closing, or at least making less supple.

"We're living like retired people," I said one day to Susan.

And most of all we'd left out what happened when the conversation shifted from having a baby to getting a baby.

Not long after we finished the house, we ordered a catalog from an agency that handled foreign adoptions. It was arranged by country. You could get a baby from Peru or Bolivia or Colombia or Romania or Russia or China or Nepal. The catalog listed the rules and regulations and restrictions in all these places—where various lifestyle misfits— homosexuals, single women, unmarried couples, people over forty, Bible thumpers, atheists—might find themselves in or out of favor. The kind of children available in each country—infants, toddlers, older kids. And prices—Nepal was the cheapest by far, but, the catalog warned, all of these prices were strictly à la carte, and some of the items were infinitely vulnerable to the vagaries of the particular marketplace you chose. You had to pay your way there, stay in a hotel while the third-world bureaucracy bumped along, and contend with all those functionaries with their rubber stamps and outstretched palms. Well, they didn't say that exactly, but the implication was clear—an indeterminate amount of baksheesh as well as patience, more in some places, less in others, would be required.

On a sultry summer day, we went to a meeting at the agency's offices in suburban Boston, We sat in the air-conditioned conference room and drank tea out of Styrofoam cups with forty or fifty other people and learned all about how you get a baby from a far-off land, about the lawyers here and there, the chartered airplanes, the fantastic tourist opportunities while you wait, the importance of bringing a piece of the child's homeland back so that she will have a memento of

her roots (which I found confusing. I mean, didn't all this business
hinge on a rootless view, on nurture over nature every time?), the
emigration papers, the immigration papers (they even handed out a
form from the Immigration and Naturalization Service, suggesting
that we get started even if we hadn't yet decided, since this form held
the key to bringing the child into the country and could take forever to
get processed), the adoption papers, the payment plan. I stopped
listening for long stretches, looked around the room at the gathered
fertility-challenged—all white, seemingly affluent, middle-aged—and
wondered for what loss they were seeking consolation. I watched out
the window as a thunderstorm gathered in the east, listened to it
crackle over the building and pull away, saw the sky clear and the
afternoon sun kindle the glass towers of downtown Boston, all prelude
to a brilliant rainbow. The facilitator directed everyone's attention to
the window. It was an omen, she said. They turned and their eyes went
dewy. They really wanted and they really believed.

When she announced—just after a glowing couple brought in their
adorable toddler in patent leather and lace, imported from China (the
toddler, that is)—that there just happened to be baby triplets available
today in Korea, there was a stir of laughter in the room, and I was sure
that someone was going to put his money where his mouth was, that
someone there (maybe more than one someone; was that competi-
tiveness lurking behind the laughter? would there be an auction?) was
going to prove to be more than a spectator. But not me. I just couldn't
imagine myself doing any of this—trekking to some unknown place to
get handed a baby plucked randomly from an orphanage, spending
my first night as a father at the Holiday Inn, changing diapers in front
of CNN while waiting for an exit visa, buying a sombrero or a floppy-
eared Himalayan wool hat for that future talk, the one where we
explain why her skin is a different color or her eyes a different shape,
struggling to keep an infant whom we hardly know happy and quiet
on the eighteen-hour flight home, the hairy Customs eyeball on our
papers, our baby, our obvious incompetence.

Or was it just adoption—abroad or at home—that I couldn't
imagine? Not just the yuppie robber-baron aspects, but also the

apparent lunacy of the thing itself, courting disaster by taking on a stranger's legacy. What would happen when a baby whose face didn't reflect mine or my wife's or the people whose faces ours reflected woke me out of deep sleep at 2 A.M.? Would I be able to resist the urge to put the intruder outside? Would he or she ever be my own?

The contemplation of adoption awakened some latent tribal impulse in me, the primordial instinct to preserve and protect my own and repudiate the rest. Freud tagged this as one of the leading follies of civilization—the narcissism of minor differences, the belief that I am better than you because I have this hooking Jewish nose instead of that high Aryan brow. But this wasn't all just the stuff of ancient bloodshed. Medical science tells us that we are literally in our progeny, in the genes we pass along. And we had good genes, Susan and I. Success genes. Lawyer and doctor genes; whose could be as good? Suddenly I was a racialist, a genetic determinist, hewing to folly with bone-deep conviction, instantly forgetting the cancer, deafness, retardation, suicide, insanity, malfeasance, and seemingly innate cruelty that ran so deep in my own accomplished family.

Or maybe I just didn't want a kid badly enough to suspend disbelief and judgment.

The catalog sat in a basket, slowly covered over by mail and magazines. We got on with our lives, each childless day a trial run for the rest of our lives, no day glorious or awful enough to move us decisively one way or another, every action freighted with life-or-life uncertainty. We got a puppy. When I drove it home and it put its head in my lap, shaking in fear, and I reached down to pet it; when it whined all night and I stuck my foot out of bed and kicked its kennel; when we had to figure out what to do with it if we wanted to go out for the day—we read all these events like tea leaves.

We went to another meeting, this time at a Jewish agency that had good connections in Eastern Europe. This was Susan's idea. She thought that my horror of otherness might be overcome by the promise of a child who came from my own ancestral homeland—descended, perhaps, from the very same Cossacks who chased my forebears all the way to America.

The social worker wore her hair in a black bun pulled back so tightly that it narrowed her eyes. She fidgeted with her long painted fingernails as she described her agency's program in her Brooklyn accent. She showed us pictures of happy couples bringing their babies home. She showed us the offices where we would be grilled for the home study. She leaned across her desk and said, "I want you to know that here we don't believe that people ought to adopt because they want to help a child, to rescue a kid from poverty or an orphanage. It's not for the child's benefit. That's just not a healthy reason. The only good reason to adopt is for yourselves. You want to adopt to make yourself happier? That's the kind of couple we want."

And speaking of enlightened self-interest, the social worker also happened to know of a lawyer who could advise us on how to strike a deal with a sister or a friend, or, failing that, who could help us round up a woman willing to be implanted with our own little zygote, willing to court complications, to sign legal documents that promise to hand the baby over right away and never look back. We hadn't put this in the file either: that we visited this lawyer, that we actually approached someone, an acquaintance, a sweet and strapping young woman, to ask us if she'd do us this big favor.

She was smarter than we were. She just said no.

It wasn't long after that that we climbed our wedding hill and made our decision. We held each other and talked about making closer relationships with nieces and nephews and all the other compensations we could find or invent. We resolved to put our feet firmly in one world, to close the door on the other one, to end the torture of decisions reversed by the minute. We bought the car and lived our lives and tried to stop the questions in their tracks when we walked by an infant in a stroller.

The next spring, Susan said to me, "Look, I just don't think I can live with this. What if I get old and look back and wish we'd done something different? I'd never forgive myself. I realized the other day that if I were alone, if it was just me, I'd do it. I'd adopt. And I'm afraid of what that means about us. I might come to see you as standing in my way."

When you're in your second marriage, and you've chucked it all (including the first marriage) to be there, and you're sure that your wife can stand anything—sure in part because she has already withstood so much—and you've long ago forgotten the fact that there was a time when you didn't even know each other, didn't share a breakfast table, it doesn't really matter how self-absorbed you are. You'll take some notice of words like these.

And of this. Later that same week, at my office's staff meeting, a colleague of mine was describing a case of hers, which involved a Catholic-school girl who had gotten pregnant and had decided to give her child up for adoption. The discussion was supposed to be therapist talk about how to handle the conflict in the family, but I could only pay attention to my ankles, to the strange energy that was creeping up my legs, not unlike the vertiginous buzz that seems equally likely to fling you off the precipice as keep you safely away from the edge, that made me want to leap up and say, "Wait a minute! What about the baby? Who's getting the baby?" But it seemed unprofessional. So I cornered her after the meeting and asked with all the nonchalance I could force. "Oh, I guess they've made arrangements with an agency," she said.

I was shocked at the soreness of my temptation, the vividness of my fantasy of letting myself into her office, rifling her files, getting the information, arranging a coincidence. I was appalled at my acquisitiveness. And most of all, I was overrun by the breathtaking purity of my desire.

So we signed up with an agency. Not the Boston one or the Jewish one, but a little agency in El Paso. Because I had one condition: we had to adopt a newborn. I didn't want to defy both nature and nurture, compounding the genetic crapshoot with an environmental one. Who knew what foster care or orphanage horror was in store for a baby while he or she awaited the bureaucrats? But most foreign governments require that children be at least three months old, often much older, before they can be exported. And most healthy newborns, the scarcest commodity in this very hot market, go to people with deeper pockets than ours, or who have more time to wait than we did—we had by then joined the ranks of the middle-aged. But in El Paso, evidently, young Mexican women regularly have children they cannot keep, and who are Americans by virtue of their birthplace—which means there are no foreign rules to abide by or palms to grease. For us it was the best of both worlds, for the children were still foreign in one important respect: they were not white. Our willingness to have a brown baby was fostered more by the fact that my brother was married to a Nuyorican and Susan's brother to a Peruvian—unions which had already given our families six more or less brown babies— than by any multiculti commitments. But there was no doubt that it gave us a leg up on the competition.

We didn't put this in our folder either—that our shrewd strategizing had led us to expect a little brown girl. That she was going to be named Lily, that we were already planning our regular root-seeking trips to Mexico. That we had turned on a dime one day when we realized that Texas might as well be a foreign country, decided to use the same agency that had done our home study (a license granted in Connecticut is recognized in Texas, so we were using a local agency to vet us for the obvious logistical reason) for the adoption itself. That we were still expecting a Hispanic girl—a Puerto Rican child from Hartford, we imagined—when the agency called with the news about a little white boy lying in an incubator in the hospital where I was born. That we had spent the next weekend reading about premature babies, learning about gestational age and critical birth weights, about ventilators and antibiotics, about emotional and social problems of premature children, trying to parlay our little bit of knowledge into some kind of certainty, that we crunched the numbers—fifteen hundred grams, thirty weeks—added up the factors, and decided to make a bid. That we had waited all week to hear something back, that when Susan called on Thursday to ask me to make dinner and I only asked her where the tomato sauce was, she started crying. That when the agency called the next day to say that the birth mother wanted to meet us (but not, of course, until Monday, when the social workers came back to work), the weekend loomed large and cruel in front of us, and we blamed her for leaving us to roast on this spit. We left all of that out.

Omissions that may or may not have anything to do with why Carrie is right now sharing this round table with us and the social workers, our family-building enterprise squarely in her delicate, pale hands.

She answers the social worker's question. "I liked the fact that you were a teacher and you were a psychologist," she says, looking vaguely in Susan's and then my direction. "I thought it would mean that if there were problems, you could handle them." It is really a good thing that I didn't tell her about wanting to shoot my cousin.

I take my first good look at her. She isn't just thin, she's gaunt, emaciated, worn beyond tired. There are dark circles under her blue eyes, setting off her high cheekbones. Her hair is long and layered, her shoulders are hunched and she holds her arms tight to her body, keeping her hands in her lap when she is not sipping her tea. She sits in her chair—a brown captain's chair with a curving top rail—without touching its back or sides, a little wisp of land in a dark sea.

For the first time, I grasp the enormity, the vast, mythic proportion of this business of taking the flesh of your flesh, placing him forever and ever in the care of someone else, walking away, never to see him again. Carrie knows what this means better than I do. She has two other children, a boy and a girl, whom she has raised alone. She tells us about them, the hard life they have had, living in rundown apartments and houses in different towns, attending unwelcoming schools. How she didn't want to burden them with knowledge of another child coming, so she concealed the pregnancy ("I carry small," she explains, and I wonder how this is possible), had to hurry home from the hospital after the delivery so they wouldn't know they had a brother, has been packing lunches and putting them on buses for the last two weeks, living in a secret twilight of grief and indecision, and (she doesn't say this, but I think it must be true) thinking every day about going to the hospital and getting her boy, whom she loves as a mother, whom she wants to do right by, whom she may give to a psychologist and a teacher so that he'll be with people who know exactly what to do to keep him safe.

She tells us about the day he was born. She'd been out four-wheeling the day before, riding around the woods in a friend's pickup truck. "It was getting bumped around that did it, I think. I wasn't ready to decide yet, I thought I had more time." She went to the hospital while the children were at school, called the one friend who knew she was pregnant to look after them, gave birth at around three that afternoon. It was an easy delivery, no doubt because it was her third and he was very small. She'd asked for the priest to baptize him. She was home early the next morning, in time to get the kids off to school. She told them she'd been sick, but she was better now. She went to the hospital once to see him, gave him a Beanie Baby, but hasn't been back in over a week.

We ask about the father. "He was a real gentleman," she says. From the South, "a lot nicer than my ex-husband." She only knew his first name. He was a big man who had the room next to hers when Welfare put her family up in a motel. She distracts us from the father with a horrifying description of living for months in a single room with two young and active children. It's not too hard to do this, because it feels so unseemly to be asking in the first place for the details of her love life. Later, Susan will tell me that she thinks it was a long affair, that Carrie knows more than she let on, that she is protecting him. I think he was a construction worker temporarily housed, who got lucky with his next-door neighbor. We both wonder what we will tell her son.

And now we have settled into conversation, the familiarity of stories traded momentarily covering over the utter strangeness of what we are doing. The dissonance is not just between the appearance of civilization and the barbaric business at hand, but also between the sympathy Carrie's suffering kindles—her poverty and single motherhood; her nomadic, fatherless childhood; her abortive attempts to pull herself up by training to be a nurse's aide, someone who can wipe and wash and push and carry old people abandoned in convalescent homes; the whole cruel apparatus of the free market focused on and embodied in this kind and hapless woman—and our inescapable wish, no, our fierce and burning need—now that we have determined that she is a kind, if hapless, woman, someone whose genes we probably don't have to fear—to capitalize on it. The thought flits through my head—I could give her the twenty-five thousand dollars, and then she might be able to keep her son. But I say nothing.

Because you have to believe that you are entitled, that you will be a better parent than she will be. Even if you know that the credentials that so impressed her, that gave you the resources to be doing this in the first place, are largely flukes, nothing you really deserved, and certainly nothing to do with bringing up babies. You have to believe this even more than you believe that you will be better than your own highly educated, well-intentioned, and vastly incompetent parents. You have to believe this and she has to believe this, or you might just as well write her the check and push it across the table and go home.

You have to have hubris, you have to be willing to be the author of your own original sin to ask another human being to give you her child. And here at the shack, I find myself more than willing. I am not only eager and greedy, I am dying for Carrie to look at me and my wife and say, "Okay. I've decided. Where do I sign?" But even though we've been our best psychologist and schoolteacher selves, lived up to our dossier, agreed to her terms—that she can get (via the agency) letters and pictures updating his progress, that we will pass along Christmas and birthday gifts—she is not ready to close the deal. And now it is time to go. We watch the social workers leave, our son's mother in tow. The boy, alone in his crib, is eleven days old.

Later, we will call the agency. They will tell us that they are sure the workers are helping her to make up her mind. That they are sure that if she decides to give him up, it will be to us. I will lie awake all night, thinking of those outstretched arms. We will get up Tuesday and pretend to live our lives and we will lay awake all night again, and when Wednesday comes, we will give up, sure that she feels as we do— unable to walk away from this urge. But the phone will ring that afternoon, and the agency will tell us that Carrie has signed the papers that assign them as guardians and, much more important, allow us to go and visit the boy in the hospital.

And the next day, at three in the afternoon, we will meet another social worker at the entrance to the hospital. She will be so well dressed that I will notice, for the first time, what I have put on for this momentous occasion: a pair of blue jeans with holes in the leg, a flannel shirt with enormous, sloppy buttonholes, stained work boots, a ratty cotton hat. We will make our way through the lobby to the elevator and up to the neonatal intensive care unit, cordoned off from the rest of the hospital by huge swinging double doors with signs warning away the diseased, insisting that all who enter wash scrupulously before handling the babies. In the hushed corridor, we will meet the hospital's social worker. Our little entourage will step through the third door on the right into a room that is home to three plastic cribs, one on each wall. A couple will be sitting in front of the one on the left, the mother holding an improbably small baby to her breast. In the far corner, a nurse will be hovering over an infant who is crying implacably. And there on the right, asleep and alone in the third crib, wrapped in a white blanket, a blue knit cap covering a head the size of an orange, his tiny and immaculate face in deep repose, will be the boy from the stained-glass window, my son.

YOU DON'T SEE THE OTHER
PERSON LOOKING BACK
Michael Lowenthal

They say animals resemble their masters, so I shouldn't have been surprised that Oscar, Tommy's Seeing Eye dog, the instant he was unharnessed, rose to his hind legs and humped my knee. But you've got to expect a yellow Lab to have some boundary issues, and Oscar was easy enough to distract. A stern "Down, boy!" and a toss of his stinky rawhide chew, and he snuffled off to a different sort of pleasure. Tommy proved significantly more persistent.

Tommy was my roommate on the Rainbow Bear Valentine's cruise for blind gay men and friends. I had decided to share a room to save on cost, and left the choice of whom to the trip's planner, a blind gay travel agent; before our sail date, he gave me Tommy's name and number. I called Tommy and we chatted amiably about our hobbies, our hometowns. He was glad to hear my voice, he said, so that when we got to the ship he'd recognize me. His voice herked and jerked with a nasal Mid-Atlantic accent, inflected upward on all the wrong syllables. In the same tone as he'd asked what types of books I tend to read, he inquired, "Do you like massages, Mike?" I answered with a lengthy, equivocating *hmm*, followed by the statement that I wasn't entirely averse to them. Tommy, not indicating if he gauged my apprehension, pushed the broom of small talk once again: Was it as cold in Boston as it was in Pennsylvania?

I didn't hear from him for more than a month. Then, three days before departure, I was greeted by a message on my machine: "Mike, it's Tommy. I was wondering if you'd bring some cream for your skin so I can massage you. And I like a rectal thermometer, if you could bring one along. I like the feel of one going up my ass, but that's entirely up to you. Anxious to see you on Sunday. Take care."

Months earlier, when a friend, apropos of nothing, asked what I thought it would be like to be gay (as we both are) and blind, my response didn't include rectal thermometers. Not knowing any blind people and never having thought about their sex lives, my immediate reaction was pity: sexual attraction must be so faint within that visual eclipse, without the sparkle of pretty faces, flirty looks. Almost as fast, though, pity mixed with a nervous sort of envy—as though *I* might be the one in the dark. This was the same brand of irrational sexual jealousy I've felt toward women, whose orgasms, unlike men's pro-creation-intended spurts, seem more purely about pleasure for its own sake. When blind people—*without* the aid of visual inspiration—feel the burn of sexual desire, is that desire, I wondered, deeper, more authentic?

But these musings applied to blind people of any orientation. For a blind person to be openly *gay*, I imagined, must require an even greater intensity of attraction. The recognition of sexual identity is complicated enough for sighted gay people; how much more fraught must it be if you have no visual experience of gender, if all you have to follow is straight society's lead? Right away I wanted to meet someone openly gay and blind, someone who, despite this double disorientation, feels his attractions so keenly as to stake his life on them. Maybe he'd validate the doggedness of my own desires.

I searched the library for information about homosexuality and blindness, but found not a single citation. I contacted Stanley Ducharme, Ph.D., of Boston University, editor of the journal *Sexuality and Disability*; in his sixteen years in the job, he told me, he hasn't received any submissions on the topic. The most extensive treatment of the issue is a subsection of a chapter of the 1933 text *The Blind in School and Society*, by Thomas Cutsforth. Writing about homosexuality among students at residential schools for the blind, Cutsforth deemed it "a problem of environmental causation . . . a perfectly natural, although unfortunate, result of the conditions under which the children live." This didn't sound much like the sexual stalwarts my imagination had conjured.

Turning finally to the Internet, I came upon a Web site for BFLAG: Blind Friends of Lesbian, Gay, Bisexual, and Transgender People. The group, I learned, was founded in 1996 and counts forty intrepid members. I joined a listserv to which many of the BFLAGers subscribe. A typical exchange:

<<My name is Alejandro and I live in Mexico. I have an eye problem called keratoconus, and although I am not totally blind I am not very distant from that. I have had a difficult time finding a boyfriend because most gays are mostly concerned about their looks and as I wear very thick glasses most of them think I do not look "attractive.">>

<<My name is Peter and I live in Sydney, Australia. I am 35 years of age and totally blind. I am in exactly the same position when it comes to finding someone. All men think about are looks. I think what's in the heart is more important.>>

If I had sought validation, now I felt accused. Would *I* ever consider dating a blind man? Does my own vision act as a kind of blindness?

When an ad was posted on the listserv for a blind Valentine's cruise group, I decided that I had to go along. I was hoping that a week among some sightless gay men might make me see something new about desire.

In San Diego I waited two hours in line to board Royal Caribbean's *Vision of the Seas*. Searching the crowd of two thousand passengers for a group of visually impaired men, I scanned a human catalog of failed attempts at beautification: women with penciled eyebrows like appliquéd licorice; face after hypertanned face. And yet everyone appeared ebullient and contentedly coupled; I, who had recently separated from my boyfriend, was the only person identifiably alone.

I found Tommy's and my stateroom on Deck 4. Although the *Vision* was still firmly moored, my stomach queased. I hadn't spoken with Tommy since receiving his phone message, but had left a return message on his machine, explaining that while I was looking forward to making new friends on the cruise, I would not be interested in any physical intimacy.

I walked in calling, "Tommy?" but he wasn't in the cabin (which was roughly the size of my kitchen back in Boston). His clothes crowded one half of the closet.

I unpacked my own clothes and set out exploring the ship, telling myself I was searching for my roommate, but hardly looking. I hiked fore and aft through the warren of tight hallways, then upstairs to the Casino Royale and Champagne Bar, to the pool, solarium, and jogging track.

Hopelessly lost, I ended up at the Viking Crown Lounge, where I spied a man at the bar, gulping a margarita, a Seeing Eye dog curled at his feet. I steeled myself and approached, preparing to offer my most neutral, nonsuggestive handshake, then remembered that Tommy's dog, he'd told me, was young and yellow. This one was black, with a light rime of gray around the muzzle, and wearing a rainbow neckerchief.

"So, this guy comes to read the meter," the dog's owner was saying to the man next to him. "And when I show him in, he goes, 'You blind people are just so amazing. You just blow me away, all the things you can manage by yourselves.' And I wanted to say, 'Yeah, that's right, guy. I can even *jerk off* by myself. Don't like to, but I can if I have to.'"

The man waggled the straw in his margarita, basking in the laugh he'd known he would earn. Although he was seated, he radiated the pratfallish energy of a physical comedian. His skin was acne scarred, and his nose was the bulbous knob seen in caricatures of Bill Clinton, but his take-no-prisoners humor was magnetic and sort of sexy.

I introduced myself and asked if he was in the Rainbow Bear group. He turned in the direction of my voice and offered his hand. His name was Howard, and his friend was Steve, a sighted Englishman with close-cropped silvering hair and an affable, snaggletoothed smile. They had met last year on a Caribbean cruise and decided to rendezvous on this trip and room together.

"And who's this?" I asked, patting the dog's head.

"His name's Harvey," said Howard. He felt for the dog's rainbow neckerchief. "He accessorizes wonderfully, don't you think?"

Was Howard what I had expected, after months of thinking about blind gay men in the abstract?

Blindness has long been associated with sexual deviance. In the Middle Ages, blinding was a common punishment for sexual crimes—a not-so-subtle symbolic castration. In literature, too, characters are often blinded for sins of sexual transgression: think of Oedipus, Tiresias, and even Peeping Tom, who was blinded after sneaking peeks at Lady Godiva. The link persists today in superstition: jerk off too much and you'll go blind. And yet, as much as blind people have been feared and shunned—blindness was often thought to be contagious—they have also been revered. In antiquity, from Greece to China to Ireland, blind people frequently served as bards. There is a long tradition of the blind as seers, soothsayers, and mystics—individuals who, lacking sight, compensate with an abundance of insight and/or foresight.

How similar this is to gay people's situation: oppressed and denigrated, accused of spreading scourge, yet in some ways celebrated and esteemed. In certain Native American tribes, gay members have been honored as shamans. And in even the most repressive cultures, gay people have been disproportionately lauded for their creative (if not procreative) talents: as court jesters, artists, and musicians.

As I had readied myself to meet men who are both blind *and* gay, I imagined them at an enigmatic nexus: fear and awe, hatred and reverence. They're doubly outcast—but might they also be doubly visionary?

Nearing our assigned dinner table in the Aquarius Dining Room, I came upon a man being tugged by a tawny guide dog, bobbling behind the animal as though it were a child and he the child's wind-tossed kite. His neck was thicker than his mostly bald head, which looked slightly misshapen, like that of an infant, or like a pumpkin left too long on the porch.

"You must be Tommy," I guessed, as he veered perilously close to a waiter balancing a tray of eight salads. He appeared just as off-kilter as his phone message had sounded.

"Mike?" he said. "How'd you recognize me?"

"Your dog," I fudged. "He's just like you described him."

The rest of our group was already at the table, and we introduced ourselves one by one. I sat next to Bill, a natty Philadelphian with more than a passing resemblance to E. Lynn Harris, whose current pot-boiler, he said, had been his afternoon's guilty-pleasure reading. (He listens to books on tape while on the treadmill.) Next to Bill was Robert, the trip's organizer, a large man (his Yahoo profile mentions a waist of fifty-four inches, leg inseam of thirty) with a whispery bass voice and glaucomatous eyes. Robert's sighted partner, Tim—partner both in their travel agency and in their eight-year relationship—was an avuncular, heavyset man who in comparison to Robert seemed tiny.

Carl was next, at fifty-nine the oldest by a decade, his Mississippi drawl and his clunky corrective glasses both thicker than any I'd previously encountered. Then catlike Doug, whose buzz cut flashed with silver, as did his blank, squinted eyes. And finally Steven, Doug's sighted boyfriend, a Texan with a wry, friendly smile. (Howard and Steve, whom I'd met in the Viking Crown Lounge, were seated at the next table over.)

I struggled to remember each new acquaintance's name, but the blind men didn't seem to have this problem. They called on one another from across the table, carrying on animated conversations while they also read about "tagliatelle gifted with portobello mush-rooms" on the special Braille menus and, learning the lay of the land, fingered their intricate place settings (five forks, four spoons, three knives). Our waiter, oblivious to their multitasking expertise, ap-peared to panic when he realized that most of our group was blind. As if the blind men were children, or invisible, he addressed only me and the other sighted guys. I wanted to feel outraged on the blind men's behalf, but in truth the waiter's gaze, directed squarely at my eyes, helped alleviate my own discomposure.

Tommy's phone call had left me on the lookout for strangeness; I kept waiting for someone to propose a group massage. But the meal was almost eerily run-of-the-mill. Like any couple, Doug and Steven debated sharing their entrées. Carl rated the quality of the ship's potent coffee. Bill, in deference to his figure, declined dessert.

A *Vision of the Seas* crew member, in full eye-patched, tricorned buccaneer regalia, came from nowhere and held a plastic cutlass to Robert's neck, growling "Argh, matey!" while a photographer snapped pictures. Robert, with no idea what was happening, defended himself against the fake blade, but the pirate was already on to his next victim. "Argh," he repeated, inflicting his punishment on each unsuspecting blind man. When my turn came, I stared at the camera like a hostage.

Dinner stretched until ten-thirty, and I was pooped. While Tommy headed to Deck 5 and its row of custom-built mulch boxes where Oscar could relieve himself, I retreated to our room. I stripped to my underwear and climbed into the narrow bunk closest to the door, which we had agreed would be mine. When I turned out the light, our cabin—the ship's cheapest sort, with no windows and a heavy, fireproof door—succumbed to darkness of a degree I'd seen only once, when I toured Alcatraz and got locked in solitary. Lulled by the ship's rocking, I dropped asleep.

It felt like weeks later when I was woken by the hands. They touched my ankle first, through the blanket, then my shin. I heard the approach of heavy breathing.

"This is my bunk," I blurted. "Yours is farther."

The breathing got louder. I couldn't see anything but could sense Tommy kneeling, shuffling closer. His hands were on my face now, and I grabbed hold of his arms. My pulse felt like a choke chain at my throat.

"I just want to see what you look like," he said.

Get away, I wanted to shout, but would Tommy think me scared of blind people? And wasn't I? Shouldn't I get over that? I kept my grip tight on his wrists, but let him rove.

"I haven't shaved in a couple of days," I said self-consciously, then wondered why *I* was apologizing.

He handled my features like a sculptor shaping clay, as if he weren't appraising my face so much as creating it. He lingered at my outsized nose, the feature that most people find unattractive, but that for those few who like it seems to be a fetish. It's what initially drew Scott, my longest-term boyfriend, to me from across a crowded room, and I'll never forget my shock, the first time we were alone, when he put his mouth over the whole huge thing and sucked it.

Might Tommy, too, have a nose fetish? If so, how could he have known my appeal without this grope? I had read about the challenges of sex ed for blind people, whose learning relies so much on tactile exploration—which in the case of strangers' bodies is taboo. In the 1970s, blind-rights activists advocated special sex ed classes making use of live nude human models, and in Scandinavia a few such courses were attempted. Elsewhere, however, the plans were squelched: models, it was worried, would be perceived as enjoying vicarious sexual thrills.

Thrills? I was clammy with discomfort and alarm. How far did I have to let Tommy go to assuage my guilty conscience?

Just as I had reached my breaking point, he abruptly concluded his reconnaissance. He moved over to his own bunk, undressed, called good night, and in seconds fell to high-horsepower snoring.

Even without the noise, I couldn't have slept. I was mad at Tommy for using his blindness to take advantage of me, mad at myself for believing that he had done so, and madder still for not knowing which was true. It was so dark I couldn't see my own hands.

I lay there, as my heartbeat subsided back to calm, and thought about things unseen but alluring. I once got a call from an editor who mentioned another Boston writer. Did I know him? His name was Vestal McIntyre. I didn't know him but I knew instantly—unequivocally—that I would, and that we'd hit it off in more ways than one. *Vestal McIntyre!* I can't explain it except to say that it was love at first name. I looked Vestal up in the White Pages, called him, and proposed a date. We met days later and climbed presently into bed. Our fling lasted months. He's still one of my best friends.

Handwriting has given me hard-ons: not the look, but the feel, the stippled loops and slashes on the backside of anything penned by Scott, who writes just as forcefully as he loves. Smells, too: the scent of vetiver, which Scott used to dab on his neck, still drives me wild. But how much are these attraction by association? They turn me on because they remind me of Scott, who hooked me with his looks when we locked eyes across a room.

The phone sex industry relies on people's ability to be turned on by the voice of an unseen partner. But most customers, I think, hear the voice and construct a visual image to go along with it—an image based on someone they *have* seen.

What if you've never seen anything?

Doug was born three months premature and kept in an incubator, where overexposure to oxygen caused a condition known as retinopathy of prematurity and left him completely blind. I sat with Doug on day two of the cruise at a retirement party for Robert's guide dog, Zeppelin, who suffers from arthritis. It was a festive affair by the pool on Deck 9, complete with a frosted rum cake and reverent testimonials ("He knocked me backward, away from the car, and saved my life!").

Doug hadn't yet spoken directly to me, but I sensed that his shyness hid a fierce curiosity, apparent not in his eyes, where we usually think of that trait as being evinced (his were cloudy and often misdirected), but in the alertness of his posture, the tilt of his head toward unfamiliar voices. When I took the initiative, he seemed eager to talk. After years in the computer field, he told me, he works now as a massage therapist. I flinched, recalling Tommy's snooping hands, but Doug, anticipating my reaction, added, "It's tricky. You say 'massage' and people assume it's something sexual." He assured me that his business is legit.

Doug was thrilled just to be sitting casually among a group of blind gay men. Until two or three years ago he didn't know of any others, despite the fact that he's been involved with gay culture since the early 1970s, when, as a senior in high school, he entered a gay bar for the first time. He'd been having sex with boys for a decade before that.

Later, when we met privately, I asked Doug how—with no visual sense of either gender, and knowing that boys were expected to like girls—he realized that he was gay.

"There was never really a question in my mind," he said. "There was always something more appealing when you said 'boy' versus 'girl.' Boys smelled better."

"Like what?"

He thought a second. "Like outside: grass and dirt and sweat."

And boys, it seems, were readily available. Throughout his early teens, Doug had frequent sexual encounters with boys, and his blindness was "not in the least bit" an issue. "In the bathrooms at school we all checked each other out," he recalled—which, for him, meant with his hands.

In college at Texas Tech in 1972, Doug overheard some rednecks talking about how "the faggots are going to be out in full force tomorrow," and after calling the student center anonymously he found himself at the very first meeting of a gay campus group. "I had to work really hard to become part of that group," he said. "I think it was mostly the blindness. People were a little standoffish."

In the years since, Doug has found most of the gay world—which he feels is overly focused on questions like "Does my butt look good in these shorts?"—similarly skittish about accepting a blind man. But he has enjoyed a number of short- and long-term relationships, all with sighted men. I asked about his current boyfriend, Steven, and in particular if he had any sense of what Steven looks like.

"I know that most of y'all pick people by the way they look," he told me. "And I know that's how I *don't* operate. I couldn't tell you what sort of jawline Steven has, or what sort of nose. I mean, I could tell in comparison to myself—his nose is a bit longer and more squared off. He's told me that his hair is sort of red-blond, but that doesn't really mean anything to me."

If he could, would he want to see Steven?

"As selfish as this sounds," Doug said, "if I could see for just ten minutes, I would want to see what *I* look like. I could be hideous or I could be okay, but I don't know. And there are *things* I'd like to see. The house I used to live in. My cat. I would like to see a giraffe, because the concept is just so bizarre. As far as how people look, it may be kind of important, but not terribly."

*   *   *

"Can you get a photo of me blowing?" Bill asked. "I know it's *personal*, but . . ."

"Of course," I said, and aimed the camera. "I'm sure it won't be the first picture of that!"

We were in Cabo San Lucas, Mexico, our first port of call, at a mom-and-pop glass-blowing factory. The shop boss had offered to let Bill try his hand at the craft, and, after private tittering about long rods and hot, stiff tools, Bill consented. When he drew a deep breath and huffed with all his might, the molten blob at the end of the rod globed. The group cheered. I snapped a photograph.

"Ooh, me too," said Howard. "If it's an oral thing, put me next!"

I'd woken that morning groggy, after another fitful, nervous-about-Tommy night, but now, leaving my roommate to his own devices, I was having a ball. These guys were cracking me up, especially Howard with his incorrigible ba-dum-bum joking. He had the same raunchy, quick-draw wit as most of my best friends, and his delivery was impeccable, in a grainy voice that trailed off like Jack Benny's at the ends of phrases.

Howard was also wonderful at guiding me in guiding him. At first I called out every obstacle: *steps coming up, maybe six of them, in about four yards, okay now three yards, you're almost there* . . . After five awkward minutes of this, Howard said, "Listen, if you just let me hold your elbow, I'll feel everything your body does and you won't have to say a thing." Instantly our balance of power improved: Howard was the craftsman, I was just the tool.

At the next stop, a stucco church in San José del Cabo, I whispered descriptions of everything I could see: the plain but beautiful woodwork, the half-dozen Mexicans, heads bowed in fervent prayer. When we reached the altar, I noted the statues of Jesus and Mary on the wall.

"What colors are they?" Howard asked,

I chided myself for not having included this information; I was still adjusting to being someone else's eyes. Mary was blue, I told him, and Jesus was pure white.

Howard clucked his tongue. "Now, if Jesus was with twelve men, should he really be wearing white?"

The confessional, I thought, would be a good bet—lots of tactile wooden latticework—so I led Howard and Carl over to it. I described the thronelike priest's seat and the bench for penitents.

Immediately, Howard dropped to his knees. "Do they have glory holes?" he said, hands scanning the wooden booth. "Bless me Father, for I have sinned a *whole lot.*"

"Yeah, Howard," Carl added, "that's why you're blind!"

Howard is actually blind from retinitis pigmentosa. He was born with 20/200 vision: legally blind but still able to see the blackboard in first grade if the teacher used special thumb-thick chalk and if he sat in the front row. By the end of high school he couldn't read even large-print books up close, and now, at forty-six, he retains only the barest light perception.

Howard's early sexual stirrings were similar to those of most gay men. "You knew the boys in your class that you just wanted to be in the proximity of," he told me. "It wasn't even a sexual thought. But there was an attraction there. You liked the way they talked." In 1970, when he transferred from public junior high to the Western Pennsylvania School for the Blind, he finally had the opportunity to act on his desires. "I appreciated it so much," he said, referring to the school's gender-segregated dormitories. "They put the girls all the way over to one side and kept them there." He had sex with a number of his schoolmates, and by the eleventh grade everybody in the school knew he was gay.

From this point, Howard felt driven to join the larger gay world. "I would walk past the Holiday Bar in Pittsburgh, which I knew was a gay bar. I used a cane to travel in those days. I had to learn which side of the street it was on. I had to ask a stranger where it was"—which should have been scary, but desire trumped fear. Since he wasn't yet of legal drinking age, his goal was not to go inside the bar, but simply "to be near there. That's all I thought of at that time."

After he graduated and moved to Harrisburg, Howard became something of a barfly. It was fun, but more important, it was his strategy for attracting sexual attention. "People would say, 'I know this blind guy who's in Harrisburg, and he has a dog.' *Everybody* in those bars knew me. They wouldn't know a lot of other folks, but they all knew Howard. And they also knew he was a sleaze. And he is!"

Was he worried that people might think: He's blind, he needs to take whatever he can get? "I've heard that," Howard said. "But if I was sighted, and engaged in the same sexual behaviors, it wouldn't be because I need to take anything I can get. They would say I was a slut."

Howard eventually fell in love and began a committed, fifteen-year relationship with a sighted man. They split up four years ago, partly due to the difficulties of maintaining a "mixed marriage."

Howard worked in the blind-social-services field for almost twenty years—most recently as the founder of a computer resource center for blind people—but his passion is the gay community. For five years he ran the gay and lesbian switchboard in Harrisburg, and at one time or another he has been involved in "every gay organization" in the city. If he weren't blind, Howard told me, he would be "a sighted *gay* person," meaning that gayness would be his prime identity. He said, "I never wanted to be anything but gay."

After touring the church, our group split up, some hunting the best tacos in Cabo, the half-dozen rest of us looking for the Rainbow Bar & Grille, which Howard, searching a gay-travel Web site before the cruise, had identified as the sole gay bar in town. (Like most of the blind men I met, Howard uses screen-reading software and is something of an Internet wiz.)

Our tour guide, Doris, declined to accompany us, but she pointed out the spot we were looking for, a block away. We trooped over, a traffic-blocking procession of men and Seeing Eye dogs. But when we got there we saw no sign and no bar, just a hotel. We turned around our human train with roughly the same ease as we might an actual locomotive, and retraced the steps to where Doris had left us. Still nothing.

We reversed the group once more, now beginning to attract attention. I jogged into the hotel lobby and asked in Spanish for the Rainbow Bar & Grille.

"Are you sure?" the desk clerk said in English, clearly thinking I'd gotten my Spanish wrong. He glanced past the open door to where the group of blind men and their dogs patiently waited. "That's a *gay* bar."

I assured him that was precisely what we wanted.

It turned out that the bar was in the next building over, with a half hidden door marked only by a tiny notice of its hours of operation, which, unfortunately, did not include now. I imagined the hilarious scene our gang would have made barging into such a determinedly concealed bar.

As we chugged off, disappointed, in search of lunch, I considered the hotel clerk's apparent surprise that a group of blind men might be gay. I could have mounted a high horse and convicted him of a multiplicity of isms, but the truth was that the men in our group barely registered on my own gaydar. Sure, both of Doug's ears are pierced, and Howard's dog wears his rainbow neckerchief, but when Doug asked me intently, "Do we blind guys 'read' as gay?," I had to tell him I didn't really think so.

The concept of gaydar is slippery at best, dependent on overgeneralizations and cultural context. (A classic conundrum for gay Americans abroad: "Is he gay or is he just European?") And yet, as much as signals can get scrambled, there seem to be some genuine means of recognition. On one level, it's all in the eyes, the practiced glance that balances dare with fear. Blind men can't receive or send such signals.

There's something else, too: the only term that comes close is "self-consciousness." Growing up with the fear of being unmasked, most gay people develop an early preoccupation with their appearance, and sometimes a delusion of being constantly watched. This self-consciousness manifests in different ways and degrees: mannered, theatrical gestures and gaits; overprimped hair and skin and clothes. The blind gay men I met, although they know they can be watched, never actually see themselves being seen and don't appear to be as prone to self-consciousness. My sample size was tiny, but none of the men's mannerisms was the slightest bit stylized in the ways that usually trigger gaydar.

But if blind gay men don't "look" or "act" gay, does this really reflect essential differences, or does it say more about the constructed nature of gay culture? Many components of the conventional gay "lifestyle" are inaccessible for blind men: noisy gay bars are tricky to negotiate; gay novels and newspapers are rarely available in Braille or audio, and most gay Web sites are not designed compatibly with screen-reading software; even porn movies, which for legions of gay men have served as sexual primers, are largely useless (try just listening to the dialogue). If much of "gay style" is a marketing contrivance or a result of aped behavior, blind men are less likely to feel its influence. As Doug told me, "I could never pick up a *GQ* or a *Blueboy* or an *Advocate*, and look at pictures and tell what people are wearing." In terms of stereotypically gay gestures, he said, "If you haven't seen it, how would you know how to do it?"

And yet, Doug's experience also suggests a more intrinsic source of gay identification. When he was a boy, not yet in his teens, he accompanied his mother to a shopping mall in Dallas. As they sat in a bakery sipping sodas, Doug was riveted by the voices of two men at the next table. "I was fascinated by the way they sounded," he said. "I don't know that I knew why. I just knew that they sounded interesting. And when they left, Mom was like, 'Those two men were fairies.'"

Doris had told us we'd need to hire taxis to the dock, but after lunch Bill suggested we walk. "How far can it be?" he said, forging ahead with his dog.

The marina was clogged with vendors hawking cheap souvenirs, but, as Bill pointed out, one benefit of being blind is that you can pretend not to notice what you choose. It was typical of Bill to emphasize the good points about blindness. A lawyer specializing in Americans with Disabilities Act litigation, he's acutely aware of the difficulties faced by blind people, but also of how much those difficulties are imposed, not inherent.

Bill told me about himself as we strolled along the water, speaking with the hyperarticulate, almost homiletic diction that I associate with certain African-American newscasters, like Bernard Shaw. He didn't fully lose his vision until he was twenty-one, by which point he'd already come out as gay, so he was able to experience gay visual cruising. "I'm really glad I did that," he said. "I'm really glad I *had* that." And yet he's adamant that his blindness hasn't limited his sexuality. He's had two significant relationships, one for five years and one for seven. Neither boyfriend was blind, but he's "not exclusively into sighted guys, that's just the way it's happened." And although he's open to having another partner, he would insist on maintaining his independence. "I would *never* live with someone I was involved with," he said. "No way."

Bill spoke with relish of influencing the men he dated, teaching them to be more aware of nonvisual sensory input. The idea that sight is necessary for sexual attraction he dismissed as laughable.

What about sex itself: is it different if you can't see?

Bill bristled. "There's no difference. If anything, being blind is an advantage. If you're prone to feeling uncomfortable, it helps, because you don't see the other person looking back."

Sometimes the best things, he implied, aren't what you see but feel, and I remembered something that had happened at the glass factory. After Bill's triumphant blowing debut, Doris had arrayed glassware on a table. Bill and the other guys inspected the samples, feeling every ridge and swell and turn: margarita glasses, beer steins, a blowfish-shaped candy jar. Everyone's favorite was a tiny tequila shot glass that featured matching dimples on either side: a built-in grip, perfect for thumb and index finger.

The shot glass was passed from hand to hand, and the more expensive, more ornate baubles abandoned. "It just feels right, doesn't it?" Bill said. Doris was dispatched to fetch three sets of four each, with clear instructions to find the indented glasses.

She returned a minute later, empty-handed. "I hate to tell you this, but that glass? It was defective. It wasn't supposed to have those indentations."

And Bill, who'd had his heart set, groaned with disappointment. He knows the difference between defective and just right.

*   *   *

"Down, boy. Down!"

I kicked Oscar's chew toy across the stateroom, trying to keep him occupied while I struggled with my tie. Tommy and I were getting dressed for the captain's reception, to be followed by the formal dinner.

Tommy stood in front of the vanity in just his forty-inch-waist Calvin Klein briefs, dabbing CK 1 on his neck. "So, Mike," he asked, "are you a skinny guy?"

My tie came out wrong, wide end shorter than the thin. "Um, I don't really know," I said. What should I have told him? That my waist is 20 percent smaller than his, or that in the urban gay circles in which I travel I'm probably considered average, with perhaps some flab to lose?

Tommy pulled on his slacks and an oxford shirt. "I might go up later and check out the gym," he said. "It's just in my stomach where I put on weight. I know I don't look near my age. I look much younger."

I wondered who had told him this, and how long ago. His chin sagged. His hair had ebbed to just a horseshoe. To me, he looked his age of forty-five.

I checked my own receding hair in the brightly lit mirror: Am I aging badly? Does it turn people off? I'd bungled my tie again. I tried a third time.

Tommy rifled through a drawer, feeling for his own tie. He asked, "Are you a hairy guy, Mike?"

I stepped away. "Hairier than some. Less than others."

"You sure are evasive!" Tommy said. He knotted his tie: perfect on the first attempt.

I *was* being evasive. Why shouldn't I tell Tommy the basic facts that, were he sighted, he'd be able to gauge at a glance? I've imparted more intimate details to strangers in bars and dance clubs. In those contexts, the exchange of such personal information is always implicitly seductive; the last thing I wanted was to lead Tommy on. And yet I felt bad for dodging his questions, as though this time I were the one taking advantage of his blindness. Maybe I also wanted to punish him.

"Well, would you look at that," he said, apparently dropping the issue. "Six o'clock and it's still light out!"

He'd told me the day before that he still retains some light perception, but obviously it wasn't much help to him. "You're in front of a vanity," I said. "Our room doesn't have windows."

Gay men are tagged as being obsessed with superficial beauty, and, like most stereotypes, this one seems based on some degree of truth. Gay culture—or what passes as such, generated mostly in urban clubs and "lifestyle" magazines—is a conformist cult of the body in which looks are paramount. How do blind men fit in to such a world?

In terms of their own appearance, some people's blindness is not readily evident, while others have conditions—cataracts, glaucoma— that make them "look" blind and may cause them to be shunned. But whether or not they appear outwardly different, blind men, simply by the fact of their blindness, call into question the ideal of "perfection" in pursuit of which so many gay men go to extravagant lengths. If sighted gay men's identities, on some fundamental level, are dependent on being *looked at*, blind gay men's presence can be unsettling: Is it really essential to expend such effort on external attractiveness?

But blind gay men are not immune from the concern with how their bodies look. Bill is a regular treadmill user, and more than once I heard Doug—disparaging himself for recently added pounds—recommitting himself to the NordicTrack. Aside from Robert, who is obese and identifies as a "bear" (a category referring to hefty, hairy men), the men I met all seemed conscious of falling short of some body-image ideal.

Weight gain can be a special concern for blind people, often stemming from restricted mobility. Another factor may be blind people's desexualization by the sighted world. Blind people rely on their sighted acquaintances to help them with outward appearances: to tell them if their clothes match, for example, or are stained. But because sighted people too frequently don't "count" blind people as sexual beings, they may not think to offer advice about cultivating attractiveness. "That's why there tend to be a lot of overweight blind people," Doug suggested. "Nobody says to them, 'Maybe that's not the way you want to be.'" When I asked Doug about his own self-perception, he said, "I know other people have much better bodies. But people don't scream and run away, so that's a good sign."

In certain arenas of the gay world, there are physical attributes more important than body-fat percentage or 20/20 vision—for example, in the chat rooms on Gay.com, of which Howard is a fervent devotee. (It takes two different software packages and a lot of patience for him to gain access to the site, but he considers it well worth the trouble.) Howard's online profile is upfront about his blindness, but when he's in a real-time chat with other horny men looking to hook up, he'll present himself simply as "46 years old, 5'10", 195 pounds," and, using standard gay lingo to describe the length and circumcision of his far-above-average manhood: "9.5 cut." "I'm going to use that asset to my advantage," he told me, "because I'm trying to level the playing field. They don't care then if you're blind."

Howard himself, although he won't be able to see his sexual playmates, certainly judges them by superficial attributes; in fact, like any gay man cruising for casual sex, that's pretty much all he cares about. "If I'm on the Internet," he said, "and I meet somebody, the first thing I want to know is height, weight, if there's any facial hair. Then I go to, 'Are you smooth or hairy?' To actually feel sexually aroused by that person, the smoothness is such an issue."

I asked Howard how he vets the men he meets in person—say, in a gay bar. Is he comfortable asking such direct questions out loud?

We were across from each other in my cabin—me on my bunk, Howard on Tommy's—but Howard stood up now and moved across and sat next to me. "My little ploy would be that I would sit down," he said. "I've finally got a bar stool. And I go, 'Boy, beautiful day out there today. I can't believe the weather!' And if the person doesn't just say 'Yeah,' if I get a sentence or two, now I realize this person's comfortable talking to me. Plus, now I know there's not an empty chair beside me.

"And if you're continuing to talk to me, then it allows me to go"—

Howard patted my thigh—" 'Now that's *exactly* it,' or 'I can't believe that, that's awful!' I'm gauging your body language. When a person tenses, I'm already reading that. I'm still trying to get a sense of the person."

What sense was Howard getting of me right now? Was this simulation itself a ploy for sex? (Howard had mentioned earlier that he found my voice intriguing.)

"I may very well say, 'You're really tall, aren't you? Because your voice is coming from way up here. You about six-two?' Then I'm going to make a point like this"—Howard touched my shoulder, a bit more forcefully than he'd felt my leg. "Now I've got stature. I've also got how he carries himself. 'Oh, he's a bar fly, he's hunched over, he's in here *every day*.' That just told me a lot.

"Now, they're going to say, 'It's okay if you want to feel my face and see what I look like.' I don't! I mean, *oh yes*, I want to touch their face. But when people say that line? That's like squeaking a Styrofoam cooler. I don't know where that ever started."

I made a mental note to explain this to Tommy.

"But under *my* initiative," Howard continued, "I'm going to find out, so my next move is probably going to be this"—he touched the side of my face. "Okay, now I know he wears glasses. If the conversation is still going on, then I'll find out if he has a mustache. I'm not going to ask how hairy his chest is, but somehow I would find out from this"—he grabbed the back of my neck—"that he's smooth.

"I'm not the one to put the pressure here"—he pressed his leg against mine—"and hold it there to find out if he moves *his* leg over. I don't do that. If we're talking and we're both starting to get touchy-feely, okay, then it becomes just as physical as anybody else, but that's *after* you've already gotten all that positive feedback that the person doesn't mind your attention."

I realized, to my surprise, that I didn't mind Howard's attention, not at all. The utter unabashedness of his scheming had the paradoxical effect of making him seem sweetly guileless. (Whereas Tommy's apparent naïveté came across as creepy.) I found it compellingly sexy that Howard had thought in such great detail about his erotic machinations. He was a man who could feel his sexual web vibrating at the slightest touch.

His hand was resting on my thigh again. I put my hand on top of his and squeezed it.

In his memoir *Touching the Rock: An Experience of Blindness*, John M. Hull writes that for sighted people, desire and vision are so closely connected that "it becomes difficult to distinguish between 'I feel hungry' and 'I want to eat that food which I see there.'" When blindness disrupts this connection, Hull says—referring to hungers both physical and sexual—desire is often merely "the restlessness of an unformed longing."

But surely the presence of a sexual partner isn't a prerequisite for arousal, just as the presence of food isn't a prerequisite for hunger. I wondered how blind gay men fantasize. Are their longings "unformed" or sharply shaped? Is desire sparked by images? By abstractions?

"If I was just going to jack off and I was thinking about somebody," Howard told me, "it would be me with that person, reliving the stages from meeting them, from the minute they walked in . . . like seeing the comic strip beginning to end. It isn't visual. I'm not seeing their facial expression. I'm not seeing the color of their hair. But I'm seeing *position*."

Doug, having been born blind, does not fantasize visually at all. Sometimes he thinks in terms of touch (like Howard, he seeks "those thin, young body types, smooth"), but mostly, he told me, it's "scenarios. Lots and lots of scenarios. People with accents. Things outside. Going to a country where I don't know the language and meeting somebody and trying to see if we could make a rendezvous happen without any spoken words." I was astonished by how quickly Doug's thoughts moved from what's readily accessible to him (sounds; the feel of skin and sun) to a dream of freedom from the limits imposed by blindness. But aren't most people's fantasies potent precisely in their combination of what's possible and what's not?

In Mazatlán, our second port of call, we stopped at a scenic outlook where I described for Doug a swan-diving daredevil. The young macho scaled a high crag—forty feet up, fifty, to the top—then stood glistening, preening for the crowd. He looked toward the heavens and crossed himself. Then he spread his arms—a soaring bird—and plunged to the rough-and-tumble surf.

Doug heard the force of my gasp, then, seconds later, my gasp of a different tone when the boy climbed out of the water right beside us. "Tell me what he looks like," Doug whispered.

Like a sportscaster calling the game-winning play, I struggled to find words fast enough: "Brown skin, dark dark brown hair, beading water, twenty-seven-inch waist, just perfect, perfectly ribbed stomach, Champion gym shorts down to his knees, clingy, you can see every thing."

"Thank you!" Doug said, matching my breathlessness. "Thank you. My god, that was great." He offered to buy me a margarita.

"Nah, my pleasure," I said—but then wondered about *Doug's* pleasure. What did my description really mean to a man who's never seen brown, who can't hold *soaring* in his hands?

"What's it like rooming with Tommy?" Doug asked. He and Steven had invited me to their stateroom one evening, the first time the three of us were alone.

"Um, it's okay," I said. I still hadn't told anyone about Tommy's phone call or his groping.

"You don't think he's kind of strange?" Steven said.

"I guess he's a little, um . . ."

"Come on," Doug said, "he's obviously got serious developmental issues."

He went on to tell me about a special telephone service that some of the blind men had subscribed to. There was no direct conversation, but individuals could exchange messages of up to a few minutes each. When Tommy joined the network, according to Doug, he had no sense of boundaries. "You'd come home and there would be a dozen messages from Tommy. He wouldn't wait for you to return the first before leaving another. And each one got more and more explicit. I mean, I'm not easily shocked. But hearing those things from someone I'd never met? I couldn't believe it."

"I almost wonder if he's slightly Mongoloid," Steven said.

I was staggered by his use of the term, but also hugely relieved to hear confirmation of my misgivings, especially from a blind man and his boyfriend. I told them that I too had gotten a taste of Tommy's message-leaving.

"Why didn't you say anything earlier?" Doug asked.

"I guess I didn't want to embarrass him," I said, which was true. "And if we were stuck rooming together, I didn't want to make things even more uncomfortable." Also true.

What I didn't add—because as it occurred to me, my throat clenched with shame—was that I'd excused Tommy's behavior because on some level I must have been *expecting* a blind gay man to be perverted.

In a way, wasn't that why I'd signed up for this cruise: to be near to men I'd pegged as lacking inhibitions? If Tommy had conformed to my sexual tastes, might his "depravity" have been just what I wanted?

That night, I couldn't sleep. For one thing there was Oscar, panting away on the floor, liable to accost me, without warning, in puppy love. A bigger problem was Tommy's snoring, a tectonically violent noise. I had a pair of earplugs saved from the courtesy kit on my most recent transatlantic flight, and I stuffed them as deep as they would go, then stuffed my whole head underneath both of my pillows, but still the noise made my brain wobble. It was the sound of an elephant giving birth to a bulldozer.

"Tommy," I called. "You're snoring."

No response.

"Tommy, come on. You're making noise." I clapped my hands twice, I pounded on the wall. "Fuck!" I yelled. "You're driving me insane."

At the last word, Tommy finally stirred, and instantly I realized my mistake, because now that he was awake would come the scratching.

The first night it had happened, the lights were out, and I assumed the noise came from Oscar's corner. In the morning, when the commotion began again, I saw plainly that Tommy was the culprit. Tommy scratched himself constantly in my presence. He lay in his bunk, sometimes in his underwear, sometimes naked, his hand on his abdomen or somewhat lower. Scratch scratch scratch. Pause. Scratch scratch scratch. It sounded as though he were trying to rescue a man buried alive inside him.

He never acknowledged this or provided an explanation. Crabs, I thought at first. Scabies? But Tommy's clawing was so compulsive that I finally concluded his itch wasn't physical, but existential.

Sure enough, now that I'd roused him, he started up again. Scratch scratch scratch. Pause. Scratch scratch scratch.

Tommy had persisted recently in his advances, copping feels of my leg during dinner and saying, that morning as we were dressing, "I'd really like the chance before the cruise is over to see what *all* of you looks like."

Each evening our cabin steward, as part of the nightly turndown, left us two foil-wrapped Royal Caribbean chocolate mints, along with a sort of terry cloth origami: a bath towel twisted into the shape of a swan or alligator. He deposited these items on my bed, perhaps thinking their presence on Tommy's bunk would confuse him, and so on the trip's first few nights I'd made a point of leading Tommy to my bed and showing him the creations. Tonight, after my conversation with Doug and Steven, I'd decided it was a mistake to bring Tommy near my bunk for any reason. I hadn't mentioned the towel art. And although I'm a chocolate lover, the moment we returned to our stateroom I'd given Tommy my mint as well as his in the hopes that it might, like Oscar's rawhide chew, distract him long enough for me to slip into bed.

Now, well past midnight, I hissed a pointed *shh*. Tommy turned over. The scratching stopped.

In the last port of call, Puerto Vallarta, we finally collided with gay culture—literally. At the Blue Chair Resort, a gay beach in front of a gay hotel, our whole gang galumphed onto the sand, plowing through clusters of bikini-waxed, Corona-sipping men. Attendants nervously arranged chairs for us on the very edge of the resort. Even so, some patrons felt the need to move.

But the blind guys could see neither this self-satisfied slice of gay life, nor the fact that they didn't seem to be embraced by it. So they ordered drinks, propped umbrellas to shade their dogs, and kicked back.

Everyone seemed to have a fine time. Howard and Carl frolicked in the water, then wandered among the klatches of tattooed muscle-men, trying to find their way back to our group. If you didn't know they were blind, you'd have thought they were browsing the hustlers.

Later, Carl led Tommy to the surf's edge, and Tommy (who, now that I'd drawn the line more firmly between us, I decided could be almost funny) asked me to hold his oversize sunglasses. He waded into the water, gut drooping over his flower-patterned yellow bathing suit. ("Is this suit blue?" he'd asked that morning in our cabin, and seemed confounded when I told him no, but donned it anyway.) When the first big wave came, it knocked him on his ass. He came up grinning wide, a jackpot winner.

I strolled up to the bar, where Bill and Doug had gone for more beers. They asked me to describe the scene and I did my best—the bright umbrellas, the haughty men, the rising surf—but I left out the part about the slinky Mexican kid two tables over, head shaved to show a dozen sexy scars, who looked at me, looked away, then looked back and finally winked. I returned his wink, ignited by arousal.

"Isn't it nice out here?" Bill said, oblivious to our flirtation. "Just the exact right amount of breeze."

"It's the best place we've gone so far," Doug said.

I looked away from Scar Guy, my fervor flash-frozen. I should have reveled in our visual dalliance, no longer taking this capacity for granted, but what I felt was profound loneliness—like when you think of something you want to confide to a cherished friend, but then remember that the friend has died.

Why should I have felt lonely? *I* wasn't missing anything; the blind men were. And yet what exactly were they missing? The chance to wink at a Mexican kid whose name I didn't know, whom I'd probably never see again?

My sadness, I realized, wasn't so much for Doug or Bill—they seem fairly contented in their lives—but for all of us, for the way we seek connection so ardently and so often fail, for the fact that a wink, even if you see it, assures nothing.

The last night, I sat in our stateroom. I'd packed my suitcase and left it with the porters. I'd filled out the customs form. I'd brushed my teeth.

Tommy was up on Deck 5 at the mulch boxes, offering Oscar a last chance to go. One more night, I thought. Just one more.

But as much as he'd made me uncomfortable, I couldn't be mad at Tommy. Howard, who knows him well, had told me that until recently Tommy attended Homosexuals Anonymous, trying to "cure" himself of being gay. And although Tommy had told me he's been in an eight-year relationship with a man, Howard explained that the man is married and only uses Tommy for sex. He said that twice Tommy has picked up strangers who have robbed him.

The door opened and Tommy clunked in. "Hey there, Mike!" he called in a childlike voice.

"Hi, Tommy," I said, and it occurred to me that he might have *given* his valuables to those strangers; he was just that good-natured, just that clueless.

Tommy unharnessed Oscar, and, as usual, the Lab frisked up and began humping my leg. I let him thrust a moment before I shoved him off. "I can't believe it," I said, mock serious. "Tomorrow I'll have to go home to my lonesome life, with no puppy dog to love me."

Tommy plopped heavily on his bunk. "Oh, I imagine there aren't very many times that *you're* lonesome, Mike."

"More than you think," I said, honestly.

"Really?" Tommy said. "I always thought it would be different if you had twenty-twenty."

FOR KEEPS: THE
CHRISTIAN C. SANDERSON MUSEUM
Albert Mobilio

Chris Sanderson saved almost everything he touched. He saved the toy trains from his childhood in the 1880s. He saved the slate board on which he did his lessons as a boy. He saved dance cards from a barn dance in 1906. The pencil he used to vote for Alf Landon in 1936. A rock from the hill where he served as an air-raid spotter in World War II. The burnt matches which lit a candle commemorating what would have been his late father's eighty-fifth birthday. A piece of the flagpole from the school where he taught. He also saved anything anyone gave him: a vial of melted ice from the South Pole; dust from a Billy Sunday revival meeting; a small wheel from a zeppelin shot down in England in 1916; a hyena's head; a hangman's noose; and a cup once hidden in a well by the great-great-grandfather of a friend. Sanderson saved everything and anything—from the shawl his mother wrapped him in the day he was born to a lock of George Washington's hair—filling his farm-house in Chadds Ford, Pennsylvania, with the flotsam and jetsam of his most intimate life, as well as that of distant times and locales. He carefully tagged nearly all of these items with handwritten notes specifying dates and contexts ("Tissue paper from box of Indian clubs"). From childhood onward, as his well-preserved stuffed animals attest, Sanderson was a zealous, perhaps obsessed, collector. For most of his eighty-four years (he died in 1966), he pursued a somewhat quixotic goal: to memorialize himself as the subject of his very own museum; that is, to become the archaeologist and curator of his own life.

There are no marble steps or columns at the Christian C. Sanderson

Museum; it is the early-nineteenth-century farmhouse where Sanderson lived for most of his life.

Although the two-story wood-frame structure sits only a hundred yards from busy Route 100 as it passes through Chadds Ford, visitors are infrequent. Still, those who come to visit the nearby homes of Andrew and N. C. Wyeth, as well as the Brandywine Battlefield, where Washington was defeated in the largest land battle of the Revolutionary War, sometimes find themselves standing on the front porch peering through the screen door. They are usually greeted by Thomas R. Thompson, a onetime friend of Sanderson's, who oversees the eight-room museum and who has made a valiant attempt at archiving the thousands of letters and notes (over a ton in weight) Sanderson left stacked in dusty piles around the house. "After Chris died, you could hardly move in here," Thompson says. "He was quite the pack rat." The understatement is almost comical. A photo of Sanderson's bed shows that he slept on barely a third of the mattress, the remainder being buried in books and papers. This and other photos of Sanderson's rooms taken before they were cleaned up recall stories about other lifelong hoarders—for instance, Harlem's Collyer brothers, who packed their Fifth Avenue brownstone with 136 tons of stuff (including fourteen grand pianos, the chassis of a Model T Ford, an X-ray machine). In 1947, when one brother was killed by a falling bundle of newspapers, his blind and paralyzed sibling, unable to make his way through the labyrinth, starved to death. But Sanderson wasn't pathological; the tenor of his collecting mania was domestic and pedagogical, not rabid.

Every day we make dozens of decisions about what things we want to keep and what things should be discarded. We sit in judgment over our own material domain: the postcard from an old friend that's been on the kitchen counter for a month, toss it; the set of unidentifiable keys, keep them just in case; assorted Post-its with various numbers and illegible names, keep for now; a coffee mug given by officemates, goodbye. It's an unending and often perplexing chore. Most decisions we make automatically, appraising the relative utility of things—does it work? do I need it?—but other decisions are more fraught. I have a birthday card signed by my mother. Generally, I would keep these cards for what I believed to be a respectful period of about a month and then consign them to the trash (with a small but nonetheless manageable pang). There's nothing special about the inscription on the card I have kept for several years, except that she wrote the words "Your loving mother and father" two weeks before she died. I keep the card, for what reason I'm not sure. It's standard-issue Hallmark individuated only by a dash of her penmanship, but I cannot bring myself to throw it away; the pang is not manageable. Sanderson, it's clear, couldn't endure even the hint of such a pang.

The personal objects he saved are familiar to us; in fact they are things we also may have saved: Easter eggs, family photos, pressed leaves, pencil boxes, china plates, baby toys, train schedules. Such things pass through our hands acquiring a brief significance and then they somehow disappear. Who still has the pencil box they clutched on their first day of school? Or the train schedule they used when they left home to live somewhere else? There was a moment when that printed piece of paper was important to us, then it wasn't; it became disposable. But if saved, of course, such a schedule might gain talismanic power. We would consider it an object of importance in our story. If there was a museum devoted solely to your life it would be there, under glass, perhaps with a Sanderson-like annotation: "Train schedule with 9:16 express circled."

Sanderson keenly anticipated his longing for his own past and he hoarded against the prospect of being alone, the dispersal of his possessions. The odder, less obviously evocative objects that he saved attest plaintively to this fear of loss. These items are so embedded with narrative that they acquire the kinetic quality of tableau vivant sculpture. There's a hat rack with his father's hat still hung on a knob—the father hung it there but never retrieved it; he died some days later in 1898. It's easy to imagine Sanderson insuring that the hat remained at the precise angle it was left. There is a nail (yes, a solitary nail) whose significance is detailed in the accompanying note: "A very precious Relic and keepsake. The nail from the middle of the front room ceiling . . . from here hung our paper, etc. for parties." *Very precious* are words you see over and over, neatly penciled on cards attached to the most quotidian things. There are several packets of "precious" burnt matches; their notes recall the occasion of their use as well invoking a lost parent: "Matches used to light candles by Dad's pictures and flowers . . . the day he would have been 85." The poignancy of these charred wooden sticks wrapped in wax paper is sharpened by the inventiveness of the aesthetic conceit. The matches are a commemoration of a commemorative act—the kind of self-reflexive, postmodern gesture you would expect from, say, Jasper Johns, not a rural schoolteacher in the 1940s. Actually, the artist Sanderson most readily evokes is Joseph Cornell; both men were entranced by the intricate sentimentality that ephemera can generate.

One of the strangest relics is a handmade Christmas star tied to a dry evergreen branch. The star was tied to the top of the tree by Sanderson's mother in 1943, just weeks before she died. What is of value here is, of course, the actual knot. Sanderson preserved his mother's act of tying it. Did he believe that something of her inner being, the domestic events of that day, were caught up in its loops? It's hard to say. But this desiccated pine branch and yellowed star joined by some rough twine pierces deeply as a reminder of how intimately things cohabit with us; how they are almost phantom limbs. This knot is a fetish object, the repository of desire and belief. Still, we tie knots every day. We hang jackets on hooks. We comb our hair. Yet we don't deliberately save the knotted shoelaces of our children or the combs threaded with our spouse's hair. To do so would be to welcome and appease an unbearable apprehension of loss.

No doubt, Sanderson was quite the odd duck. (In a photo from Thompson's biography, *Chris*, he is seen "playing with one of his rats.") Yet he was also a schoolteacher, square-dance fiddler, amateur historian, and expert Indian club juggler, in short, the kind of quaint figure (he played Rip Van Winkle in town pageants and, of course, saved locks of his fake beard) who populates the small towns of an idealized American past. Indeed, in a painting by his friend Andrew Wyeth, he looks like a little like Ichabod Crane (wire-rimmed glasses, a sweater vest, and a tweed jacket) as he holds a map and lectures. A devoted son who never married and lived with his mother till she died, Sanderson (bachelor scoutmaster and pack-rat eccentric) would probably arouse suspicion these days. But life in the early part of the last century meant he could leave a note on his open front door reading, "Walk in yell upstairs (not well)." It was also a time when many Americans shared Sanderson's straightforward, if not naive, enthusiasm for American history: historical commemorations engaged whole communities and figures like Lincoln and Washington were held in uncomplicated reverence.

But Sanderson's fascination with history is marked by an idiosyncratic passion that can't simply be attributed to patriotism. He gathered up anything with even the slightest trace of historical value (restaurant place mats with maps of Gettysburg, presidential campaign buttons, a bit of the plane that crashed into the Empire State Building) and he created his own artifacts. An inveterate attendee of public celebrations and memorial ceremonies (he was in Washington, D.C., for every inauguration from Theodore Roosevelt's to Lyndon Johnson's), he recorded his attendance in hundreds of notes which employed the officialese of government documents: "It is now 11 p.m. May 31, 1926. Have just returned to my boarding house at Roselle Delaware, today I attended the opening of the Sesquicentennial, 150th anniversary of the Declaration of Independence." Pressed in the folds of the note might be the flower or ribbon he wore on his coat, or the bill from the boardinghouse. He drew public history into the realm of his own private myth just as he enlarged his private myth to embrace history. From his years living in the house that was Washington's headquarters for the Battle of Brandywine, Sanderson saved some charred wood, which he duly noted was the "remains of a fireplace log used Christmas eve 1919." Through the mundane experience of warming up at a fire, Sanderson connected to the first president, the blackened log a token of their intimacy across the centuries at the same hearth. He also collected the detritus of the battlefield—spent shells, aircraft pieces, flag shards, bomb fragments. If there's something decidedly inglorious about this assemblage of metal scraps (an antiwar activist could hardly devise a more grim depiction of battle as mere detonation), that surely wasn't Sanderson's intent. For him, the burnt, broken odds and ends of the past—rather than, for instance, a mint-condition uniform—offered the surest conduits into history's inner drama. They are as small (and as *used*) as the soldiers they equipped, and thus bear witness to human scale on the larger stage.

In the spring of 1968, when Robert Kennedy's funeral train passed through my town on its way to Washington, D.C., I was one of the many kids who—in hope of fabricating instant historical treasure—set coins on the railroad track. Not being much of a pack rat myself, I've long since lost the tongue-shaped pennies the train left behind. But standing in Sanderson's house surrounded by a congeries of similar cultural debris, I wonder what relationship, if any, those flattened bits of copper bore to Kennedy, or to the event of his assassination. Certainly thinking about them evokes little about the macro-history. (Televised images hold sway there.) Rather, what I mostly recall about the day was pressing my parents—who were not Kennedy enthusiasts—to hurry to the station as the car radio tracked the train's approach. I may have vivid memories of the flag-draped coffin and Ted Kennedy waving from the back of the train, but the history I would want to remember more clearly—which I simply cannot—is what my parents said, how we got along, if my mother wore a dress for the occasion, and what exactly I was thinking as I stood between them, the bell clanging as the big engine slowed for the crowd. All of that's gone. If I had saved those coins, noted the date and time the train passed, could they now conjure for me—like Proust's madeleine—some fresh habitation of my own lost time?

What is perhaps the most curious and affecting item in the house evidences Sanderson's talent for synthesizing public and private narrative, as well as devising fetish objects meant to ward off impending loss. It is a 1940 photo taken by Sanderson of his mother on the anniversary of Lincoln's assassination. Curled on her side, clutching a handkerchief in one hand, the other hand tucked under her head, Hanna Sanderson mournfully contemplates a portrait of Lincoln draped with a small American flag. A note written by Mrs. Sanderson decodes the dramatic scene: She had been nine years old, "sick with some childish ailment," on the morning of April 15, 1865, when her father returned from the village post office with news of Lincoln's death. And now: "Today, April 15 between 9 and 9:30 a.m., Christie took my picture as I lay on that same sofa and at the same end as on that distressing day 75 years ago." Private grief at public tragedy is memorialized in a photo that commemorates their intertwined nature. As with all of Sanderson's mementos, emotion is particularized. Important to both mother and son is the fact that she lies "at the same end" of the couch (probably holding the same handkerchief). The theatricality of the enterprise, with its attendant suggestion of the ersatz, is redeemed by this fervor for exactitude, for particularity. Sanderson's emotional precision—his knowing sense of what Stendhal called the "small truths" (*les petits fails vrais*)—animates his keepsakes with visceral tension. As the image of this elderly woman posing as a child eerily recollects one death, it also prophesies another. On the wall close to the photo are two other images—Sanderson's photo of his mother on her deathbed two years later, a nineteenth-century American flag draping her body, and Andrew Wyeth's painting, based on that photo, titled *Death on a Christmas Morning*. Mortality, with its sly insinuations into the everyday laid bare—the hat you hang tomorrow may the last thing you ever touch—haunts this house and invests a burnt match, a nail, and some knotted twine with a lyric melancholy. Things can, indeed, be "very precious."

It's a kind of magical thinking—ancient and vigorously abiding—to believe that something of ourselves, those we love, and those we esteem inheres in mere objects. This wishful desire to memorialize flesh within the inanimate is our hedge against separateness from others and the body's frailty. (The lowly candle that lit your first birthday cake could easily outlast your great-grandchildren.) From museums to monuments, from attics to family scrapbooks, the sum of consecrated things is vast and the number of candidates even greater. My son's crowded room needs clearing, but he claims every broken toy to be "special" to him. And, truly, many are special to me, too. In this way, a world of would-be relics presses in upon us: an unplayable copy of Jimi Hendrix's *Axis: Bold as Love,*, the cover of which you once fell into headlong, being stoned for the first time; an unwearable hand-me-down tie of your father's; or a headless action figure all vie for canonization, for their place on some shelf. Sanderson could not resist their clamorous demand. Objects spoke insistently to him of their power to mitigate loss, to salvage something durable in the face of unrelenting decay. That's why his memorabilia collection may amuse, transfix, and even unnerve us, but ultimately it is a source of formidable sorrow. It's not just the sadness which so readily springs from Sanderson's poignant, evocative *objets*. Surpassing that feeling is a nagging sense of waste which mounts to heart-withering distress over this life spent on the verge of mourning. Within all these strangely sacred things resides a too familiar kernel of fear. It went unresisted by Sanderson until it overwhelmed his being, until he became his own archaeologist or, put another way, the exhumer of his own grave. Of course, we all must shore some fragments against the ruins. They will prove the necessary charms that one day will summon our long-lost selves. My son can keep his headless Batman and three-wheeled race car. But he also needs to learn to let go of some "special" things; he needs to learn that the pang is manageable.

CONTRIBUTORS

Russell Banks is the author of the novels *Rule of the Bone* and *Cloudsplitter*, among others, and *The Angel on the Roof: New and Selected Stories*. Two of his novels, *The Sweet Hereafter* and *Affliction*, were adapted as prize-winning films. He lives in the Adirondack Mountains.

Jo Ann Beard is the author of *The Boys of My Youth*, a collection of autobiographical essays. She lives in upstate New York.

Amy Bloom is the author of two short-story collections, a novel, and a collection of essays. She teaches at Yale University and she is at work on a novel.

Charles D'Ambrosio is the author of *The Point and Other Stories* and *Essays: New and Collected*. His fiction and essays have recently appeared in the *New Yorker*, *Harper's*, and *Nest*.

Jeffrey Eugenides is the author of the novels *The Virgin Suicides* and *Middlesex*, for which he was awarded the Pulitzer Prize for Fiction.

David Gates is the author of the novel *Jernigan*, which was a finalist for the Pulitzer Prize. His novel *Preston Falls* and short-story collection, *The Wonders of the Invisible World*, were finalists for the National Book Critics Circle Award.

Panagiotis Gianopoulos has published fiction and nonfiction in *Nerve*, the *Hartford Courant*, the *Journal News*, the *Brooklyn Rail*, and the

Northwest Review. He was a recipient of a 2003 New York Foundation for the Arts Fellowship for nonfiction literature. He lives in Manhattan with his girlfriend and their daughter.

Gary Greenberg is a psychotherapist and recreational journalist residing in Connecticut. He once contemplated writing an entire book about being Joel's father, but then he realized that one day Joel would be able to read. He did once write an entire book about self-help books, but he doesn't understand it anymore. His essays and articles have appeared in *Harper's*, the *New Yorker*, *Rolling Stone*, and *Mother Jones*, and his work has been included in *Best American Science and Nature Writing.*

Kathryn Harrison has written five novels: *Thicker Than Water, Exposure, Poison, The Binding Chair*, and *The Seal Wife*. Her autobiographical work includes the memoirs *The Mother Knot* and *The Kiss*; a collection of personal essays, *Seeking Rapture*; and a meditation on the meaning of pilgrimage, *The Road to Santiago*. She has also written a biography, *Saint Thérèse of Lisieux*. She lives in New York with her husband, the novelist Colin Harrison, and their three children.

Ann Hood's most recent book is her short-story collection, *An Ornithologist's Guide to Life*. She is also the author of seven novels, including *Somewhere off the Coast of Maine* and *Ruby*, and a memoir, *Do Not Go Gentle: My Search for Miracles in a Cynical Time*. She lives in Providence, Rhode Island.

Gerald Howard is a book editor in New York City.

Michael Lowenthal is the author of the novels *Avoidance* and *The Same Embrace*. His short stories have been anthologized, most recently, in *Best New American Voices 2005, Lost Tribe: Jewish Fiction from the Edge*, and *Bestial Noise: The Tin House Fiction Reader*. He teaches writing at Boston College and in the low-residency M.F.A. program of Lesley University.

Richard McCann's fiction and creative nonfiction have appeared in the *Atlantic*, *Tin House*, and *American Short Fiction*, and in anthologies including *The Penguin Book of Gay Short Stories*, *Survival Stories: Memoirs of Crisis*, and *Best American Essays 2000*. He is the author of *Ghost Letters* and editor (with Michael Klein) of *Things Shaped in Passing: More "Poets for Life" Writing from the AIDS Pandemic*. *Mother of Sorrows*, his collection of linked stories, will be published in January 2005. He co-directs the M.F.A. Program in Creative Writing at American University in Washington, D.C.

Christopher Merrill's books include *Only the Nails Remain: Scenes from the Balkan Wars* (nonfiction) and *Brilliant Water* (poetry). He directs the International Writing Program at the University of Iowa.

Albert Mobilio is the recipient of a Whiting Writers' Award and the 1998 National Book Critics Circle Award for reviewing. His work has appeared in the *Village Voice*, *Harper's*, *Grand Street*, *Cabinet*, *Bomb*, and the *New York Times Book Review*. His books of poetry include *Bendable Siege*, *The Geographics*, and *Me with Animal Towering*. He teaches writing at New York University and is the fiction editor at *Bookforum*.

Rick Moody is the author most recently of *The Black Veil*.

Jean Nathan's book *The Secret Life of the Lonely Doll: The Search for Dare Wright* has been optioned by Killer Films. She lives in New York City.

Francine Prose is the author of ten novels, including *Bigfoot Dreams*, *Primitive People*, *Household Saints*, and, most recently, *Blue Angel*, which was a National Book Award finalist for 2000. Her short fiction, which has appeared in such publications as the *New Yorker*, the *Atlantic Monthly*, and the *Paris Review*, is compiled in two collections, *Women and Children First* and *The Peaceable Kingdom*. Her nonfiction has appeared in *Tin House*, the *New York Times*

Magazine, Harper's, Elle, GQ, the *Wall Street Journal,* and the *New Yorker.* She is the recipient of numerous awards and honors, including Guggenheim and Fulbright fellowships and a PEN translation prize. She lives in New York City.

Sara Roahen currently lives in New Orleans, where she writes about food and restaurants and indulges her taste for another regional drink, the Sazerac.

Katie Roiphe is the author of *The Morning After* and *Still She Haunts Me.* She holds a Ph.D. from Princeton in English literature. Her articles have appeared in the *New York Times,* the *Washington Post, Vogue, Esquire,* and *Harper's,* among other publications.

Elissa Schappell is the author of *Use Me,* which was a runner-up for the PEN/Hemingway Award, a *Los Angeles Times* Best Book of the Year, a *New York Times* Notable Book, and a Borders Discover New Voices selection. Her stories and essays have appeared in or are forthcoming in *The KGB Bar Reader, The Bitch in the House, The Mrs. Dalloway Reader, Sex and Sensibility,* and *Lit Riffs.* Her articles have appeared in *SPIN, Salon, Nerve, Vogue,* and the *Paris Review,* among other publications. She is co-editor with Jenny Offill of the forthcoming anthology *The Friend Who Got Away.* She is also a contributing editor at *Vanity Fair* and editor at large of *Tin House* magazine. She teaches in the low-residency M.F.A. program at Queens University in North Carolina.

David Shields is the author of eight books, including *Black Planet: Facing Race During an NBA Season,* a finalist for the National Book Critics Circle Award; *Remote: Reflections on Life in the Shadow of Celebrity,* winner of the PEN/Revson Award; and *Dead Languages: A Novel,* winner of the Washington State Book Award. His essays and stories have appeared in the *New York Times Magazine, Harper's,* the *Yale Review,* the *Village Voice, Salon, Slate, McSweeney's,* and *Utne Reader.* He lives with his wife and daughter in Seattle.

Abigail Thomas worked in publishing as an editor and literary agent for twenty years before morphing into a writer. She has published two collections of stories, *Getting Over Tom* and *Herb's Pajamas*; a novel, *An Actual Life*; and three books for children. Her most recent book is a memoir, *Safekeeping: Some True Stories from a Life*.

Sallie Tisdale's next book, stories about various women in Zen Buddhist history, will be published by Harper San Francisco in 2005. She is also at work on a book about winter, and works part-time as a nurse.

Ken Tucker is critic at large for *Entertainment Weekly* and pop music critic for National Public Radio's *Fresh Air with Terry Gross*. He is the author of the forthcoming *Kissing Bill O'Reilly, Roasting Miss Piggy: 100 Things to Love and Hate About Television*. Tucker's essay on "There Stands the Glass" received an ASCAP-Deems Taylor Award for Music Criticism.

Eliot Weinberger's books of essays include *Works on Paper, Outside Stories, Karmic Traces*, and *9/12*. He is the editor of *The New Directions Anthology of Classical Chinese Poetry* and has translated Octavio Paz, Jorge Luis Borges, Vicente Huidobro, and Bei Dao.

Lisa Zeidner is the author of four novels: *Customs, Alexandra Freed, Limited Partnerships*, and, most recently, *Layover*. She has also published two books of poems. Her stories, essays, and reviews have appeared in *GQ*, the *New York Times*, and many other publications. She is a professor at Rutgers University.

A NOTE ON THE TYPE

The text of this book is set in Linotype Sabon, named after the type founder Jacques Sabon. It was designed by Jan Tschichold and jointly developed by Linotype, Monotype, and Stempel in response to a need for a typeface to be available in identical form for mechanical hot metal composition and hand composition using foundry type.

Tschichold based his design for Sabon roman on a font engraved by Garamond, and Sabon italic on a font by Granjon. It was first used in 1966 and has proved an enduring modern classic.